IMAGES
of America

LISBON

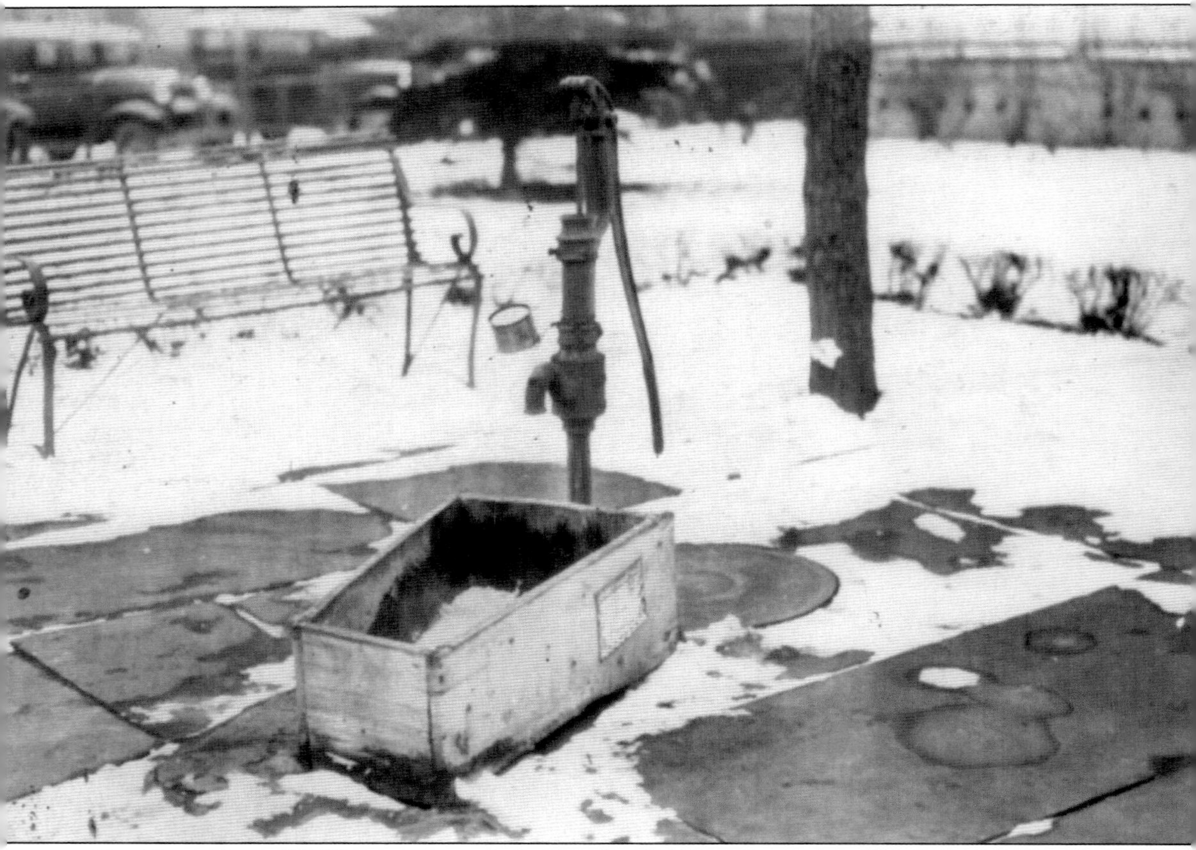

The Town Pump. Well known to residents—and probably to visitors as well—this old pump sat at the focal point of the town square. Residents of all sorts gathered there, drinking from the common cup and sharing their stories. As times have changed, it is now in a quiet spot near the Train Station Museum of the Lisbon Historical Society. (Courtesy of the Lisbon Historical Society.)

On the Cover: Classic Victorian. Lisbon is blessed with many traditional Victorian homes. This home is known as the residence of the Gaileys and the Hostetters, who were prominent residents. The classic home with its porches, rounded gazebo, and roof accents exhibits many of the characteristics of the architecture of the 19th century, just as the residents are representative of the clothing of the time and the decorations celebrate the centennial of Lisbon in 1903. (Courtesy of the Lisbon Historical Society.)

IMAGES
of America

LISBON

Ruth Gerrard Cole

ARCADIA
PUBLISHING

ISBN 978-1-4671-1470-7

Published by Arcadia Publishing
Charleston, South Carolina

Printed in the United States of America

Library of Congress Control Number: 2015935784

For all general information, please contact Arcadia Publishing:
Telephone 843-853-2070
Fax 843-853-0044
E-mail sales@arcadiapublishing.com
For customer service and orders:
Toll-Free 1-888-313-2665

Visit us on the Internet at www.arcadiapublishing.com

This book is dedicated to my father, Rev. Paul T. Gerrard, and my husband, Wendell Cole, for their love of and service to Lisbon.

Contents

Acknowledgments

Individuals and organizations have made this book possible. It is with deep gratitude that I thank Gene Krotky, curator of the Lisbon Historical Society, for her extensive knowledgeable work with photograph, vertical files, and other historical information, willingly shared; Mary Ann Gray, also of the historical society, for her willingness to use her printing and scanning skills for all of the photographs from start to finish in the process and in the book; and the Lisbon Historical Society Board of Directors for their continued support. Society president Heidi Blosser, Leah Rudy, Kris Kibler, Barry James, Lisa Wycoff, Mary Anne Creatore, Diane Clapsaddle, and society treasurer Carol Tsilimos have each worked and will continue to help in this book project from searching for photographs to offering advice. Longtime Lisbon historian Ken Everett has been very generous in supplying images, and Bob Bye, Gregg Weber, Charles Stauffer, Tom McKenna, JoAnn Tolson, and Ashley Pike have given real help. I would like to express my appreciation to Dr. Richard Shale and Joyce Pogany, who have been involved in writing Arcadia books, for their inspiration and guidance in exploring the possibilities with the Lisbon book. There are others whose enthusiasm has made this book happen. Thank you. And my husband, Wendell Cole, past president of the society, has been my total support through the process from the earliest idea through examining photographs, photographing the contemporary, proofing copy—simply being there with every stage and question. The Lisbon Historical Society with its tremendous resources and generosity lending its significant collection of photographs and informational files has truly made this book possible. My heartfelt appreciation to each and every one of you, named and unnamed.

I would express my gratitude to Arcadia Publishing as well. Although there are, undoubtedly, many of you with whom I have not been in direct contact, I would want to express great appreciation to the publishing house for your excellence in organization and your outstanding personnel. Particularly in this process I would name Betsey Poore for her care and guidance through the initial proposal and acceptance stages, Jonny Foster for his advice and continued direction through the publication and marketing phases, and Liz Gurley for being my faithful, constant editor—always willing to answer with wisdom and experience yet another question. Thank you, one and all.

Unless otherwise noted, all images are courtesy of the Lisbon Historical Society.

Introduction

In a creative writing class in college, I wrote a poem with its central image focusing upon Lisbon's town pump that was situated prominently in the heart of town, the village square. The opening line was, "The old men stand by the village pump and drink together from their common cup," representative of the community in its tradition, old landmarks, and togetherness. Over the years, many have gathered in the town square, in good times and bad, war and peace, and celebration and mourning, as crowds viewing entertainment and ordinary folk sharing daily visits.

Lisbon is a town of strong family ties, awareness of the lives and events of the citizenry, and a general sense of well-being in spite of economic stresses, national emergencies, gains, and losses. Founded in 1803 and named New Lisbon, the natural contour of the land gives a sense of shelter and beauty. Bounded by a creek on the south and west sides, a stretch of flat land on the east, and steep hills on the other two sides, the town has been isolated, yet involved. Prominent citizens have been born, educated, and launched from the little community. Major events have changed the everyday course of life. Buildings and people stand tall through more than two centuries of existence.

Visitors to the town are struck by its natural beauty—the sloping hills that guide into the community, the open spaces, the obvious marks of the past. They are amused and amazed by the citizen's references to homes not by street and house number but by former residents. They remark frequently about the beautiful Victorians that still dominate much of the area as well as the rows of houses and businesses; the Victorians are the product of the prosperous years in business in the late 19th and early 20th centuries.

And they always remark that there is so much history in Lisbon. Indeed, there is. The early settlers came with great hopes into this forested land. They hoped to carve not only a community, but also a city. Lewis Kinney built his Old Stone tavern in 1805 as a major stop for those who made the journey westward. Shops and businesses arose to accommodate the early settlers. Churches were critically important to these God-fearing pioneers. Education began in a log building and grew with the community.

Memories have been abundant from the earliest days; still they are passed down through the generations. One source has always been the family tales of arrowheads found from the days of the Indians. A few legends persist in that realm. More stories come from the days of the Underground Railroad and possible sites along its route on the eastern edge of the town. The most persistent tales come from the advance of Gen. John Hunt Morgan and his Raiders, the farthest northern advance of Confederate forces during the Civil War. The stories seem to center upon the grandmother who, as a little child that morning, had been told by the soldiers not to fear their presence, for they only sought water. The question arises as to how many stops were made or whether one grandmother was the ancestor of generations.

Names have shaped community pride. There was the founding pastor of the Presbyterian church, Clement Vallandigham. Not only did he found a church, he also established a family. One son,

Clement L. Vallandigham, became well known nationally for his Southern sympathies in terms of state's rights. Called a "Copperhead," he was at great odds with President Lincoln, who eventually banished him to the South. One theory persists that Morgan and his Raiders did not destroy Lisbon on that fateful July 1863 Sunday because of Morgan's admiration for Vallandigham. For a brief time, Lincoln's secretary of war, Edwin Stanton, practiced law in the community, a great point of pride for Lisbon.

The names continue. Sen. Marcus A. Hanna, born and educated in Lisbon, became a great national figure in his years in Cleveland industry and national government. He chose to support and promote another man with Lisbon ties, Pres. William McKinley. Both the grandparents and parents of the future chief executive resided in Lisbon; his mother and father were born in the community. It is said that McKinley was always warmly received in the town. The Fighting McCooks of Civil War fame left their mark in the stories of their dignified professions and military records. John H. Clarke, associate justice of the US Supreme Court, was a native of the community. His heritage lives on as he lies buried in the local cemetery entered by gates donated by the Clarkes. Of the Van Fossan family, the US District Court tax judge Ernest Van Fossan served in Washington, DC. The Reverend Dr. Kenneth Neigh, a Presbyterian minister, served as vice president of Chicago's McCormick Theological Seminary and director of the National Board of Missions. Nationally recognized, these citizens were launched from the little town nestled in the hills.

The Victorian homes are to admire and recall, sometimes to lament the loss, other times to admire the ageless beauty. Row houses and old brick structures, many dating to the early 19th century, are still in use around the heart of Lisbon. In the downtown area, the old stores and community buildings abound, a fair number still occupied. Historic businesses are fondly patronized or remembered. Industries and inventions are recalled. Many conversations start with naming a residence or a place with a discussion of some story that occurred in past or recent times.

The community togetherness is bound by events: the county fair within the county seat, the annual Johnny Appleseed Festival, the sports, the school activities, the major celebrations of wars ending, and historical benchmarks in Lisbon's centennial, sesquicentennial, and bicentennial make the times and the memories. Alumni return regularly for class reunions. Conversations center upon memories of classmates, neighbors, games won and lost, contests with music, and funny and sad events. Most of all, there are the big moments over which to reminisce—fires, snowstorms, landmark changes.

And yet the times have made a great difference. In 1895, the name shifted from New Lisbon to Lisbon. As the 20th century progressed, like most small towns in the United States, the commerce had moved nearby or totally away. Except for the courthouse and some stores and restaurants, the commercial and business section is largely north of the community, but there is downtown renovation of classic buildings, some for different purposes in the 21st century.

The little poem ends with the line "Once more they pass their chalice now and weep." For a community whose gifts are its greatest pride in its timeless traditions, serious links among people, and sense of a place to return, the heritage of Lisbon is togetherness, yet it evokes a sense of nostalgia, a lost time in national history. In a sense, frozen in time, Lisbon is a living symbol of small-town America—another time, another place, yet a vital part of America's heritage.

One

Establishing a Village

In the founding of a community in any age and time, there are certain essential needs. With that given, it is appropriate to look at the beginnings of Lisbon. The founding fathers of this Ohio village recognized the basic requirements. And they began.

Officially begun in 1803, actual incorporation occurred in 1825. Prior to that later date, so much was in place. Lewis Kinney, considered the official founder, built his stone house in 1805. Still standing, it is the landmark of the community—originally an inn, later serving many other purposes. Other places for transients as well as homes for the residents followed shortly. A log cabin served as the original school while churches of various denominations were built in early times. As there was the need for a jail, that, too, was established.

Commerce is critical to survival. Businesses and industries that matched the needs of the day quickly formed. In those early years, there were tanneries, potteries, and brick factories. In the village, a central market for supplying needs quickly evolved with grocers, pharmacists, and clothing stores. Mills for wool and feed appeared. With the farms surrounding the little hamlet, the needs of agriculture were met. Hope for great expansion arrived in the form of canal plans.

And the people came. Doctors, lawyers, ministers, workers—most in families with children—populated the growing community. Names of that day remain in their descendants. Homes built in that time still stand. Government was critical, and the village soon became the county seat with a series of courthouses. To this day, that is a vital part of community life and leads to connections with other county seats and state government. Cultural needs expanded. Late in the first century, a beautiful library was built, and two opera houses graced the village. The town center's village square sported a gazebo—today, a near replica graces the little park.

Within the confines of the 19th century, Lisbon achieved her identity with all the self-sufficiency, pride, and opportunities of an American small town.

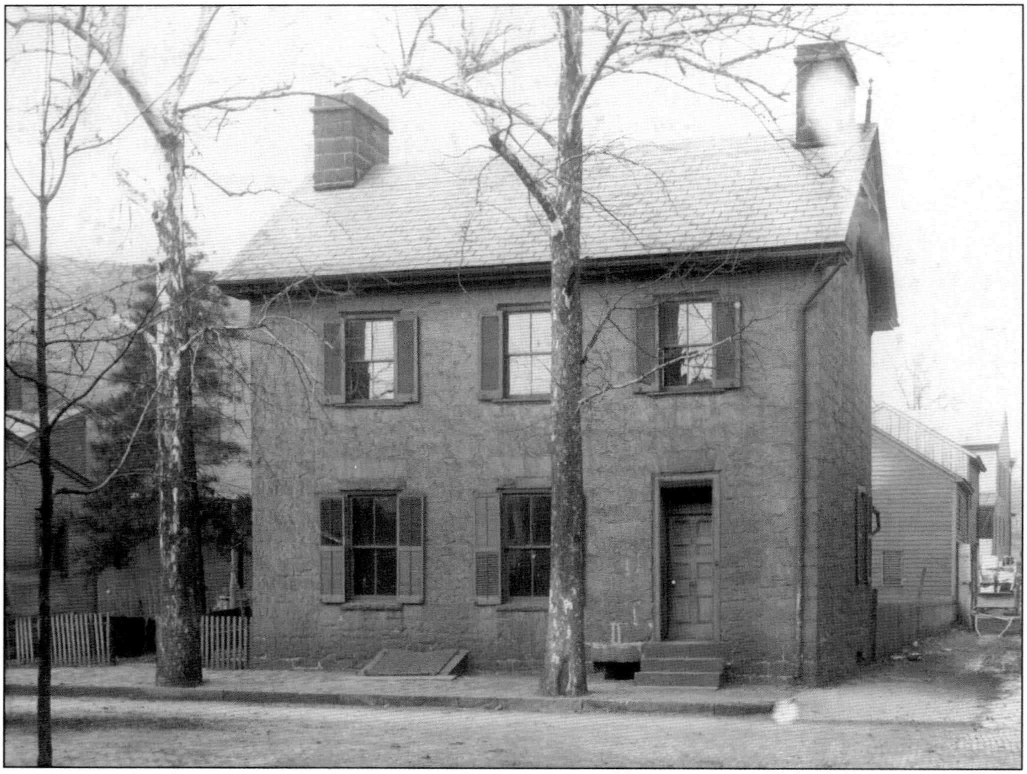

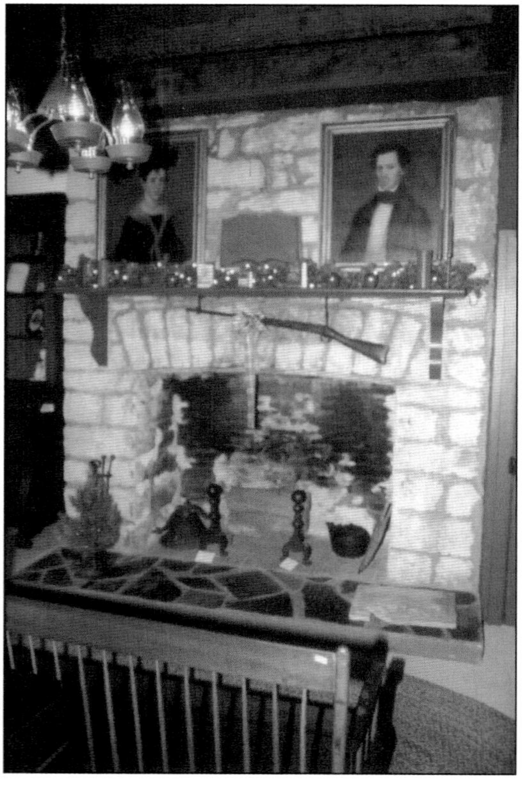

Lisbon's Old Stone House. This 1805 building is definitely Lisbon's oldest house, probably constructed by founder Lewis Kinney although some credit Christian Smith. Its years have been spent as tavern, private residence, and church. In 1952, the house became the property of the Lisbon Historical Society. Restored to its 19th-century origins, the stone structure is a major attraction with its period furniture, portraits, and artifacts. Today, it is considered the oldest stone house in Ohio.

Stone House Interior. Adults and children step into a bygone world as they experience a basic but beautiful lifestyle on a tour of the house built more than two centuries ago. Decorated for Christmas in this photograph, the mantle also showcases the portraits of Benjamin and Rachel Hanna, parents of Dr. Leonard Hanna and grandparents of Sen. Marcus A. Hanna.

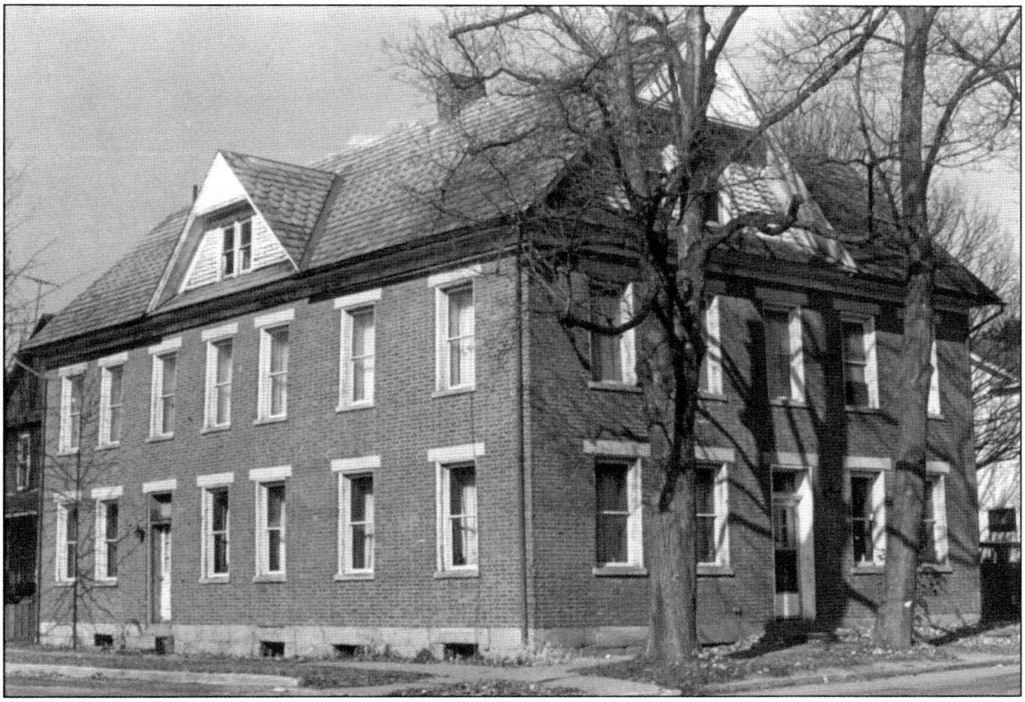

ANDERSON FARMERS HOTEL. From early days, not only was this hotel interesting for its place for travelers through the community, but also for its links to one of the most important figures in Lisbon's history. This was the home as well as the family business of David Anderson, a most important educator in the Lisbon schools for over 50 years.

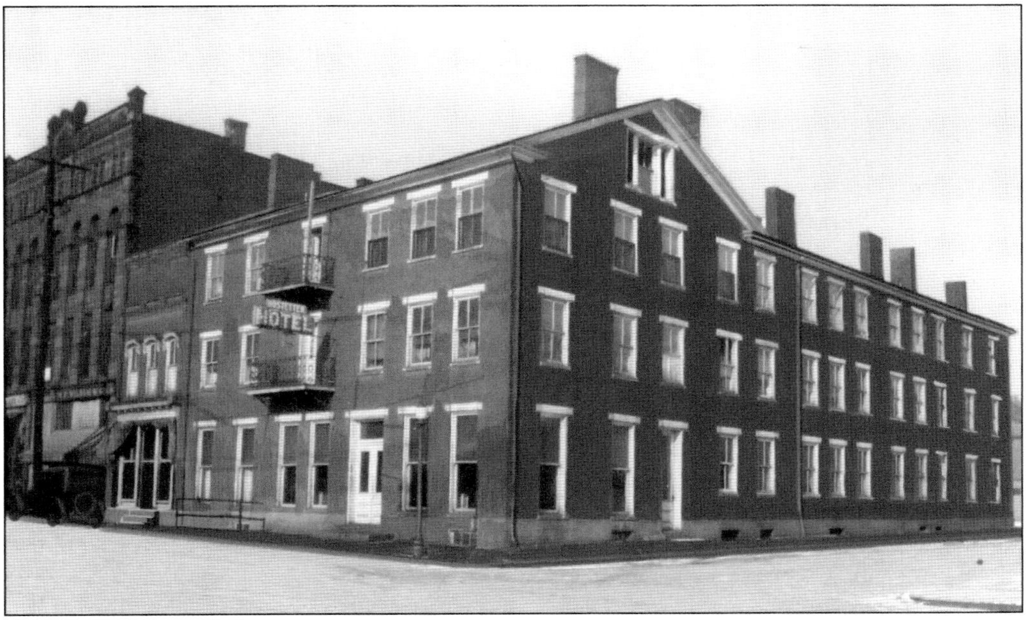

CROSS KEYS HOTEL. This old hotel began as the Cross Keys, changed to the Watson House, and ended as the Wick Hotel. Important to the community and the county, it stood until the late 20th century. Both its dining room and guest rooms were heavily patronized by permanent residents and travelers. Pres. Benjamin Harrison recommended it.

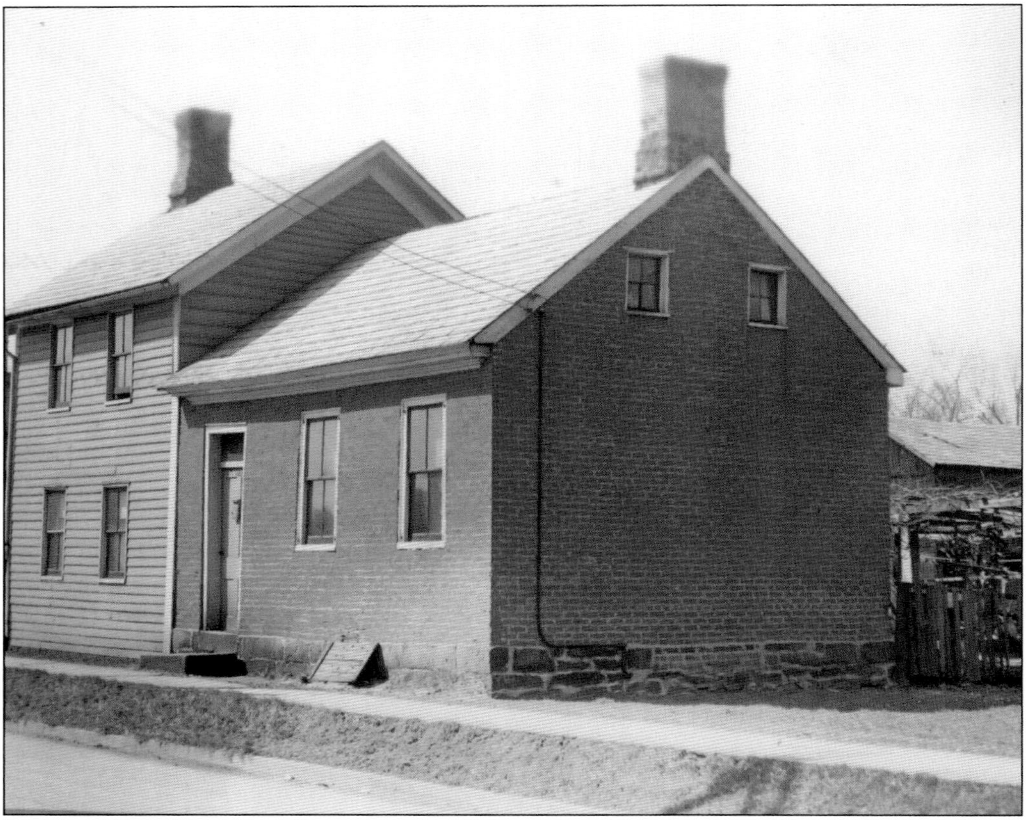

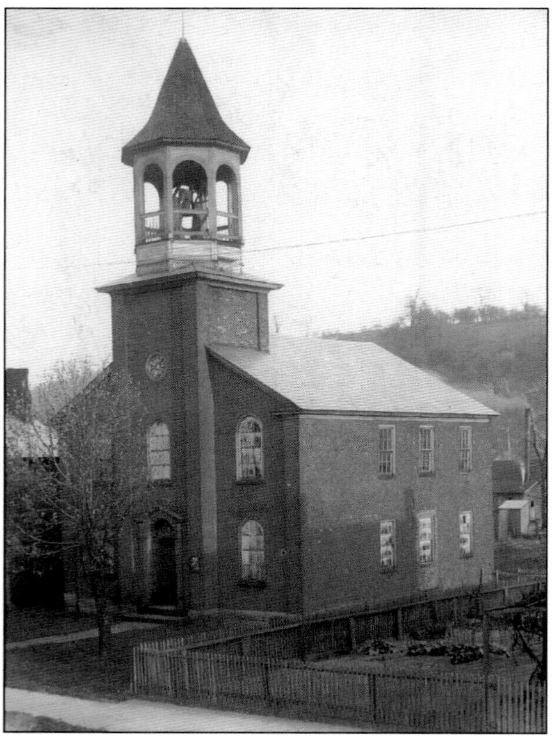

An Original Schoolhouse. As Lisbon began to provide education for its youth, this brick building on Maple Street served as a very early schoolhouse. James McKinley, grandfather of the president, taught here. As new buildings were erected, this structure became a family home even into the 21st century, when it was demolished in order for the residents to construct a new dwelling on the site.

German Lutheran Church. This early church in Lisbon was home originally to combined German Reformed and Lutheran congregations. Built in 1833, services were discontinued in 1860. This was the first church built in the southern portion of town. Later, it housed the Holiness Mission and an automobile garage; the building no longer stands.

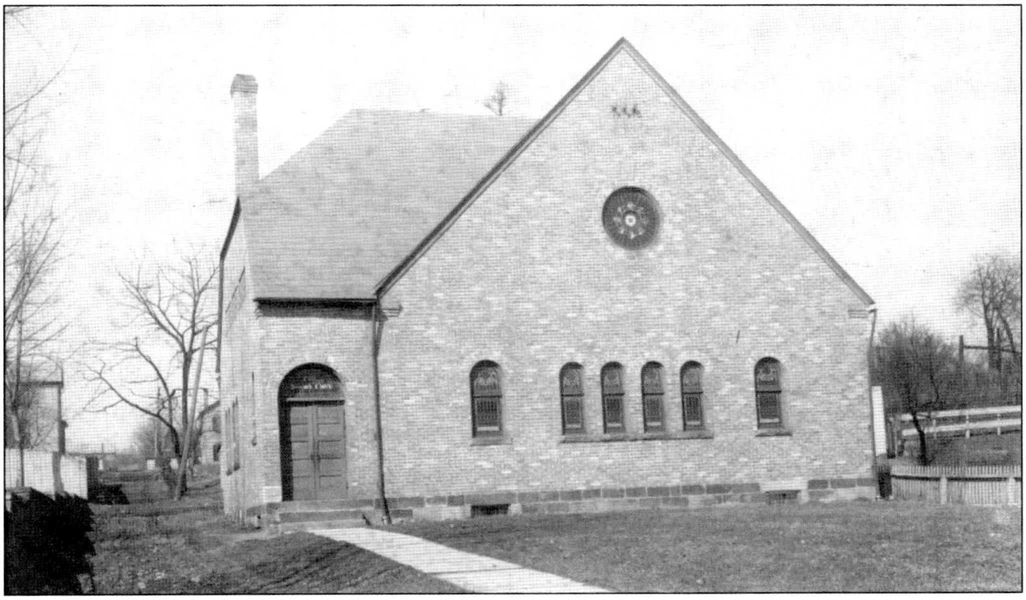

OLD REFORMED CHURCH. This clear photograph depicts the original Reformed church on West Walnut Street, now named West Lincoln Way. Later, it became the American Legion Hall, known to many veterans and their families; today it houses a day care for children. The original structure of the building is still quite evident.

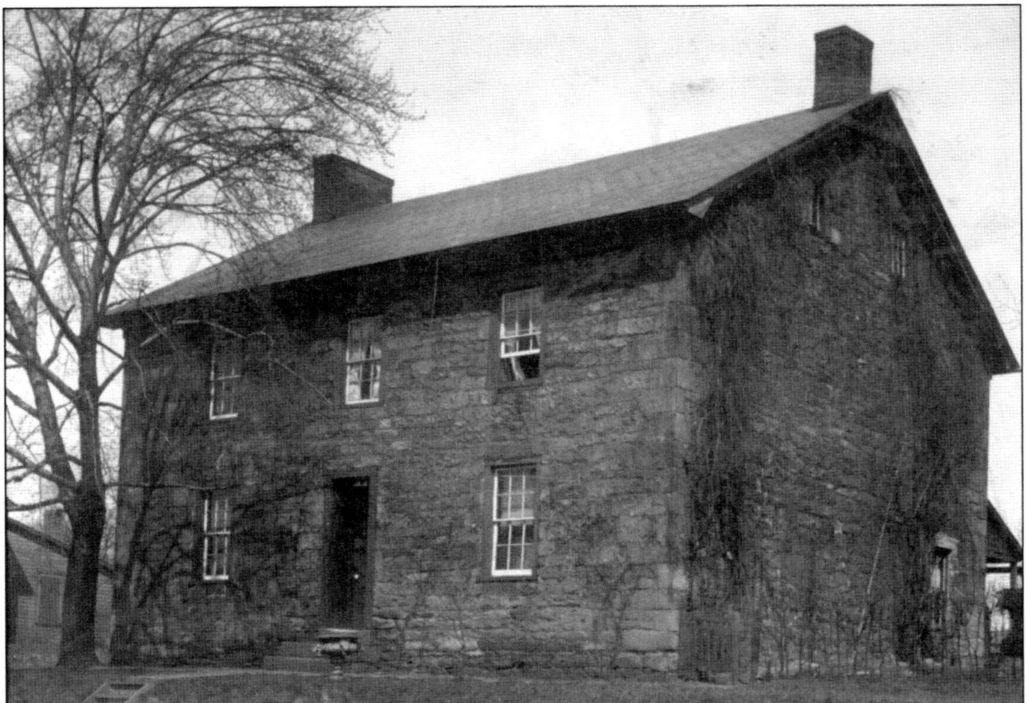

THE OLD JAIL. A necessity for every community, this solid stone building, constructed in 1808, remains at the corner of Chestnut and Beaver Streets. After its service as the village jail ended, it became a family home, distinctive with its powerful block structure. It is said that prisoners were separated by a mere curtain.

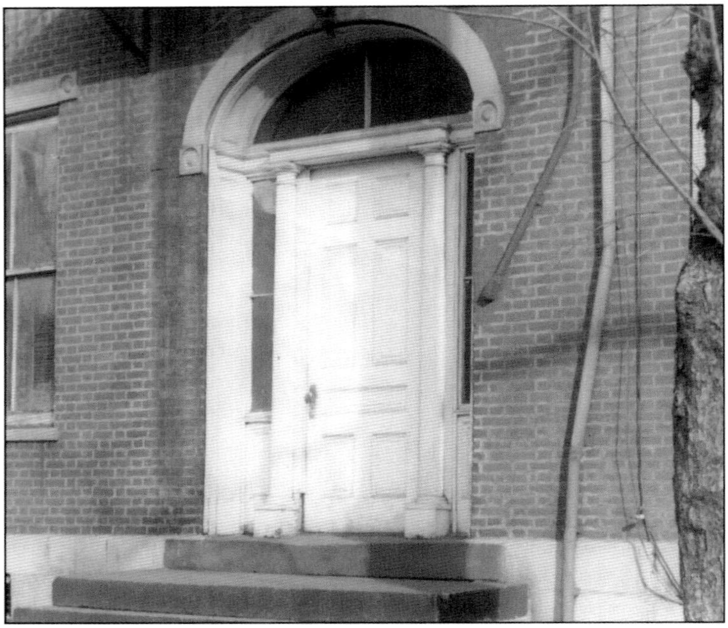

Canal Office Doorway. One of the greatest hopes of the growing village was the potential success of the canal. Chartered in 1828 and completed in 1848, the Sandy and Beaver Canal proved unsuccessful. The old doorway pictured here led to its offices. While that building has burned, remnants of the canal stretch across the countryside just south of Lisbon.

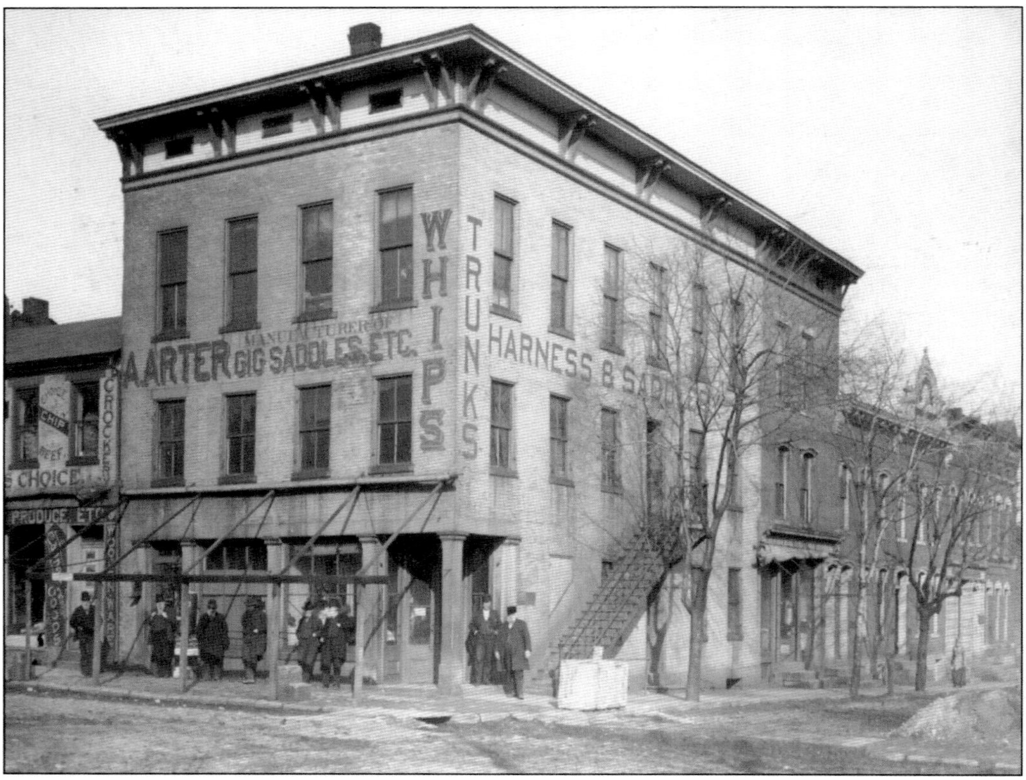

Legendary Arter Building. Originally called the Corner House, this large building was constructed in 1822 by Benjamin Hanna. Known as the birthplace of Marcus A. Hanna, it has had a varied history. Benjamin Hanna used it as his family's residence and the Arter Saddles Company was housed there, but today it serves as an insurance company. With its 20th-century renovation by developer Dean Rose, it is most attractive on the village square.

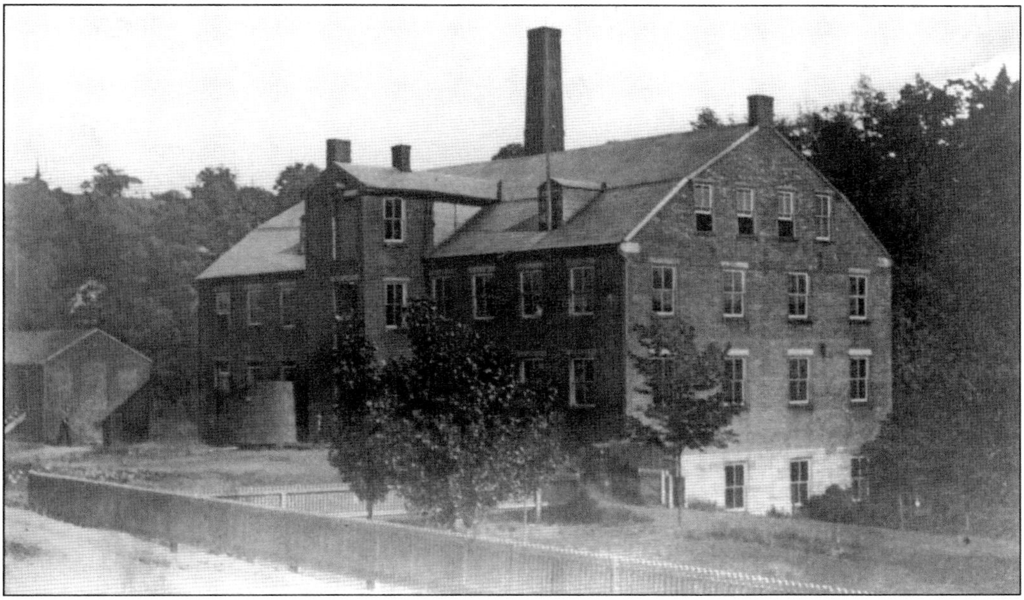

New Lisbon Woolen Mills. As part of the early industry of Lisbon, these woolen mills were built in 1847 by Dr. John McCook and destroyed by fire in 1898. Town founder Lewis Kinney was also the proprietor of a woolen mill. These mills were part of numerous diversified early industries.

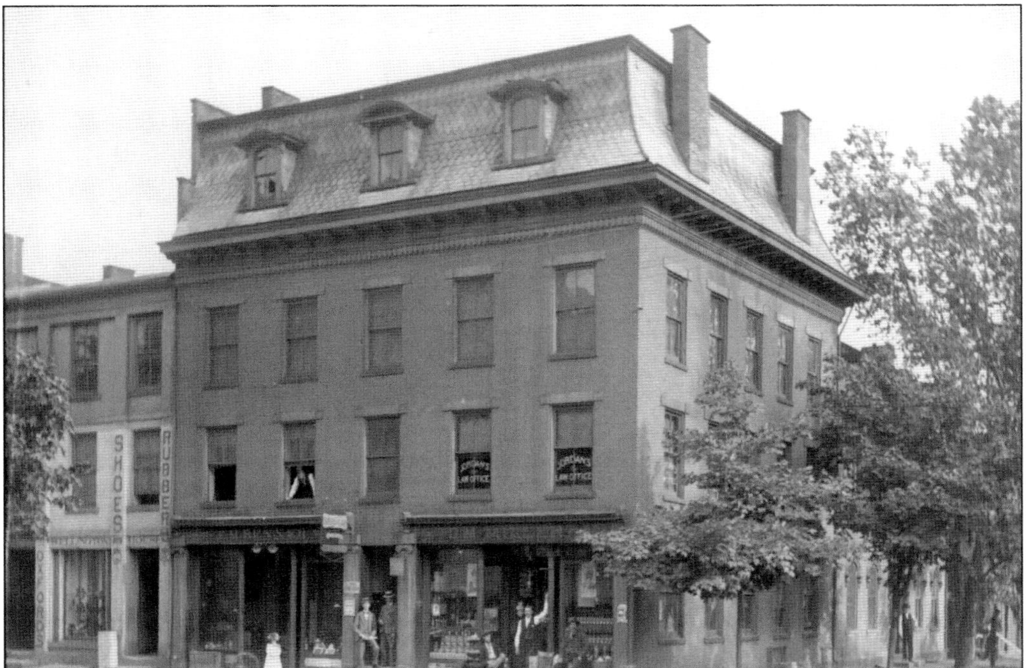

Historic Benner Block. Pictured here is the Benner Block building. Built in 1849, the block housed numerous endeavors, including the Benner Jewelry Store, the D.A. Miller Store, and the Jordan Law Office on the second floor. Over the years, it became the still-central Morgan's Drug Store. Occupying the southeast corner of the village square, it is a true landmark.

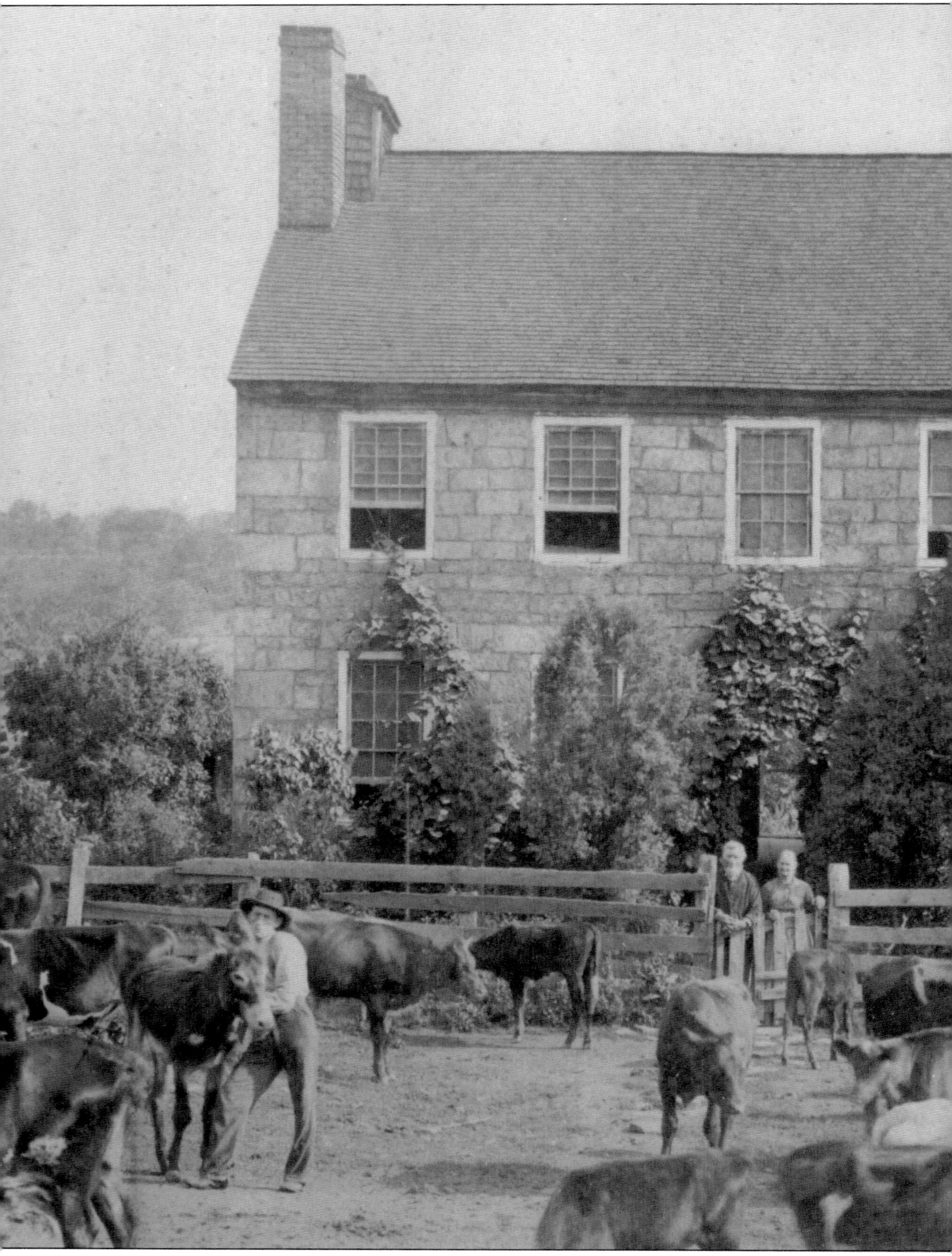

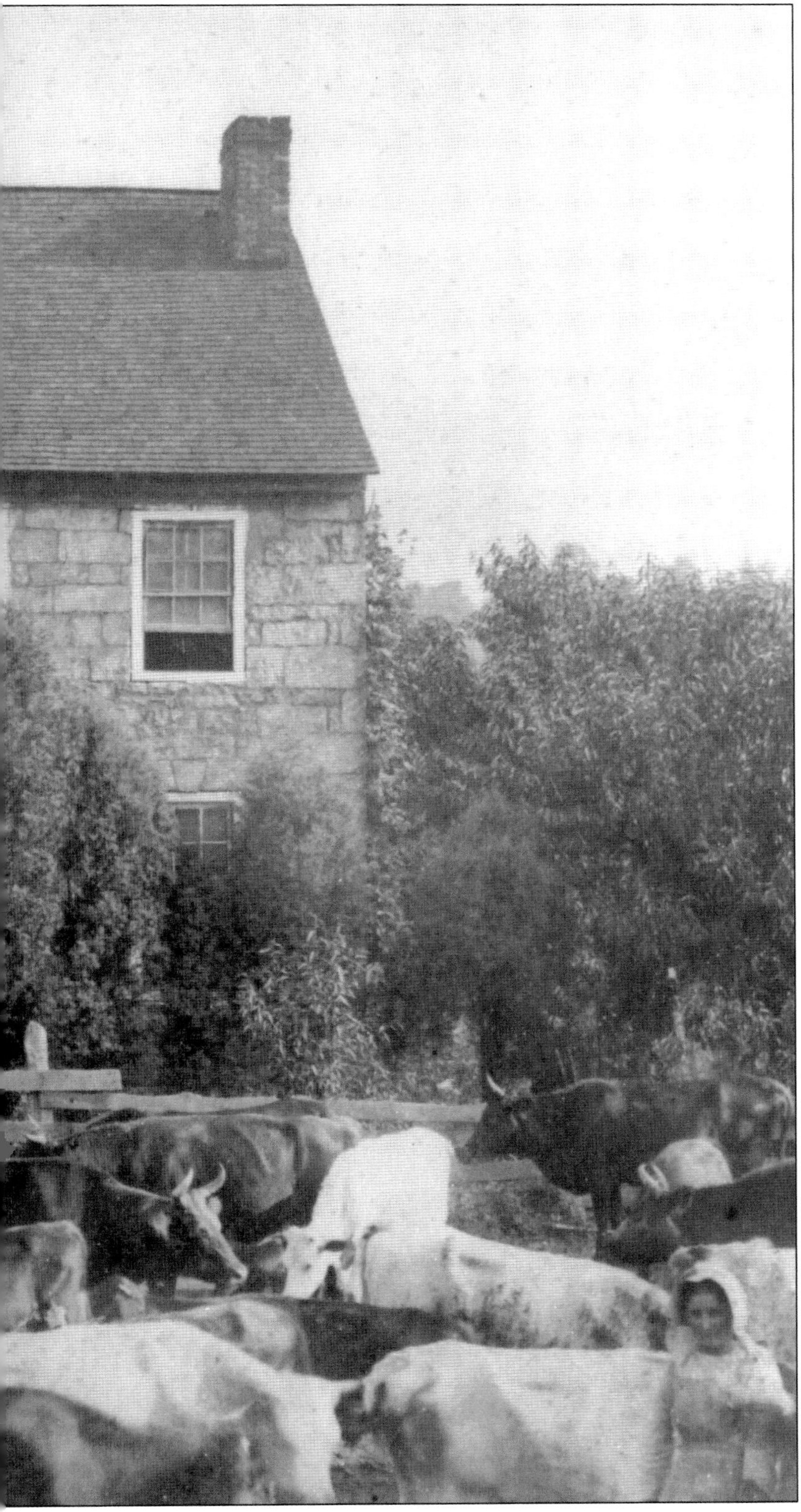

McKinley Home. Depicting and blending are perfect words to describe the McKinley Home, a short distance from the village limits. Pictured here is the definitive stone structure, still a major part of current life. Standing in the gate are Ed and Catherine Broughton, early residents of the home. Clearly linked to the home were James McKinley and his wife, the parents of William McKinley, born in 1807. William married Nancy Allison, and while they resided in Lisbon for some time, they left before their son William, the future president of the United States, was born. The home is a blend as well, since the cows represent the agriculture of the area and the Rebecca Iron Furnace is nearby. Since 1923, the home and surrounding area have been the Boy Scout reservation.

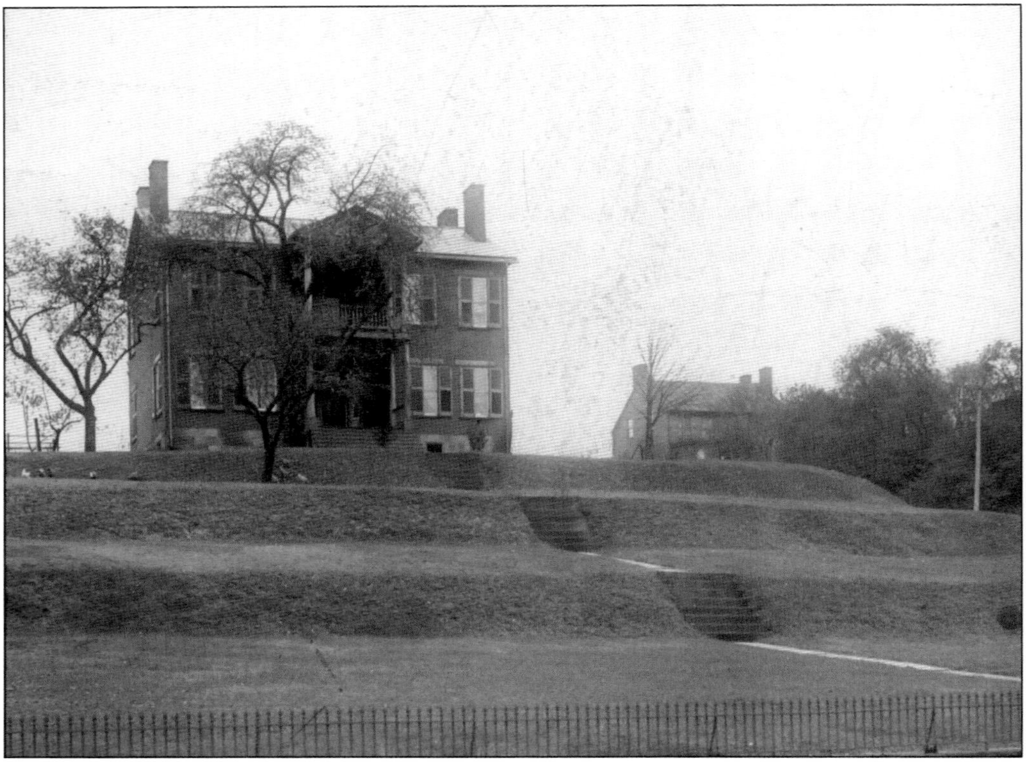

TRADITIONAL LISBON HOME. Joshua Hanna was the original builder of this home that stands on the northwest corner of Chestnut and Jefferson Streets. While it is the location of the Fraternal Order of Eagles today, it holds many memories. Always considered a part of the Underground Railroad, it was the home of R.B. Pritchard and has been a popular spot for sledding with its terraced lawns.

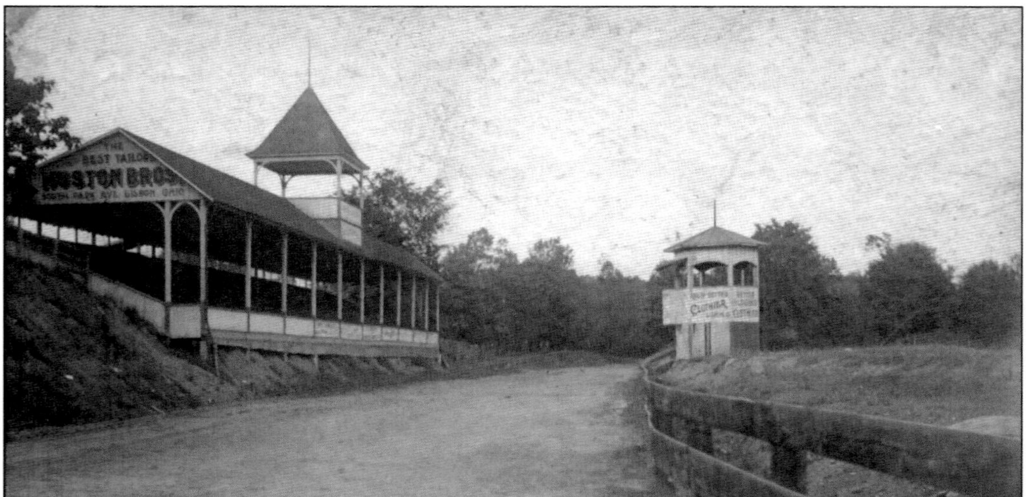

COLUMBIANA COUNTY FAIRGROUNDS. The village's position as county seat provides an important area in the county's fairgrounds. Each year, the summer fair attracts great crowds. The grandstand is a popular gathering place for animal judging, races, and stage entertainment. Recently, the 19th-century grandstand was replaced.

Second Columbiana County Courthouse. The first county courthouse was a log cabin that stood on the site of the present courthouse. The second one, shown here, was built in 1811 with a cornerstone laid in the northwest corner of the square; today the cannon sits there. This building, finished in 1817, was used until the construction of the current structure.

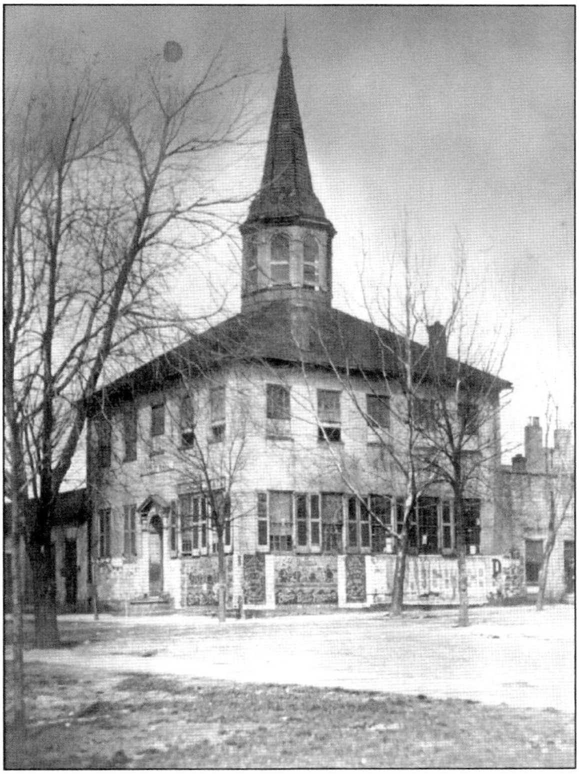

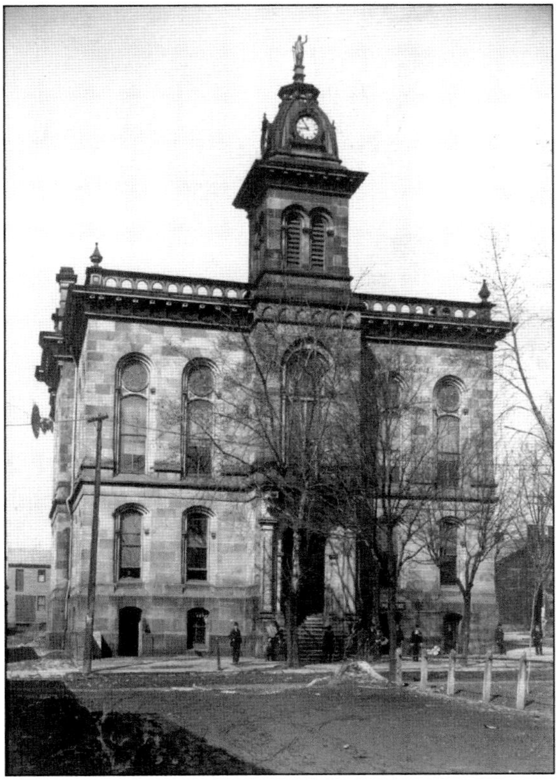

The Current Columbiana County Courthouse. The Columbiana County Courthouse, built in 1871, was constructed of native sandstone at a cost of $150,000—including furniture. It was expanded in 1934. The building continues to be a landmark, consuming the fourth quadrant of the village square while the other three are given to the central green area.

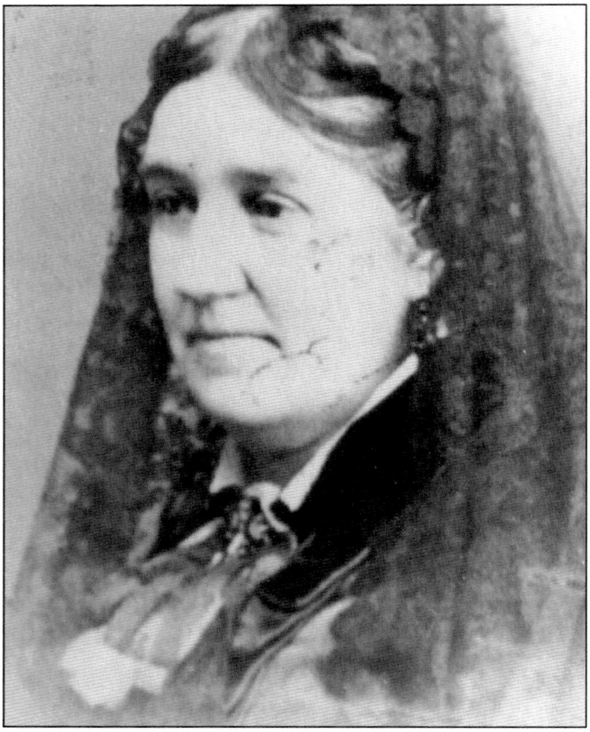

Virginia Cornwell Lepper. In the interests of memorials and cultural opportunities, Virginia Lepper gave the community its library. An earlier member of her husband's family established the first newspaper in the county, the *Ohio Patriot*, first in German and later in English. She carried on the literary tradition by establishing the library in memory of her husband.

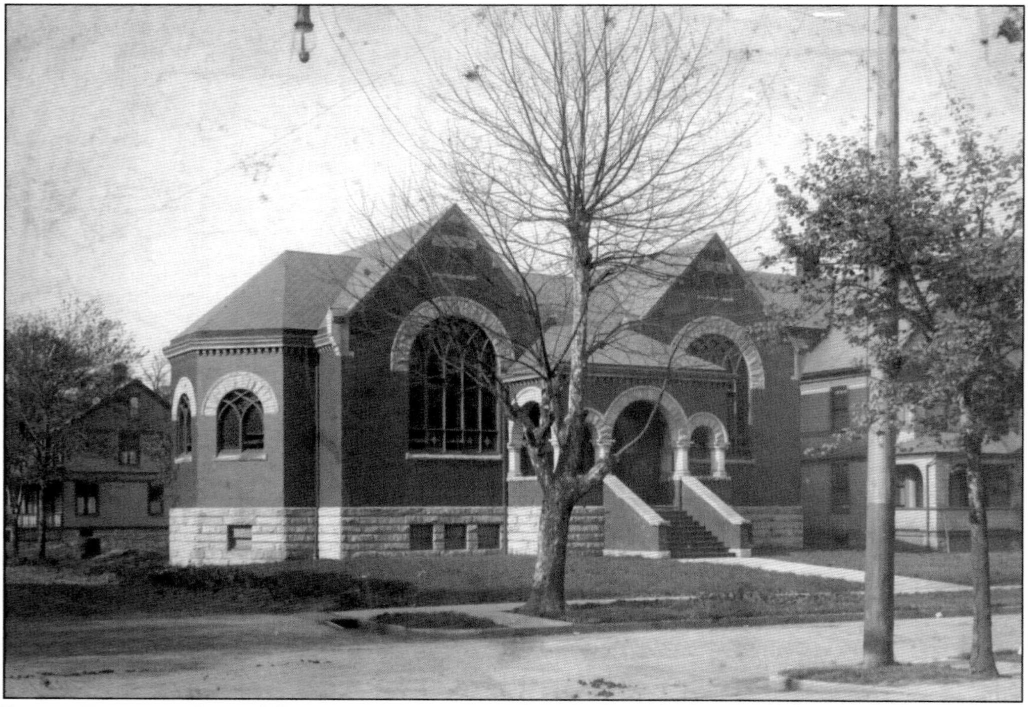

Lepper Library. One of the most picturesque buildings in the community, the library stands at the northeast corner of Vine Street and East Lincoln Way. Modeled upon an English country church, the building, with its great use by community and county, including the bookmobile, has experienced two major additions since its 1897 construction.

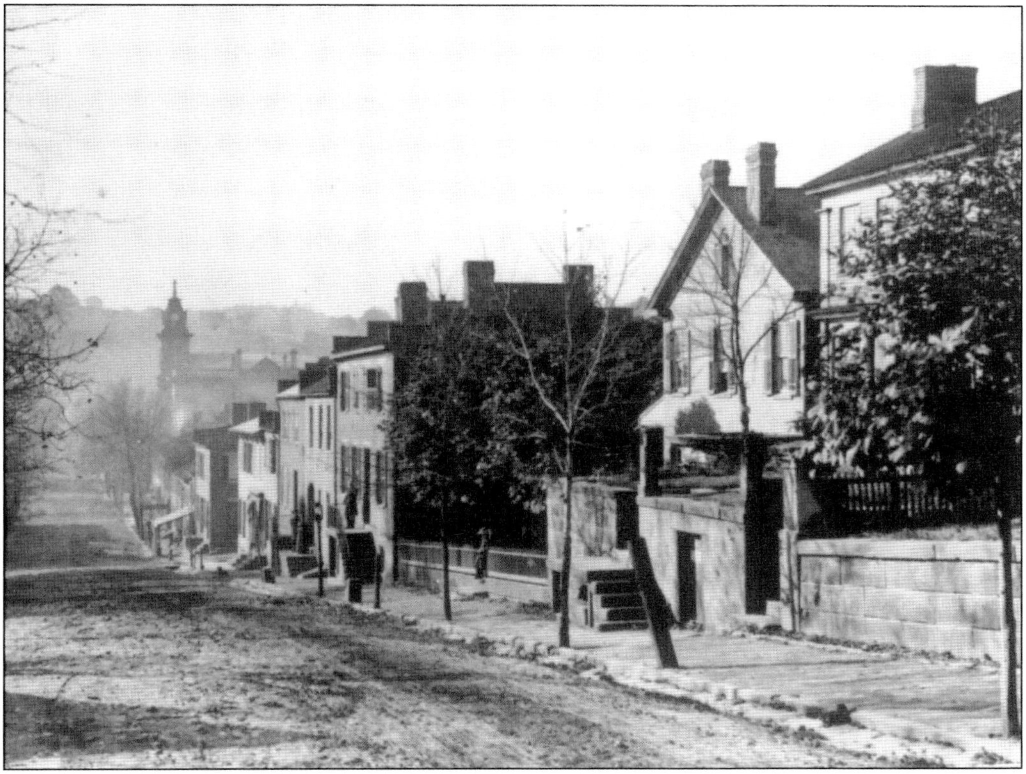

View of North Market Street. This 19th-century view of North Market Street gives a perspective on the growing village with its rows of buildings, brick walls, and old houses. The present courthouse stands tall in the southern distance, much as it does today, although all of the homes pictured are gone.

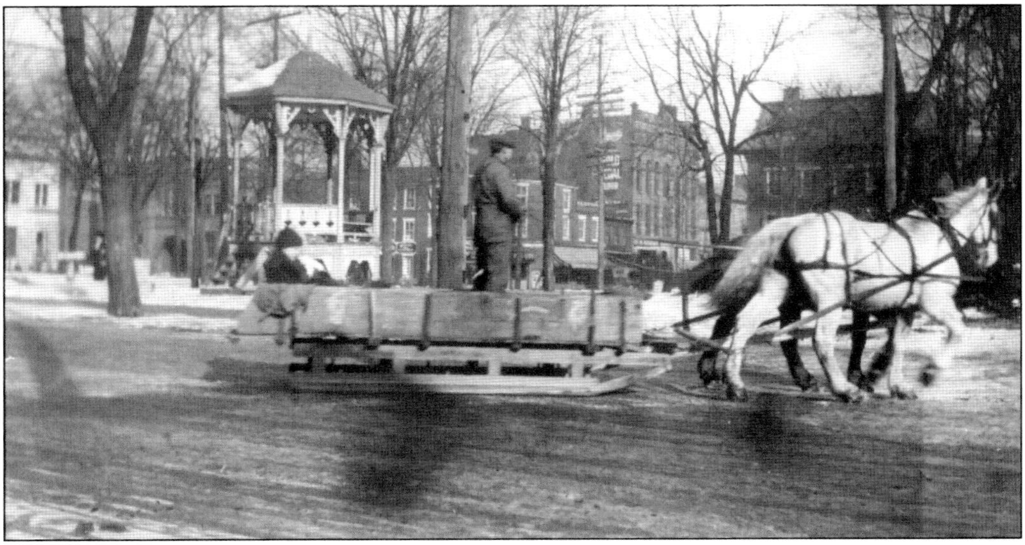

Village Square in 1900. Although the first century was concluding and the name was now Lisbon, the square was an interesting blend of familiar buildings, the old gazebo, and the horse-drawn sleigh. The hitching rail still bordered the park at that time. Some of the buildings shown on the distant right continue in daily use.

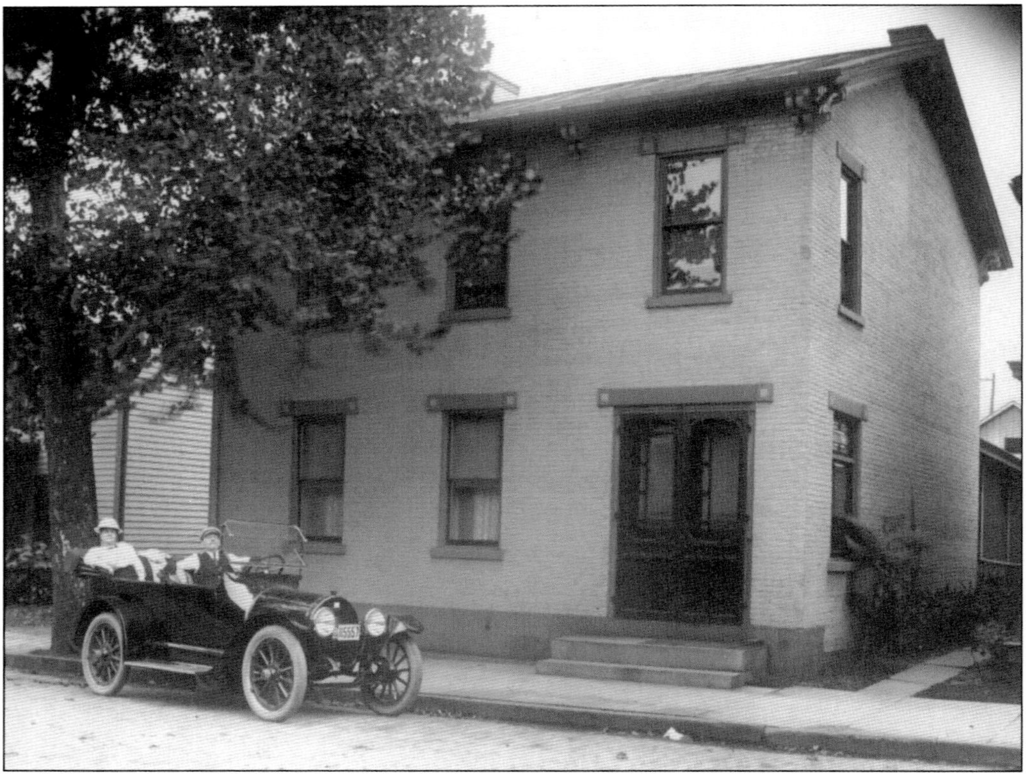

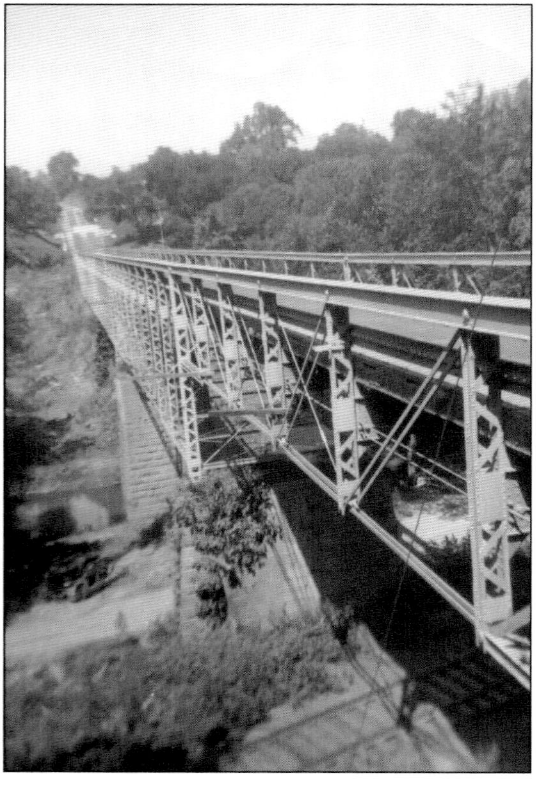

TURN OF THE CENTURY. As Lisbon progressed into the 20th century, the town possessed a new name and the main east-west street, called Walnut, had become Lincoln Way, part of the Route 30 Highway system. Soon cars would be replacing the familiar horse and buggy, but the traditional buildings would survive for many years. Mr. and Mrs. John Holton are pictured here in their horseless carriage.

OLD CANTON BRIDGE. Leaving the community via one of its steepest hills, the valley is spanned by the well-known Old Canton Bridge. The structure, replaced years ago, is a strong span over the valley that provides a home for the local park, Willow Grove, as well as the much-used Greenway bicycle trail.

Two

Economic Support

Obviously, every community needs an economic base, and New Lisbon was no exception. In the historical records of the 19th century, the diversity and number of businesses and industries is amazing. Early on, the emphasis was upon providing for local needs. Mary Firestone wrote of the early endeavors in her sesquicentennial history. The Indians in the surrounding area traded with the local citizens as well as provided hides for tanning in the numerous local tanneries. Best known were those of John Arter and Daniel Harbaugh. Blacksmithing was a critical need. The brickyard was an important early industry, and a pottery came along shortly afterwards. Natural resources promoted these enterprises along with the beginnings of the iron industry. The best known among the furnaces graced the McKinley Homestead with the name of Rebecca of New Lisbon for Gideon Hughes's wife. Industry was obviously stretching beyond the daily needs.

However, there was the continuing mission to supply each and every need of local residents. Clothing stores, shoemakers, hatters, drugstores, and grocers came into being. Notions and essentials came from a Mr. Gailey's store while a real luxury could be purchased from a manufacturer of pianos and organs. Financial needs were met with the earliest banks begun by the Firestones and the Hepburns. And final needs were met by the establishment of Erastus Eells's funeral home.

Into the 20th century, a great range of industries continued and flourished. Well known were R. Thomas Pottery, Wright Manufacturing, the tin mill, the copper company, feed mills, and insurance companies. Lisbon has been known as the home of the cash register and the soda straw. Lisbon Salesbook and Chester Hoist became important names in industry.

And the natural resources were surely developed in the advent of many mining companies. Early mining was from deep mines, and strip mining was very important in the 20th century. Familiar names in the business included Meek Coal Co., Miller Coal Co., East Fairfield Coal Co., and Industrial Mining and Engineering. In the 21st century, there are still major companies manufacturing hoists, patterns, and dog food. And the natural resources of shale oil and gas have evolved.

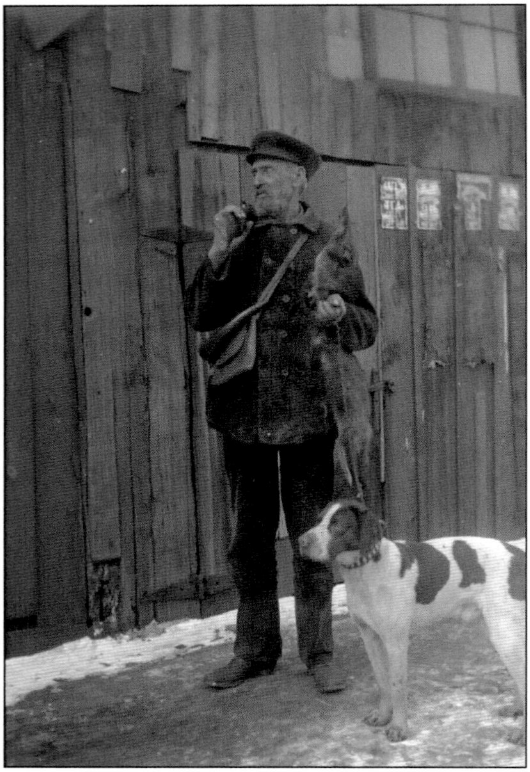

THE FOX HUNTER. With the woods and fields around the community, hunting remained an important part of local life. To this day, hunting remains a popular sport, if not the provision of necessary food. Pictured here is John Cleckner, age 86, posed with his hunting dog and his prey, a fox. The man, known for his storytelling, is seen standing in front of Richardson's Blacksmith Shop, an important part of the community in the time before automobiles.

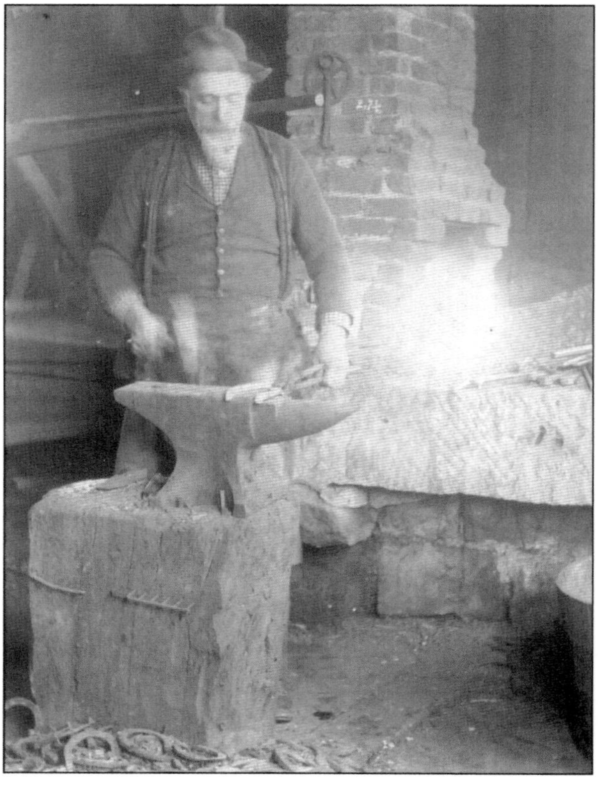

TRADITIONAL BLACKSMITH SHOP. Shawke is an important name among local blacksmiths, with four generations in the family business. This smithy, although unnamed, illustrates well the serious work that they performed in a community filled with owners of horses. An age of such craftsmen passed with the times.

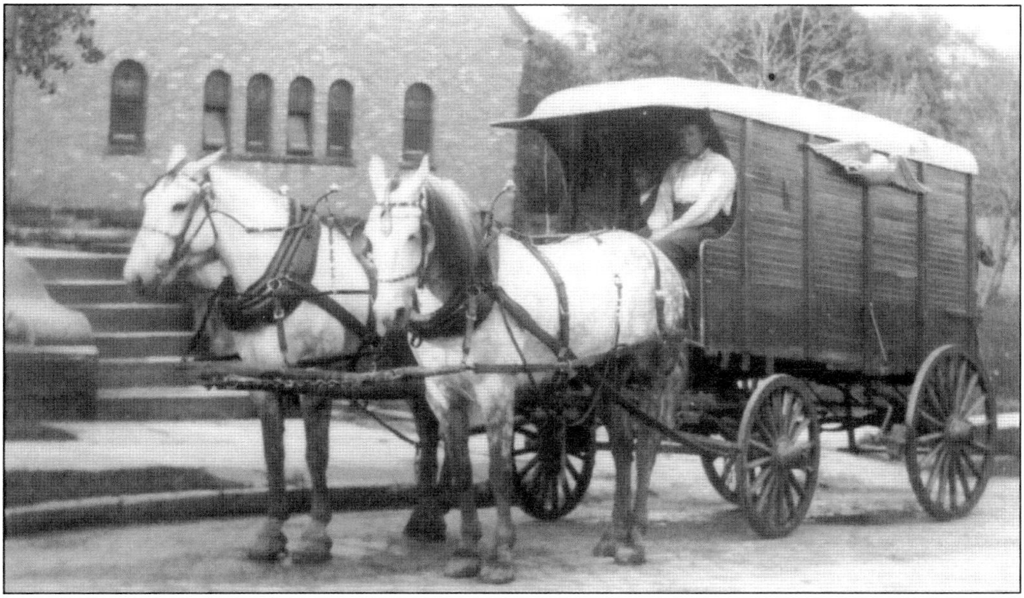

EARLY ICE WAGON. In the time before electricity, refrigeration, and other modern conveniences, the ice wagon was a vital part of daily life. Horse-drawn, this wagon passes in front of the old Reformed church, long before its conversion to the American Legion Hall after World War I. The horses, too, were replaced with a truck as the automobile age began.

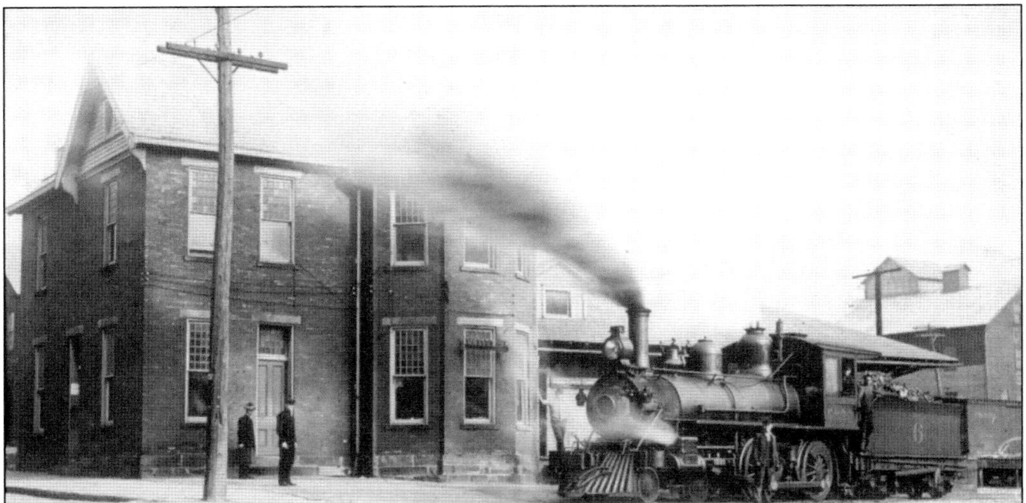

OLD UNION DEPOT. The trains passed through the community to a limited degree. This building on the south end of town, South Market Street, served as a train depot, then as office space, and finally as a community building, with the beautiful restoration sponsored by county engineer Bert Dawson. On the outside is provision for those about to embark on the bicycle trail.

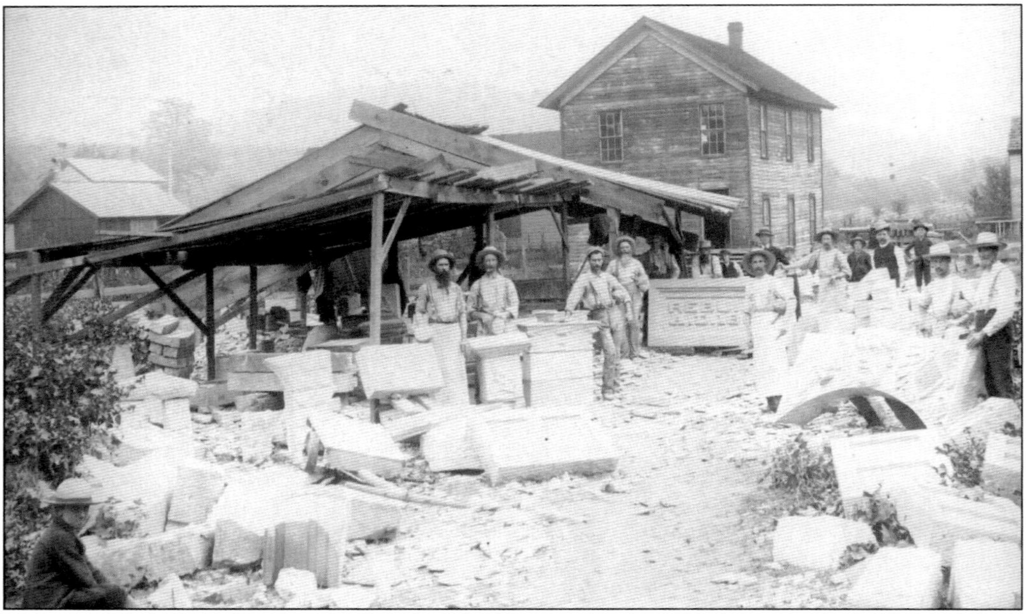

CRAFTSMEN CUTTING STONE. Craftsmen of the 19th century were skilled in their work. Ern King designed the stone, and George Force was in charge of this specific operation happening on North Vine Street on Harbaugh property, designed for the construction of the Masonic building. While the stonework property is filled with homes today, the well-crafted edifice still stands on East Lincoln Way.

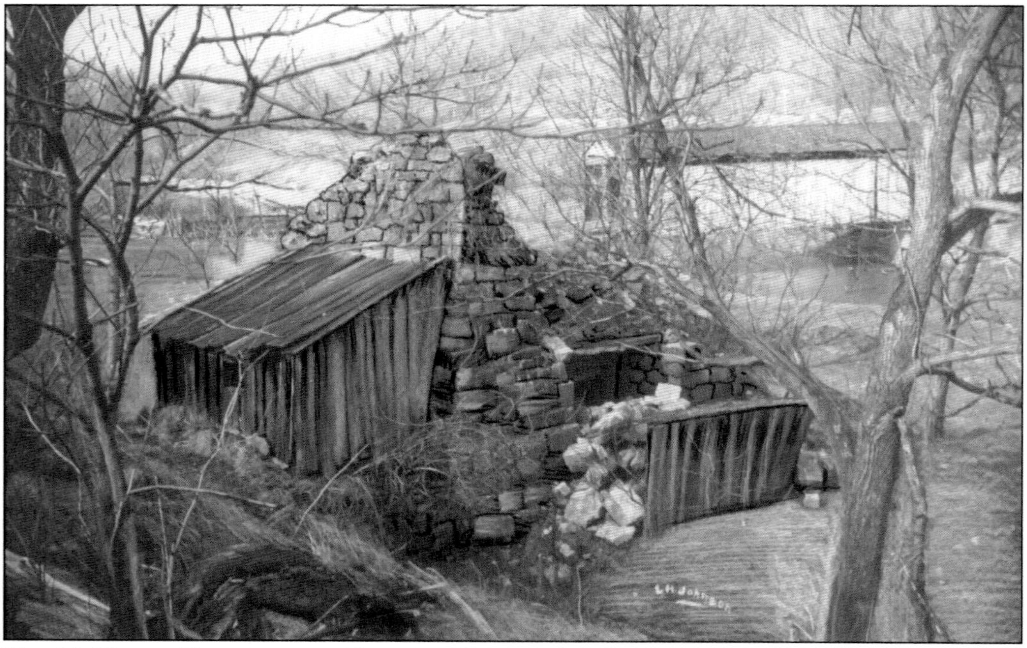

THE MCKINLEY FURNACE, THE REBECCA. From early times, iron manufacture in furnaces was an important part of the local economy. This old furnace was part of the McKinley Homestead; remnants still stand today. Various practical items were produced, and the industry spawned several other small manufacturing businesses. A covered bridge spans the Little Beaver Creek in the background.

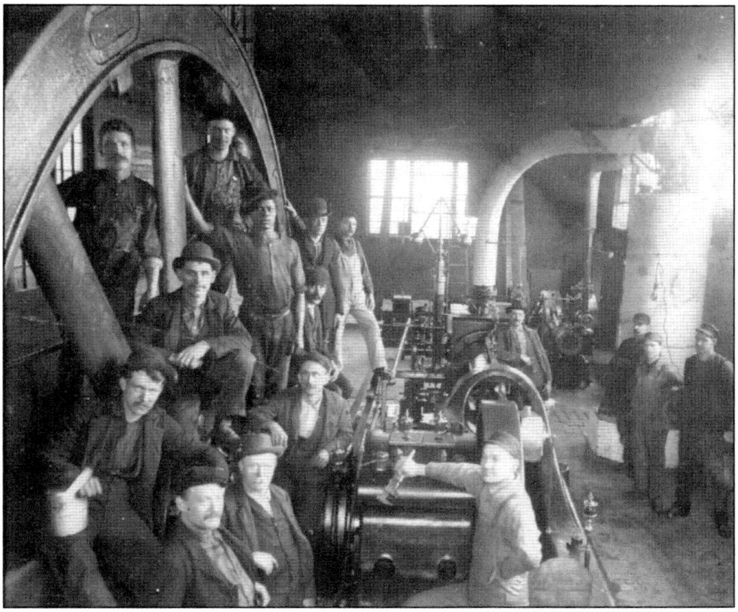

Tin Mill, 1890s. Another early manufacturing company was the tin mill, later known as National Brass and Copper. Workers shown here include, in no particular order, Dick McGee, Wes McCord, Bill Geller, Tim Collins, K.V. Reed, Joe Cox, a Mr. Robinson, Henry Hollinger, Phil Jones, and Lou McGee.

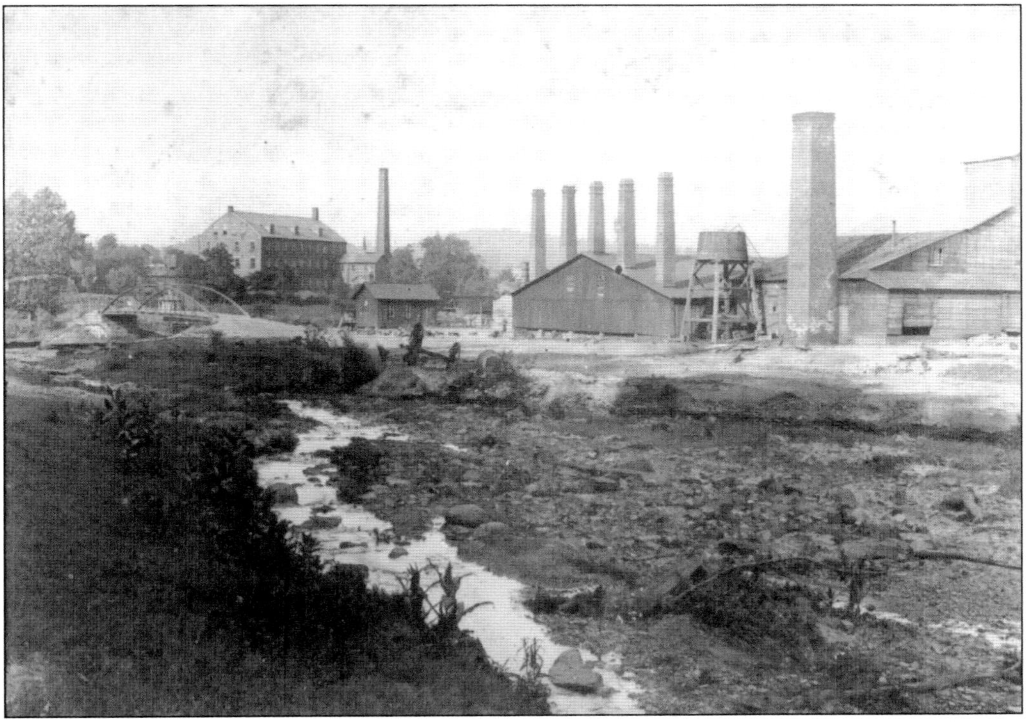

Old Brickyard. The Morrow Brick Yard, begun in the 1840s, was a project of two well-known names: Henry Morrow and Jacob Harbaugh. In this photograph, the buildings stand where the bricks were carefully made by hand, giving the operation a good name for its quality work. The plant was in operation from its founding until the 1890s. H.W. Morrow is also known for his involvement in the invention of the soda straw.

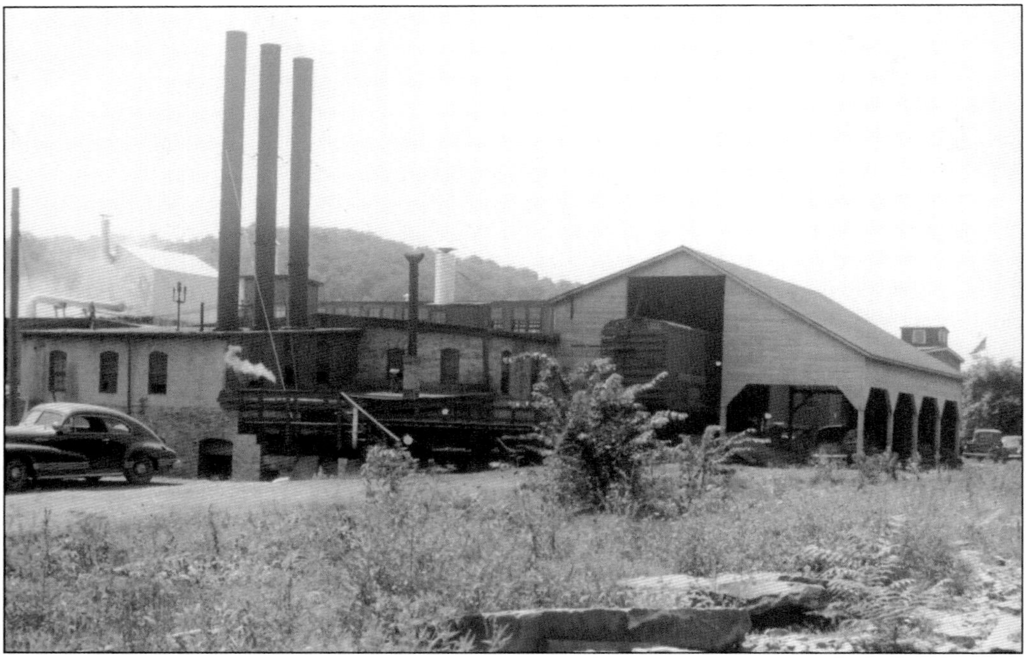

R. Thomas & Sons Co. A well-remembered company in Lisbon is the pottery known familiarly as R. Thomas. With the business originally coming from East Liverpool, the first product was dinnerware. In time, the entire company moved its operations to East Washington Street in Lisbon, where it remained until its sale to H.K. Porter & Co. and eventual removal from the village.

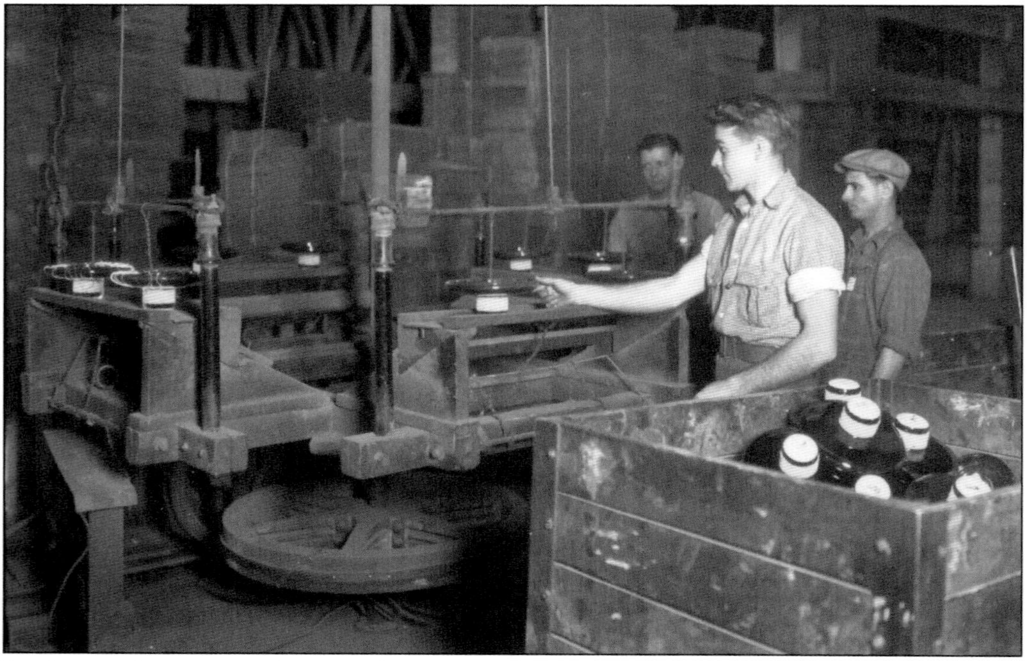

R. Thomas Insulators. In time, the company became well known for its porcelain insulators. George Westinghouse came to Lisbon to establish a national insulator contract for the internationally known product. Management personnel, who became part of Lisbon citizenry, were largely descendants of the original Richard Thomas.

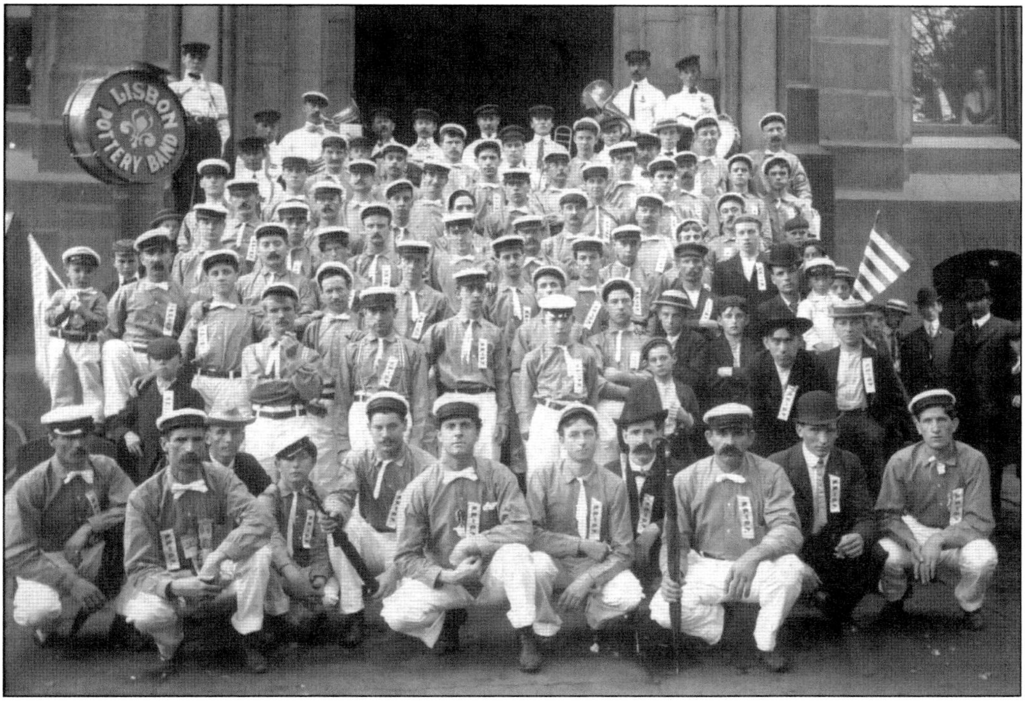

R. Thomas Pottery Band. An important benefit of R. Thomas employment was the opportunity to share in numerous activities. The Pottery Band, pictured here on the courthouse steps, included Oscar Altodefer, Jack Bevans, Claude Albright, Lou McGee, Charles Allcorn, Walter Brown, Fred Bowman, Bob Piero, Del Gilbert, Ern King, "Little Buck" Wilson, "Pop" Challis, and Ad Albright.

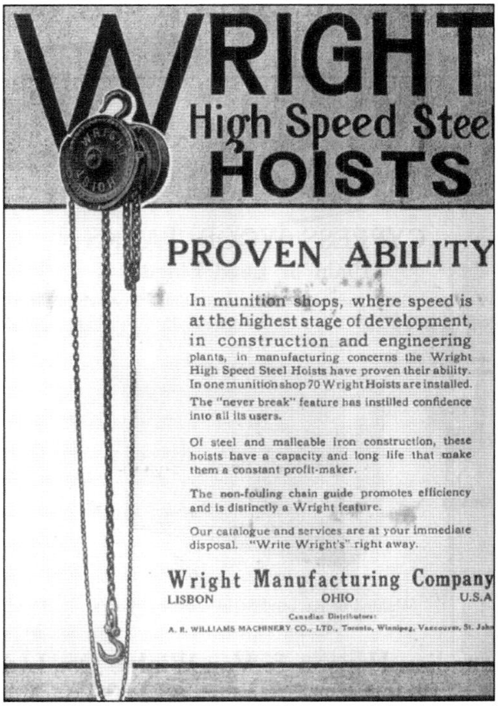

Wright Manufacturing. Diverse in their manufacturing endeavors, the Wright family operated several businesses, including service as a World War II supplier of machine gun parts. Employing 200 workers at one time, the three brothers, Hal, Charles, and William, carried on the family tradition begun by their grandfather and father. This hoist advertisement depicts their business efforts. (Courtesy of Kenneth Everett.)

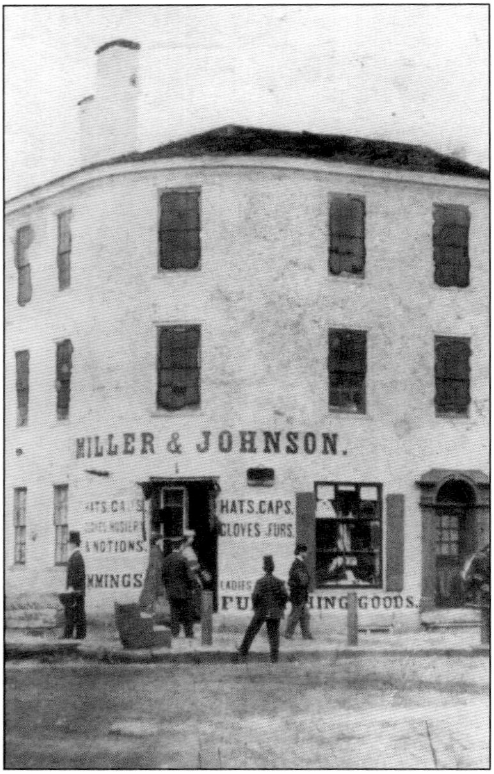

THE ROUND CORNER. The Round Corner is a local landmark. At one time, the slogan was "Always a square deal at the Round Corner." Housing many businesses over the years since it was built in 1817, it is shown here as Miller and Johnson during the Civil War era. Then, as in years to come, it is obviously a clothing store. Today, the building is undergoing serious restoration by owner James Smith and houses a Subway restaurant.

THE SANDY BEAVER CANAL BUILDING. This Lincoln Way structure has had a varied history. Not only did it house the offices of the Sandy Beaver Canal, but also many stores—from clothing to groceries—over the years. At one time, Camille Firestone taught piano in the large apartment in the rear of the first floor. At the time of the fire that destroyed the building, it was home to Hiner's Ice Cream Shoppe.

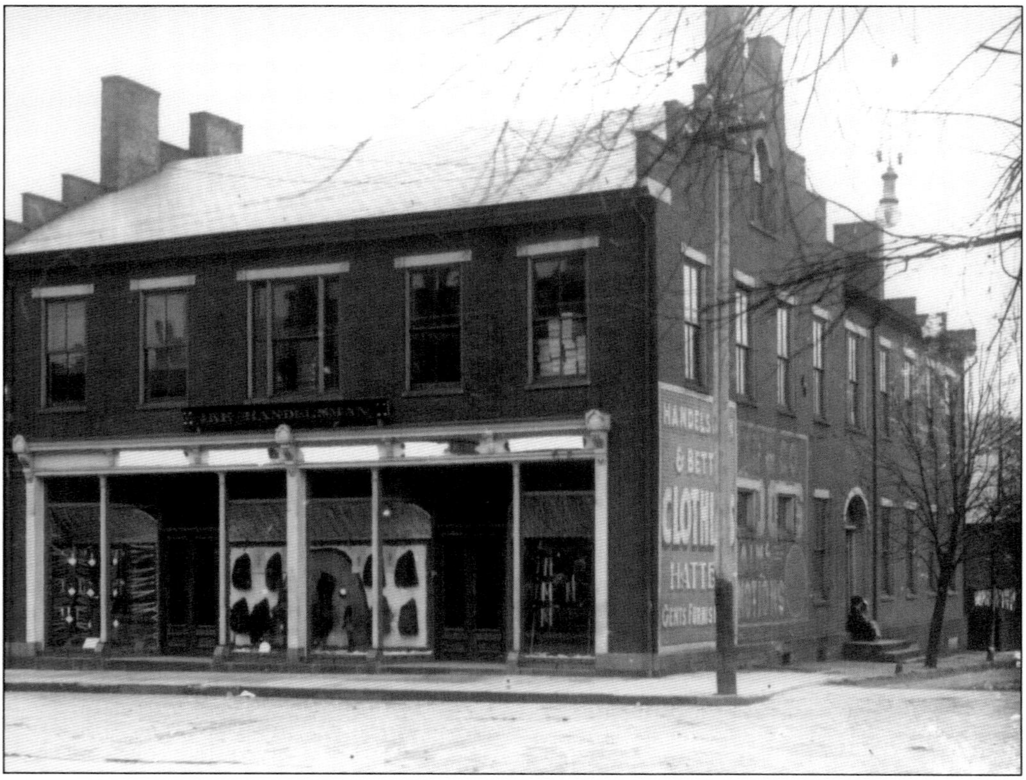

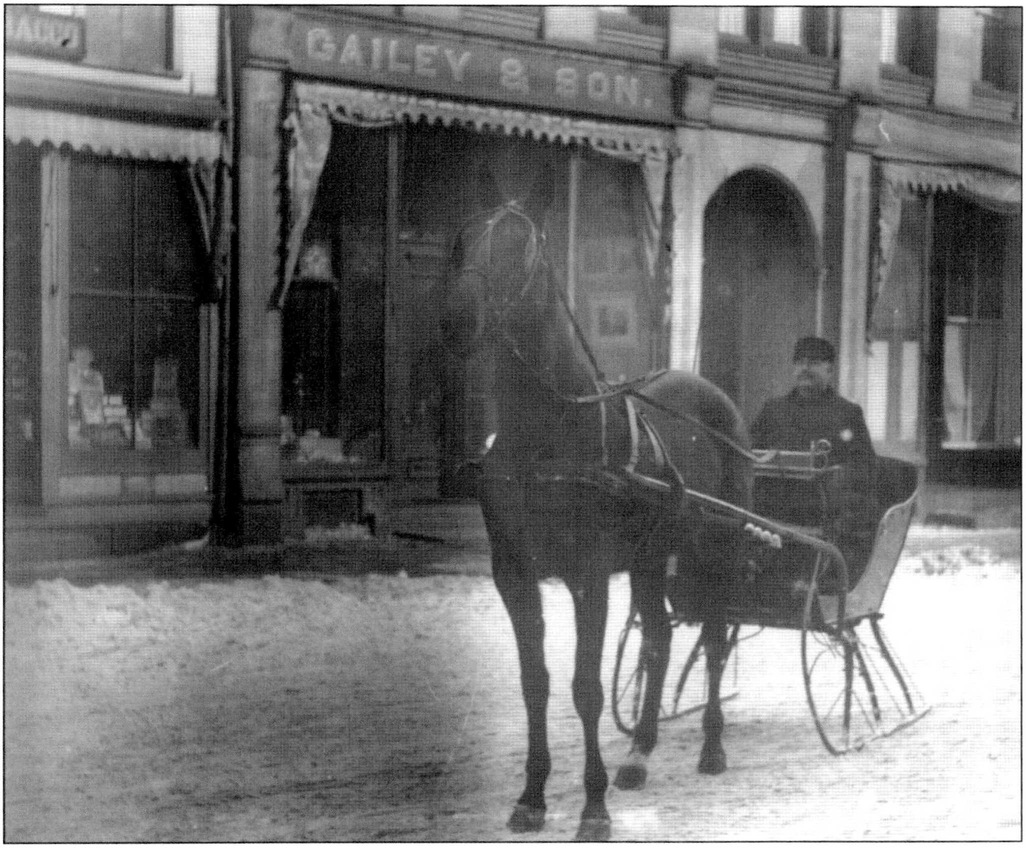

The Gailey Tradition. A Mr. Gailey's store and Victorian home were an important part of early Lisbon. The early merchant, pictured here in his sleigh, owned a store with many special artistic effects that was well patronized. Patrons were especially fascinated by the art gallery that Gailey maintained in his business.

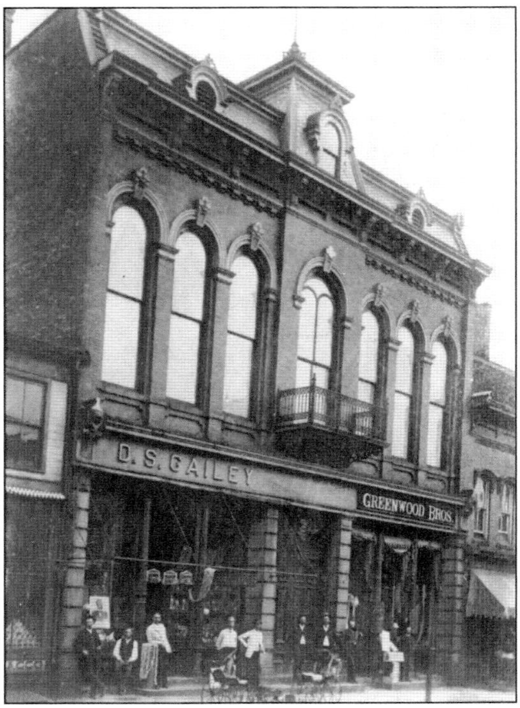

The Gailey-Firestone Building. After this building, the old opera house, burned, a large new edifice was constructed on the site. Containing shops on the first floor, the second and third floors housed the Masonic order until recently. The building is very finely crafted.

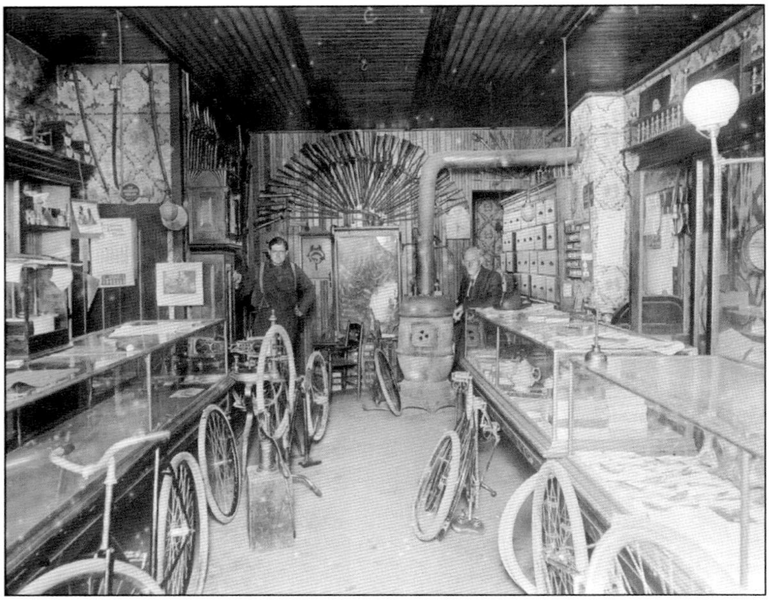

Corbett's Bicycle Shop. Popular both before and after the advent of the automobile, bicycles were an important part of American culture, including the community of Lisbon. Shown in Corbett's shop with its inventory are Will Corbett (left) and W.F. Kemble (right). Today, bicycles are still sold in the community, appearing regularly on the Greenway Bicycle Trail.

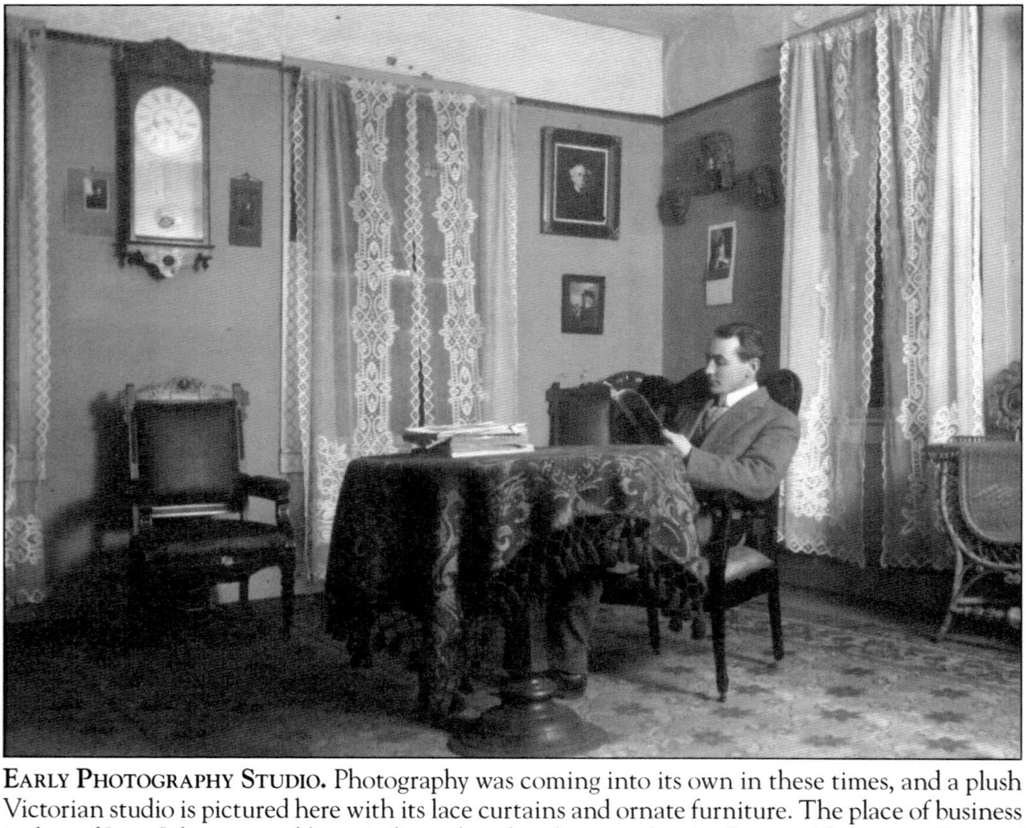

Early Photography Studio. Photography was coming into its own in these times, and a plush Victorian studio is pictured here with its lace curtains and ornate furniture. The place of business is that of Lem Johnson, and he is indicated as the photographer in that establishment. Some of his work is still in circulation.

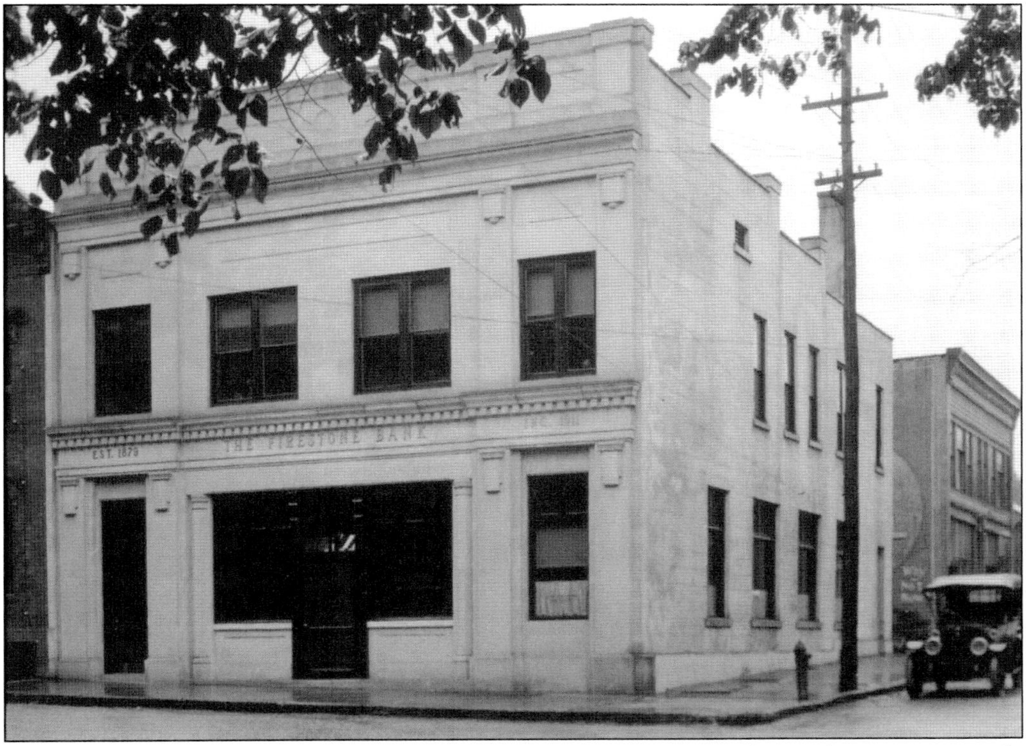

EARLY BANKING IN LISBON. One of the earliest continuous banks in Lisbon is the Firestone Bank, now part of Huntington Banking System, but it retains its early site and name. Begun in 1879 by S.J. and D.W. Firestone, it has stood on the same corner since 1883. Several generations of the Firestone family assumed the presidency over the years, including Ross W. and Leland Starr Firestone, followed by Haifley descendants.

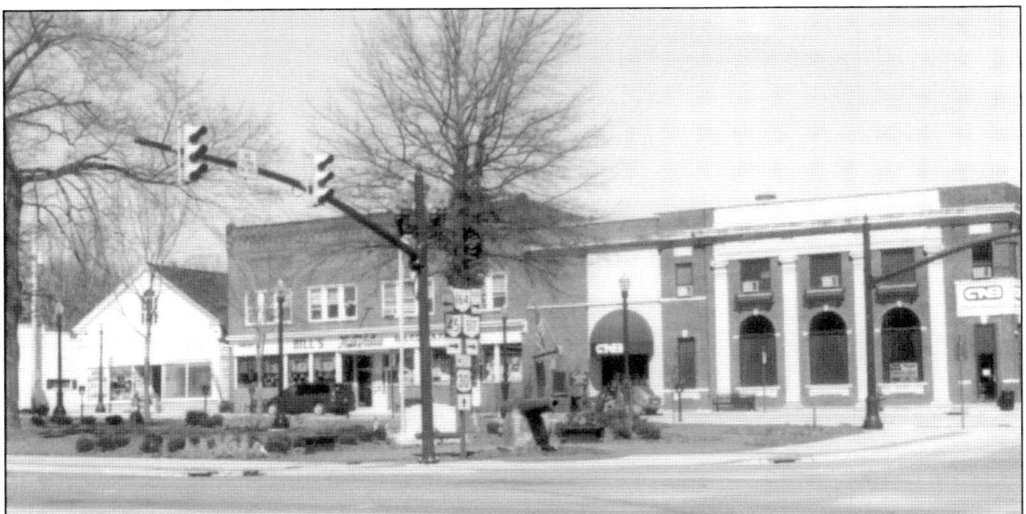

MORE BANKING COMPANIES. In 1908, the People's State Bank, shown at right, was organized by W.H. Hepburn. It was called Will Hepburn's bank at that time; his son Dallas continued in the role of bank president. Shortly after Dallas's sudden death, the bank became a part of the Farmer's National Bank of Salem. Today, the building houses the county's law library.

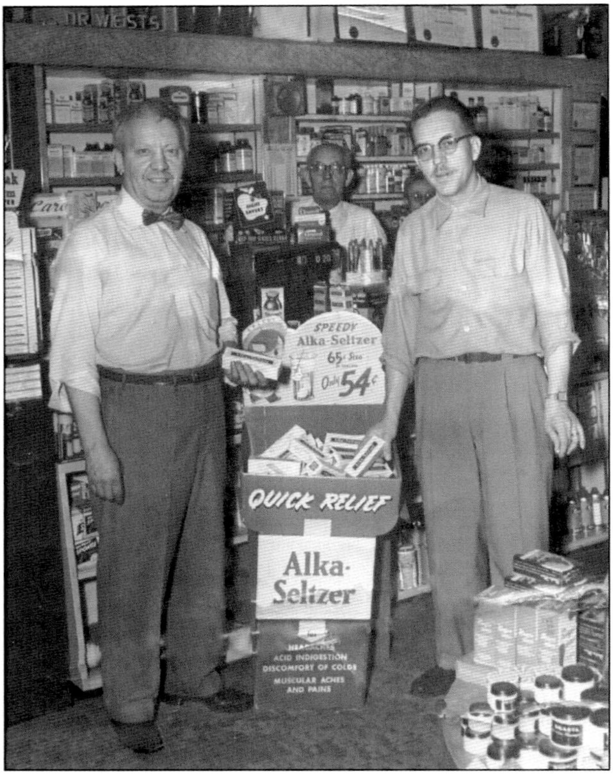

Early Lisbon Pharmacies. Numerous pharmacies and pharmacists were part of the Lisbon scene from early in the community's history. The name Nace is long associated with a North Market Drug Store, and these three pharmacists, from left to right, Felix Butch, William Morgan Sr., and William Morgan Jr., are seen working in Morgan's in the Benner Block.

Hamilton's Drug Store. Long a part of the community in the oldest brick building in the State of Ohio, Hamilton's Drug Store was founded by Martin Helman in 1806. It is known as the site of the first soda fountain in Ohio. Passing through various owners, it evolved into Hamilton's Drug Store and was sold to pharmacist Adam Rudibaugh in 1926. With the Rexall franchise, it was very well stocked.

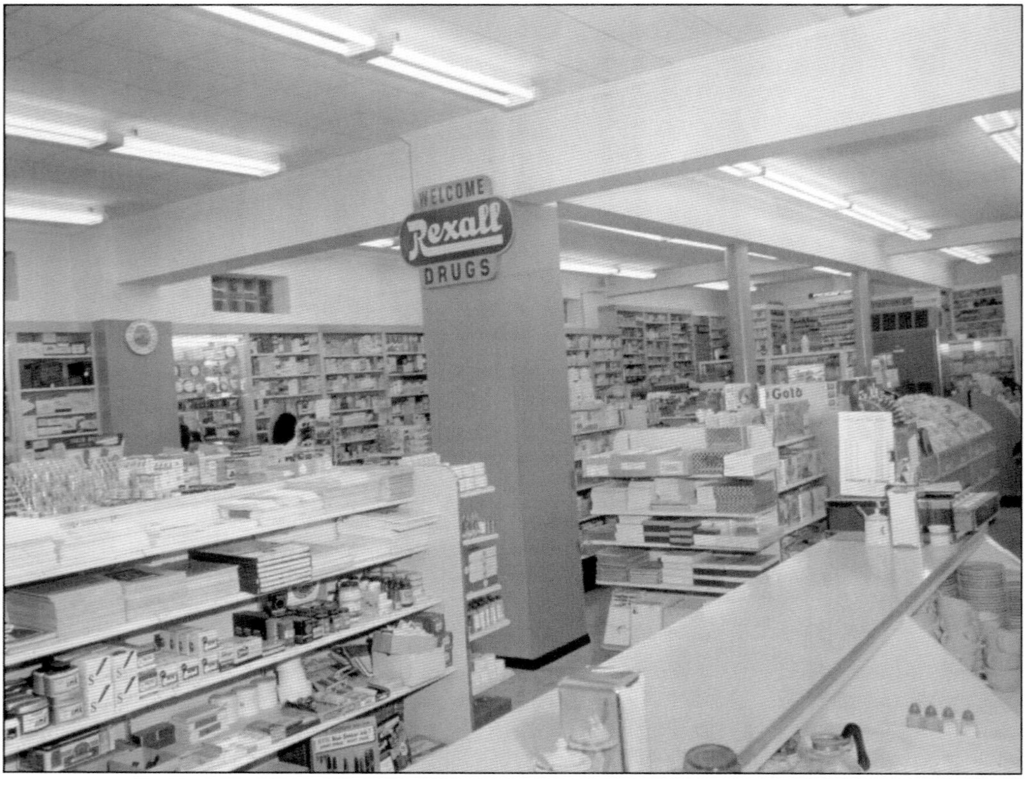

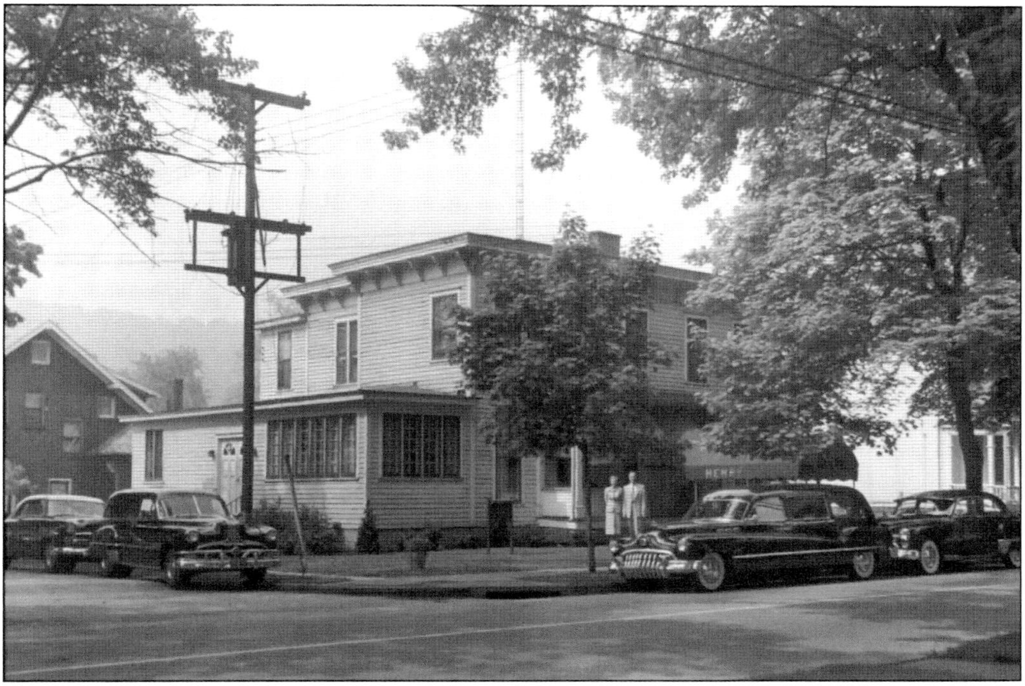

Henry Funeral Home. Founded by Frank and Ruth Henry in 1935, this funeral home still operates as Weber Funeral Home on East Lincoln Way. Pictured here is the original building with the founders, the Henrys. It was purchased in 1971 by Dan Weber, a licensed funeral director; since 2002, the establishment has been owned and operated by his son Gregg Weber, who continues the Weber name, licensure, and traditions. (Courtesy of Gregg Weber.)

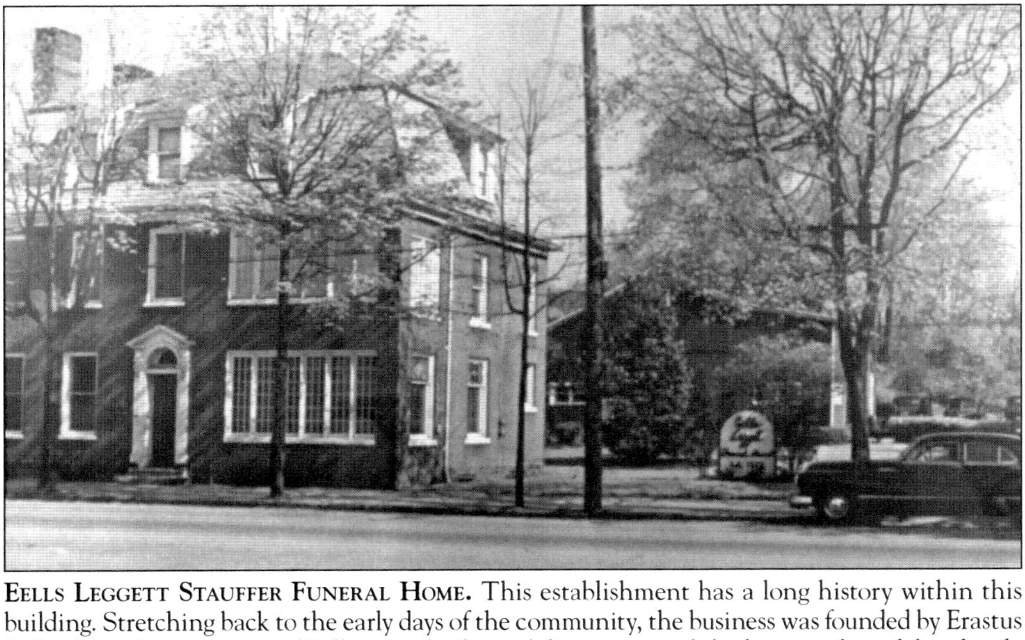

Eells Leggett Stauffer Funeral Home. This establishment has a long history within this building. Stretching back to the early days of the community, the business was founded by Erastus Eells. Several generations of Eells were the funeral directors, until the last member of that family was gone. In 1947, Robert Leggett and his son Lynn became the licensed owners; now the company is the mortuary establishment of Charles and Stacey Stauffer, both licensed funeral directors.

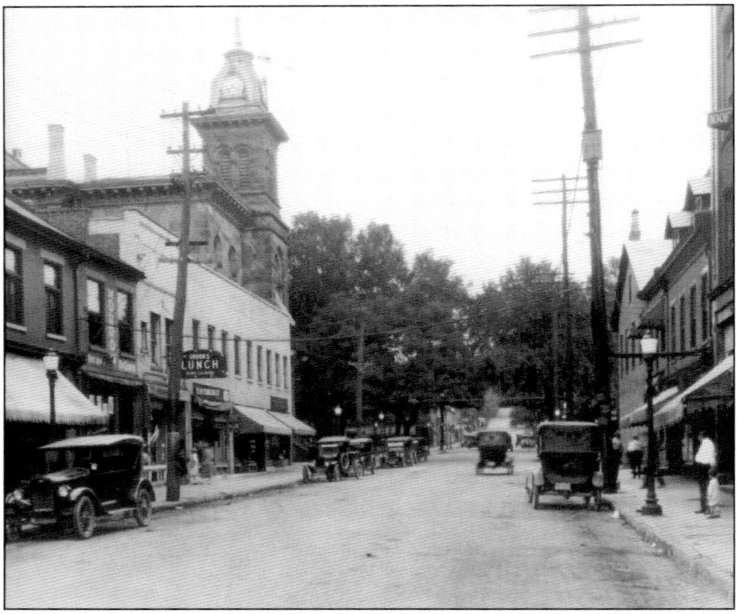

STORES AND CARS. As early cars line South Market Street below the courthouse, Crooks Restaurant can be seen. Later, Isaly's could be found nearby. Isaly's, originating in Youngstown, Ohio, was always a popular gathering sport. Today, other longtime eateries are Pondi's and Mary's Pizza. Across the street is Bye & Bye Hardware, long a fixture in the community, family owned and operated from 1896 to the present day.

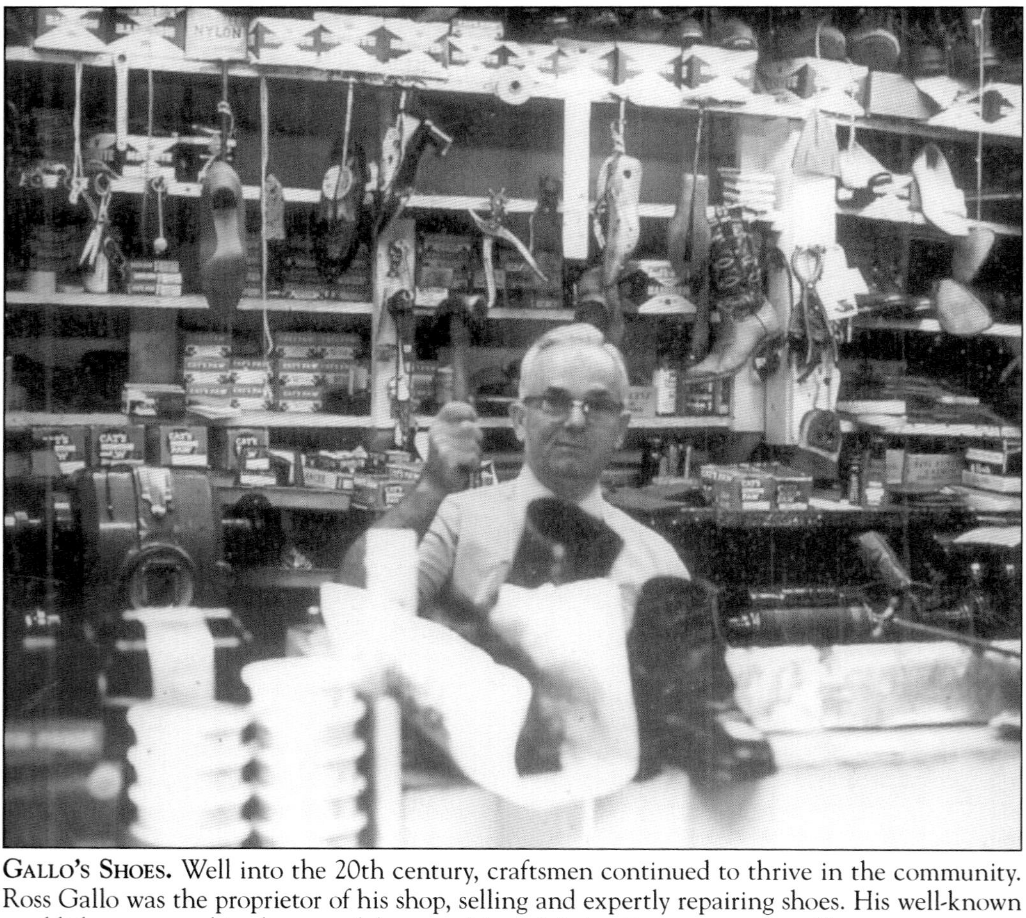

GALLO'S SHOES. Well into the 20th century, craftsmen continued to thrive in the community. Ross Gallo was the proprietor of his shop, selling and expertly repairing shoes. His well-known establishment stood in the row of shops on North Market Street, near the village square.

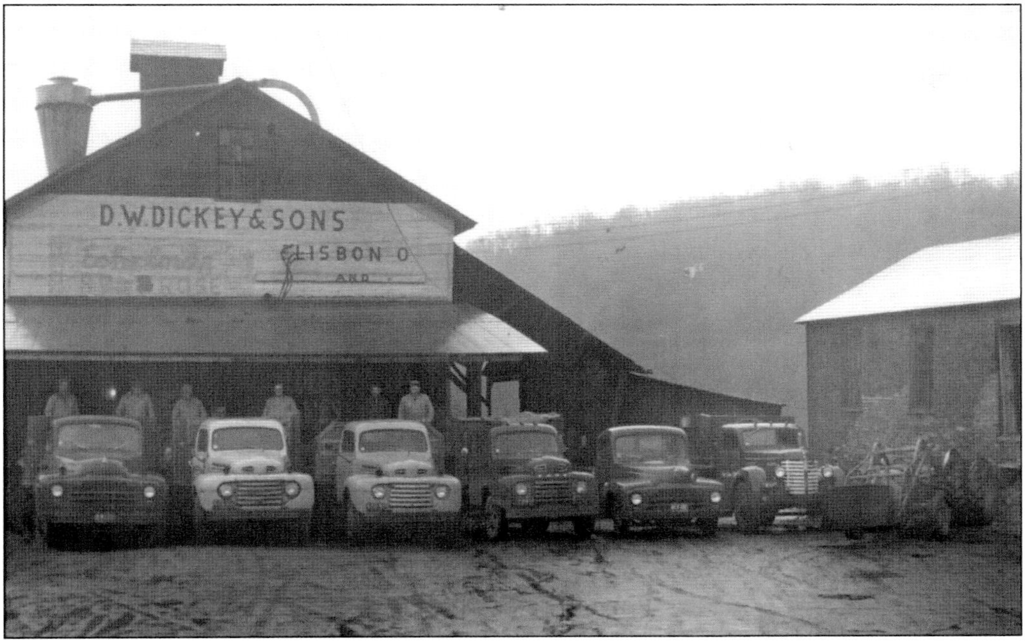

D.W. Dickey & Sons. In its history, Lisbon was home to four feed mills: Law's, Farmer's Exchange, D.W. Dickey, and Farm Bureau Cooperative Association. The only one that survived is D.W. Dickey, now sold and renamed Agland Co-op. In addition to new office quarters on the northern edge of the village, the current D.W. Dickey Company has offices and plants in several other locations, a significant enterprise with concrete and building supplies.

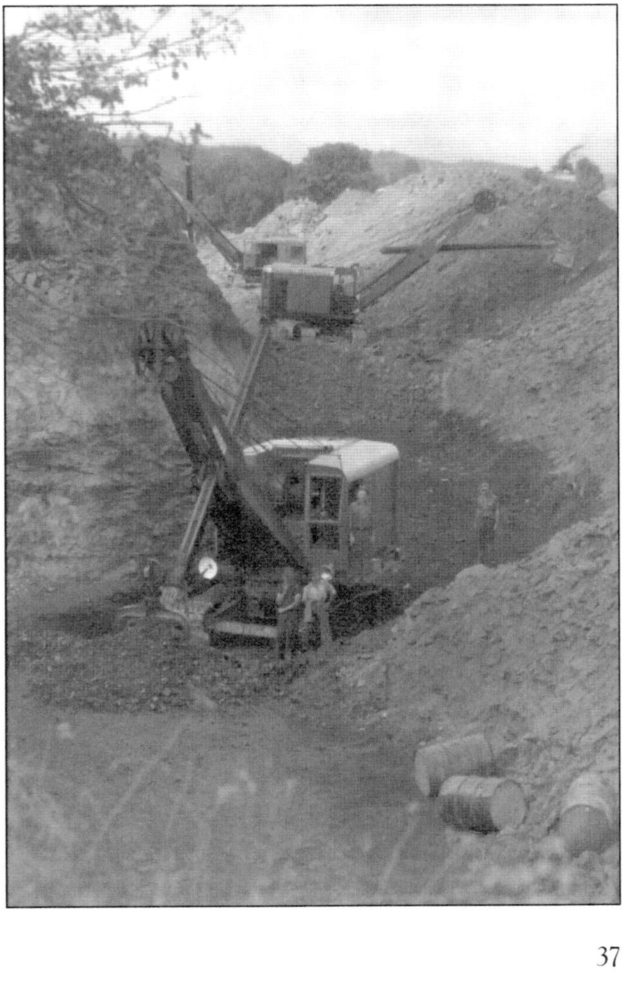

Lisbon's Coal Mining Operations. Coal mining, originally deep, later heavily involved in strip mining, became a large part of the local economy. Pictured here is a vigorous extensive mining operation with the Buckeye Coal Mining Company. Owner Harold W. Kepner can be seen standing on the stripping shovel with several workers. (Courtesy of Wendell Cole.)

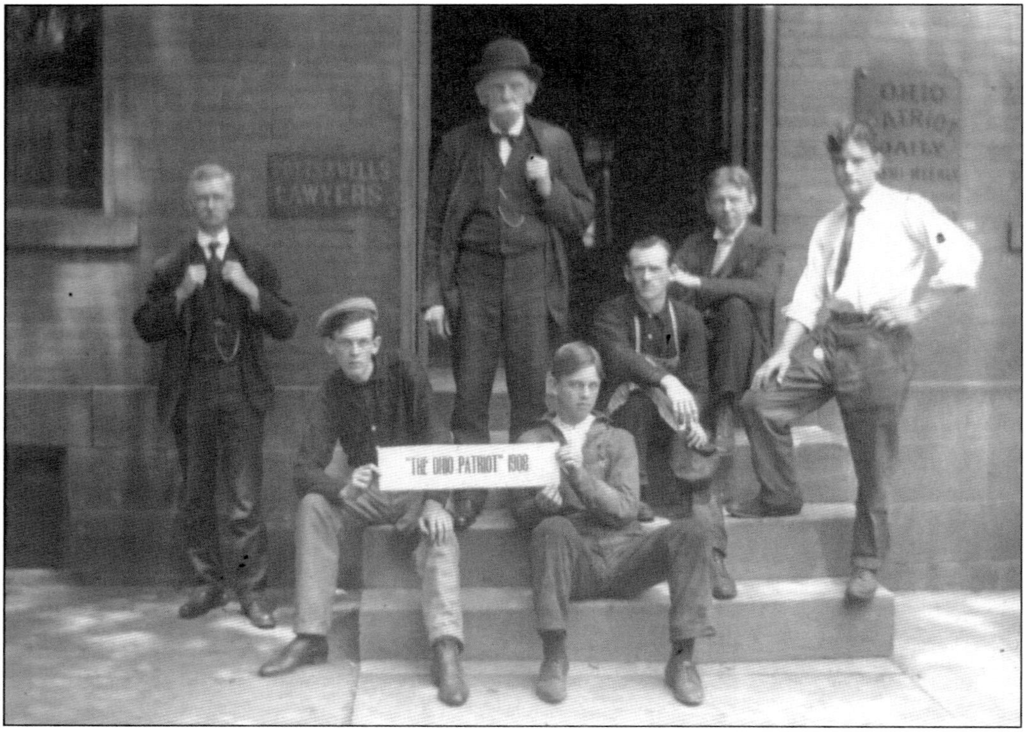

The Ohio Patriot. In a round building, John Frost published an abolitionist newspaper, the *Aurora*, in the antebellum 1830s and 1840s. A major newspaper in the evolution of print in New Lisbon was William Lepper's publication *Der Patriot Am Ohio.* Published first in German, then in English, the *Ohio Patriot* was an important newspaper for many years.

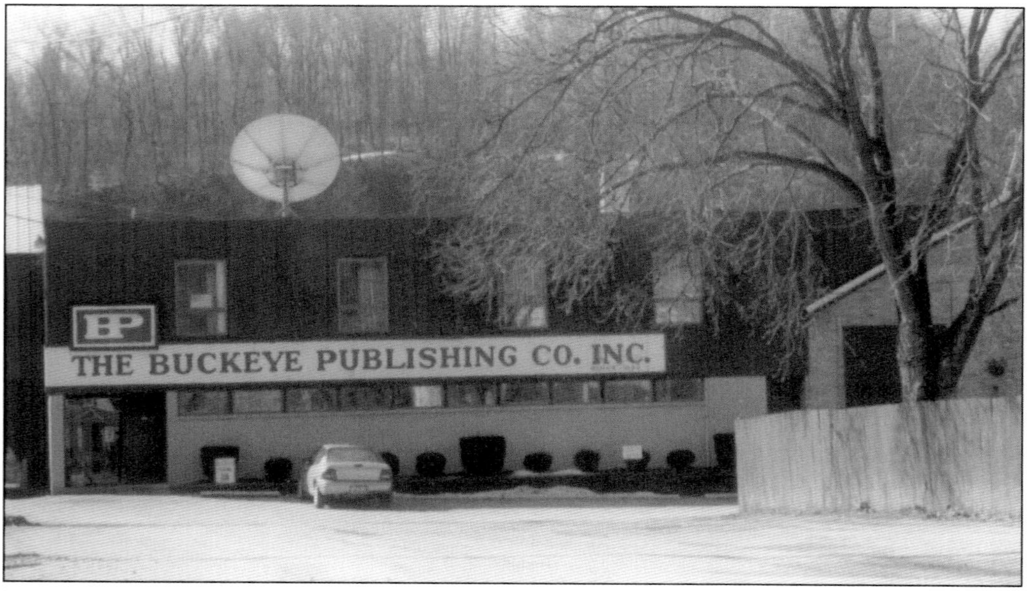

Lisbon's Newspapers. Lisbon has had a long history of newspapers, which tied together all that was occurring in the village and the nation. Notable was the *Buckeye State*, an early enterprise of the Frew family established in 1867. The Frews also published the still-current *Morning Journal.* Under the name of Buckeye Publishing, it is a very active press.

Three

Notable People and Historic Homes

Just as people are known by their homes, in Lisbon they are certainly known by their families. Many names have been the essence of the community from its earliest days. Local citizens are descendants just as they are related by marriage throughout the village. It is important for newcomers to ask questions, be careful of comments, and learn the relationships, as the locals take pride in their ancestry.

However, this gives solidarity to the community. The ties create faithful bonds, care, and concern for individuals and families. Any crisis leads to immediate help and understanding. Most of all, these bonds are the true togetherness of the village.

Throughout its history, there has been a mutual parenting for the young. People have known the leading citizens since birth and watched their growth to adulthood. While they may have their favorite stories, they also have great pride in accomplishments.

Some well-known people born in Lisbon or of parents who had been residents are Marcus A. Hanna, a native, and his political protégé, William McKinley, of Lisbon parentage. Clement Vallandigham and John Clarke were natives, as were many of the Fighting McCooks. Others such as Edwin Stanton came to the community from elsewhere.

Most of these people built homes in the village. That is its very fiber in these long-standing residences with family names attached: Moore, Pike, Billingsley, Eells, Blocksom, Van Fossan, Bennett, Taylor, Firestone, Wright, Frew, Binsley, and Bye. Their children grew in the community; many married other residents, and some of their descendants remain.

Their professions built the community with merchants, inventors, doctors, lawyers, ministers, civic leaders, factory owners, and workers. From these early families comes a strong stock of pride in place. They know the stories of who made a difference.

Another critical piece of a community is a cemetery. After some early cemeteries in Lisbon, the community cemetery was established in 1823 on land donated by Dr. Joseph Springer. Sitting atop one of the several local hills is a 50-acre final resting place complete with a chapel, mausoleum, and headstones depicting the village life forever.

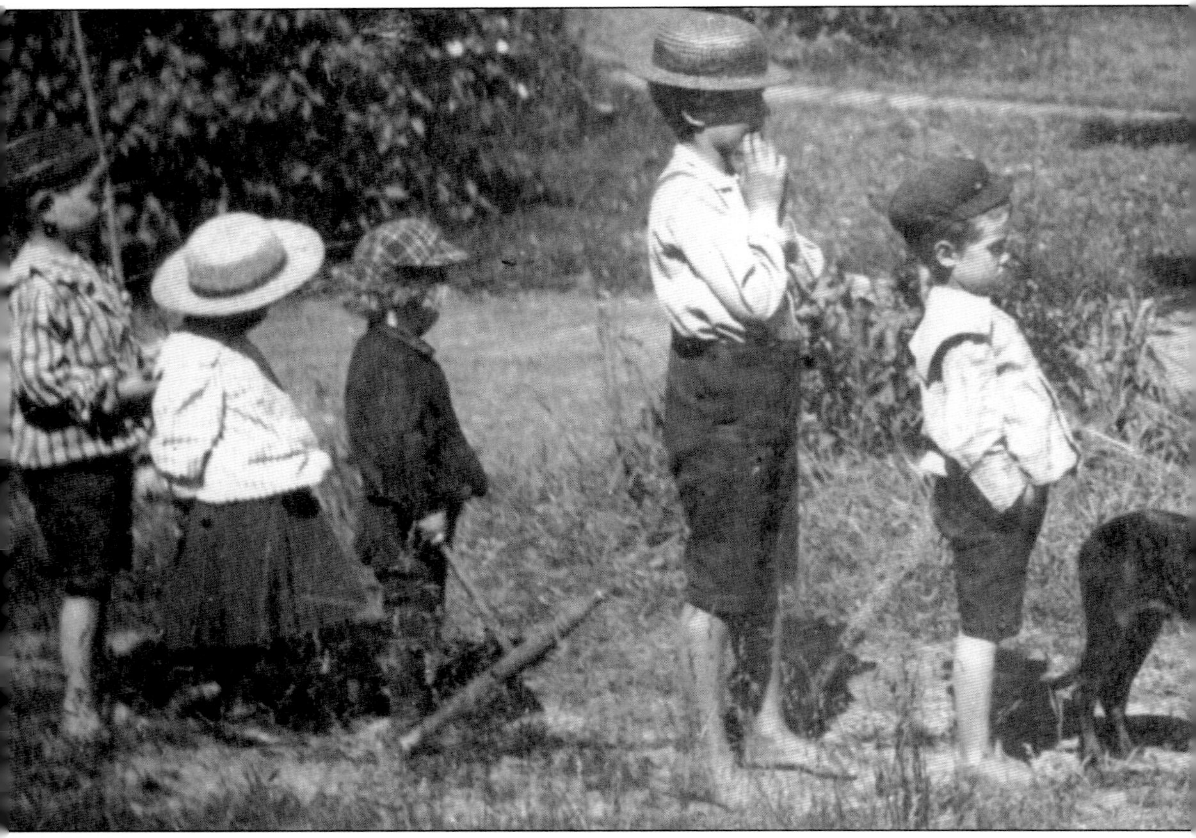

Dressed to Parade. In 1918 or 1919, this group of young boys—and possibly one little girl—form a parade complete with Ralph Frew's dog. Some of the names given include John Frew, Bill Frew, Jack Williams, Mince Harris, Charles Wright, Ralph Frew, Jim Frew, and Robert Clark. It is likely that Bob Dorrance is also included in the group. They were to become important members of the

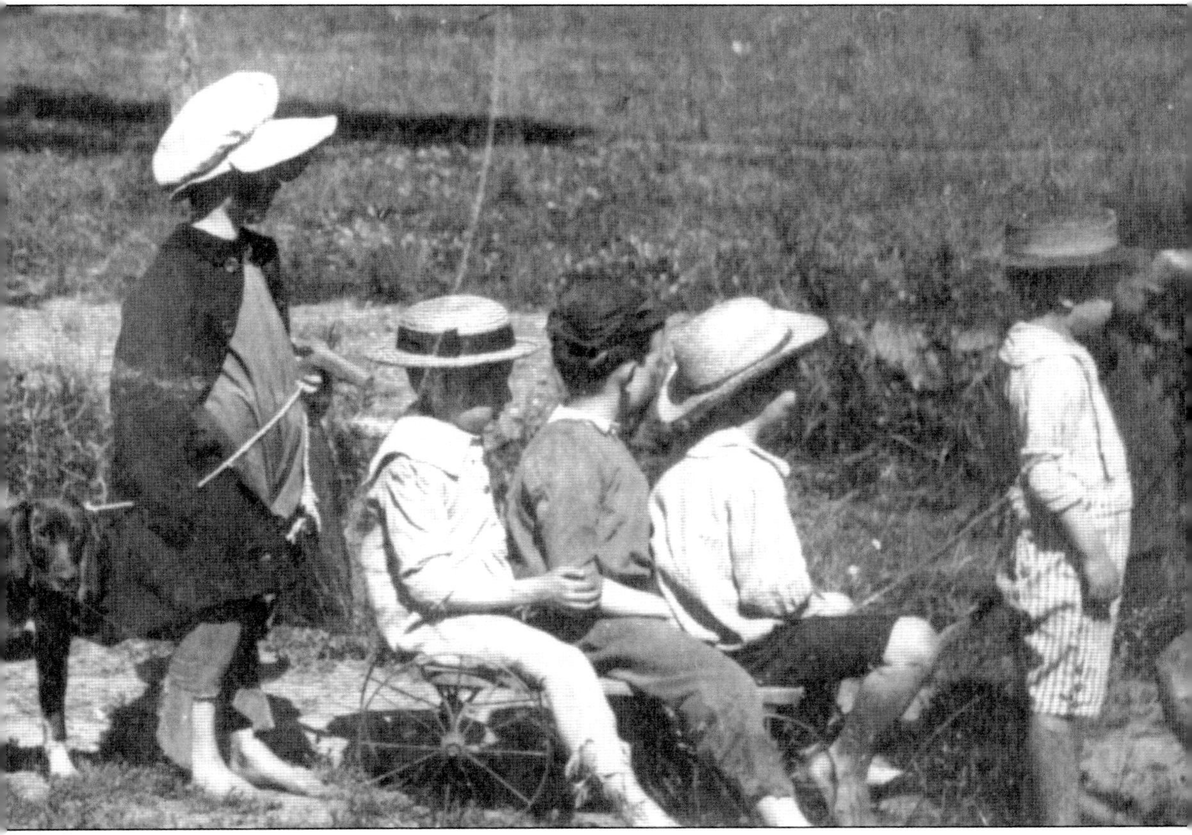

community, with the Frew family's involvement in the newspaper, Jack Williams and his gasoline station, Charles Wright and his several enterprises within Wright Industries, and Bob Dorrance, carrying on the family furniture business.

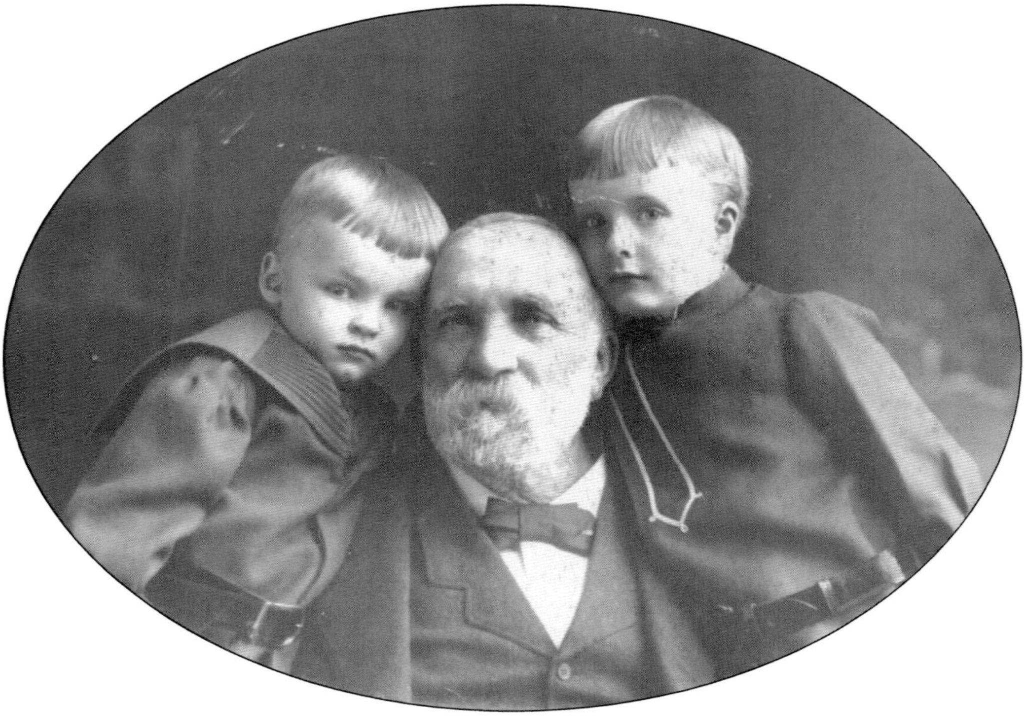

The Firestone Family. Known throughout the community as a family of active citizens and bankers, S.J. Firestone poses with his grandsons on December 26, 1901. On the left is Leland, and on the right is Gerald Howland. In time, Leland Firestone became president of the Firestone Bank, serving for many years.

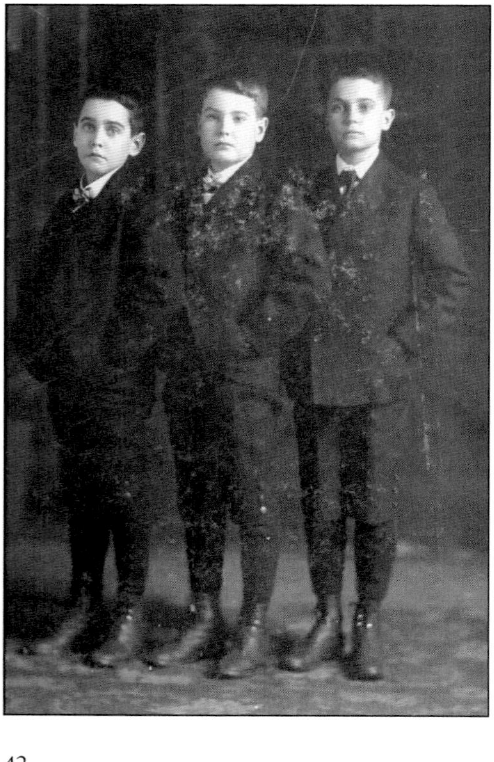

The Brothers Wright of Lisbon. Wright Industries is described as an important part of the local economy and has great diversification. Hal Wright's sons, these three brothers, Wid (left), Hal (center), and Charles (right), were major contributors to that reputation. All three lived in the community, maintaining homes and families as well as supporting many workers with employment opportunities.

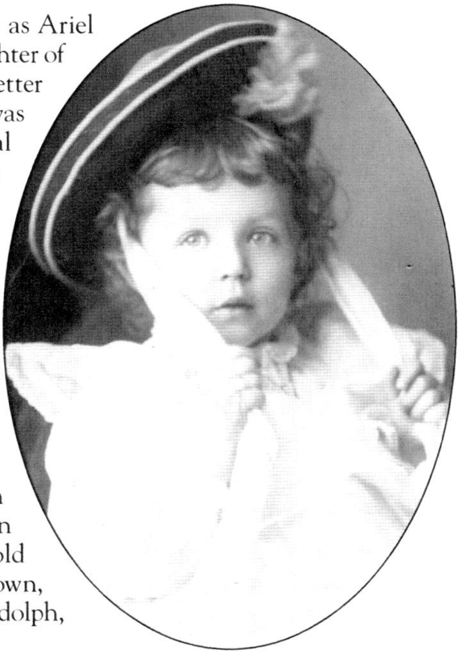

Ariel Gailey Kearney. Known to the community as Ariel Kearney, this child grew to become much loved. Daughter of merchant Frank R. Gailey and Emma Josephine Hostetter Gailey and wife of coal broker Graham Kearney, she was a very talented pianist who accompanied the annual minstrels and many other events in Lisbon with great skill and enthusiasm.

The Moore Family. In this photograph taken on January 8, 1898, the seven Moore children pose in order of height and age. Beginning with 16-year-old William, who later became a prominent attorney in town, they descend to Eva, 14; Mary, 12; Frank, nine; Randolph, seven; Charles, five; and Ralph, four.

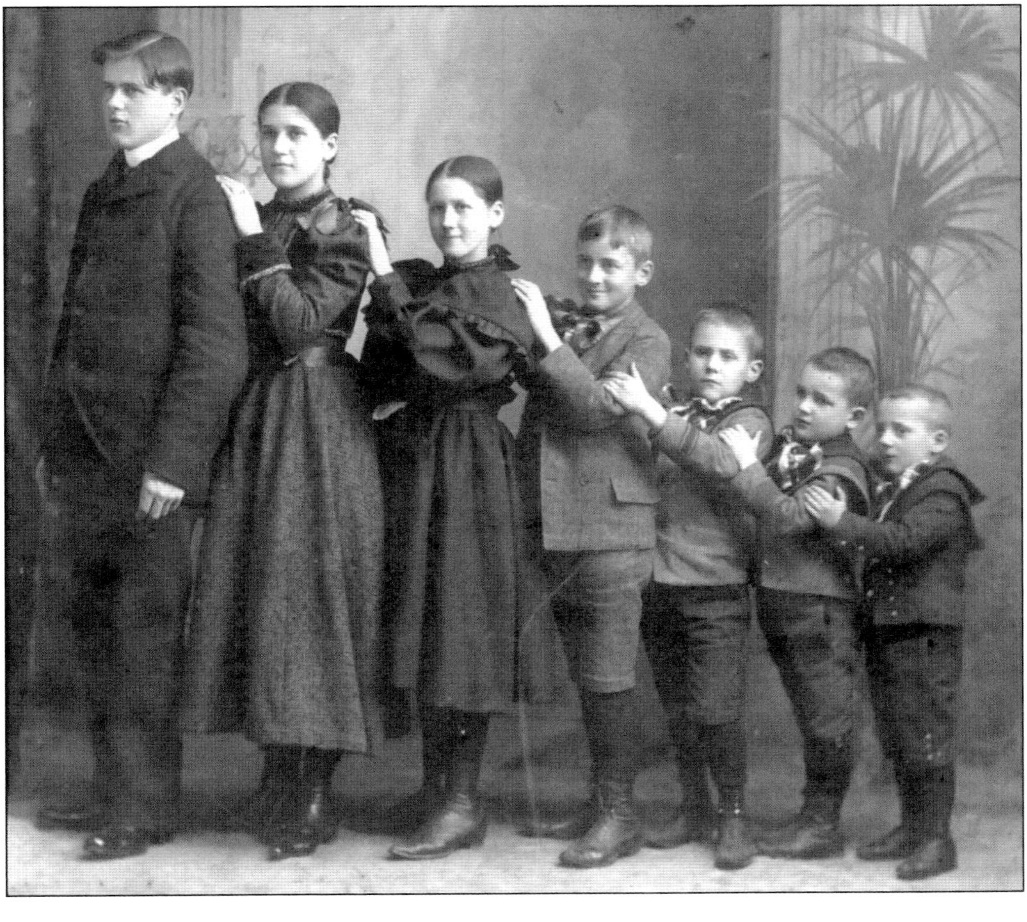

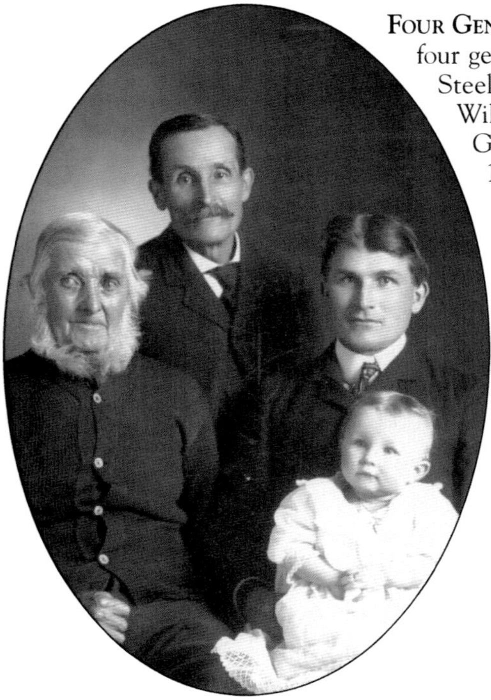

Four Generations Represented. In this oval photograph, four generations of the family of local dentist Dr. John Steele are represented. Clockwise from left they are William Dimbleton, William Steele, Dr. J.S. Steele, and Graham Steele as a baby. They were well-respected 19th- and 20th-century residents of Lisbon.

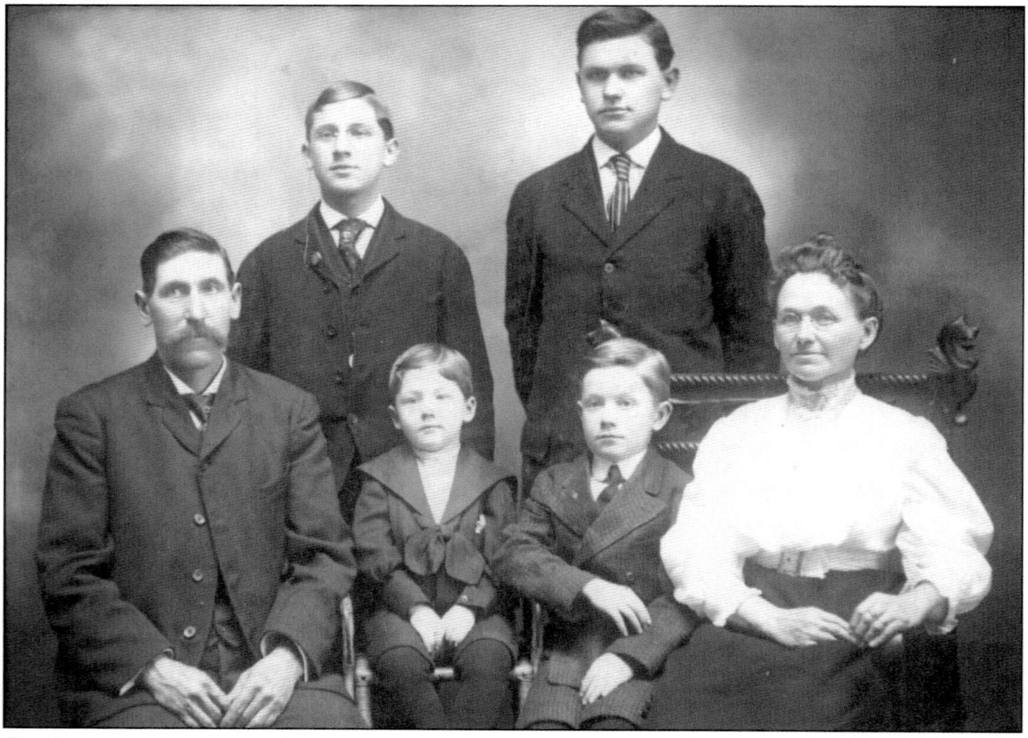

The Pike Family. This early-20th-century photograph shows all four sons of the Pike family with father Will and mother Annie. From left to right are (sitting) Will; Clyde, who became a salesman and the father of Roger, Tom, and Gary Pike, who served as principal of McKinley School; Orlan; and Annie; (standing) Dalton, who later became Lisbon's chief of police, and Roy.

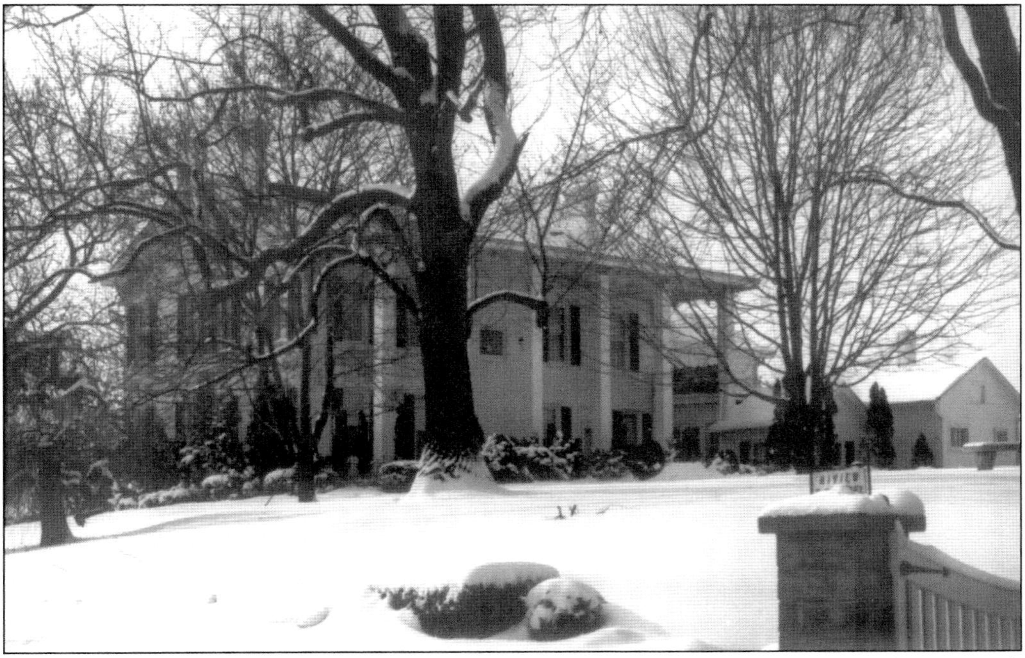

A Hanna Homestead. This 1827 home of Benjamin and Rachel Hanna stands proudly on North Market Street to this day. Benjamin Hanna was the early president of the Sandy and Beaver Canal. Known for its white brick and majestic pillars, it has housed several families since that time, including members of the Firestone family. Today, it remains as a family dwelling.

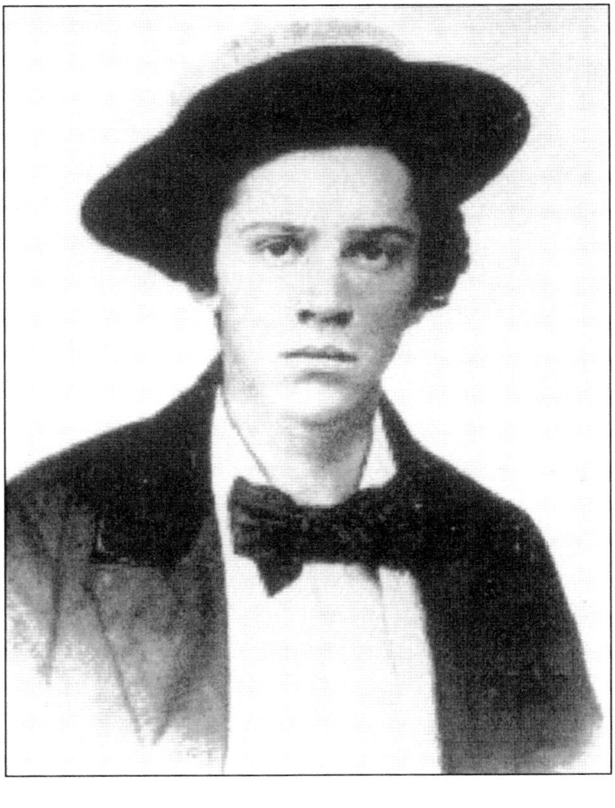

Marcus Alonzo Hanna. This rare photograph features 15-year-old Marcus Hanna, the second child of Dr. Leonard and Samantha Hanna. He spent his early years in Lisbon before moving to Cleveland and engaging in various business enterprises that led to wealth and political influence. He was both a US senator and the chief force behind the McKinley presidency.

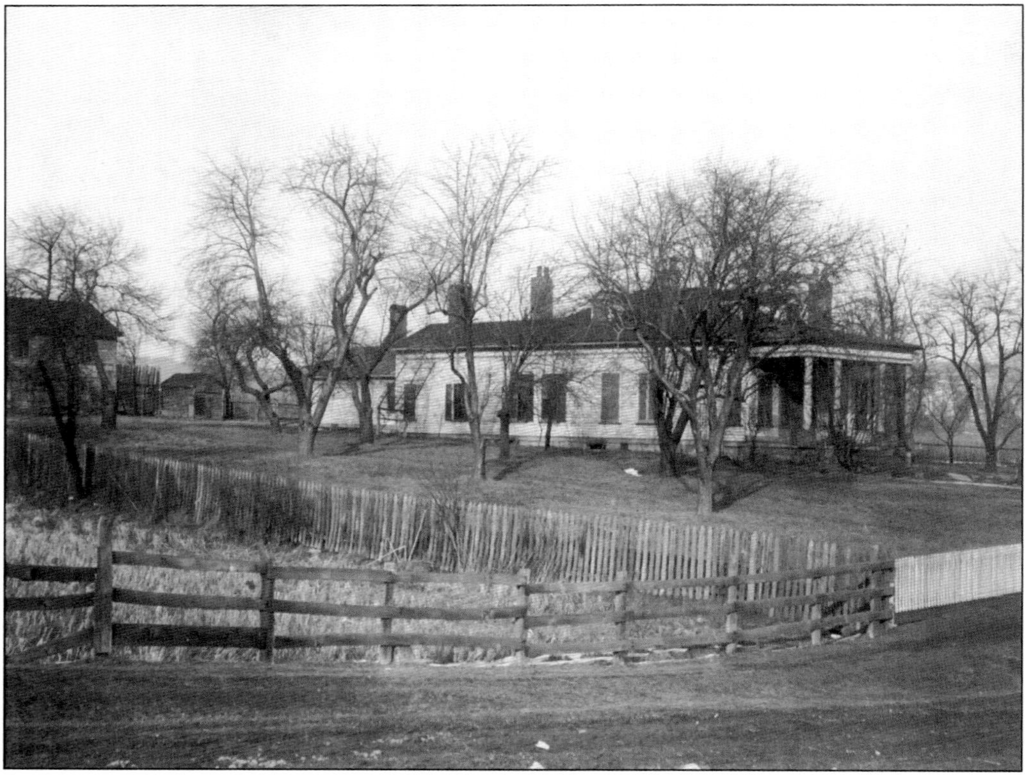

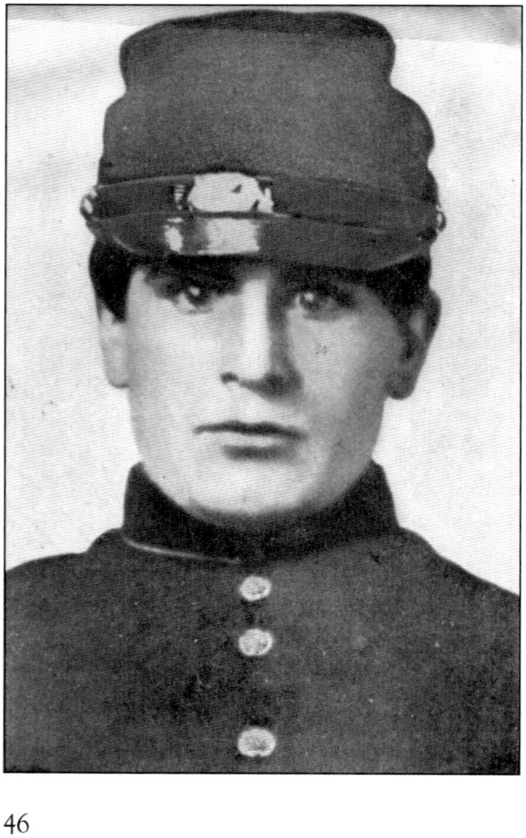

THE HANNA HOMESTEAD. This was the East High Street Lisbon home of Dr. Leonard Hanna and his family in the days of their son Marcus's early youth. It is said that the future senator played among the apple trees in the days of carefree childhood. Of the Hanna's seven children, he was to become the best known.

FUTURE PRESIDENT MCKINLEY. While Pres. William McKinley was born after his parents moved to Niles, Ohio, he maintained many links to Lisbon as well as the nation. In addition to teaching, he enlisted at age 18 in the 23rd Ohio Volunteers during the Civil War and quickly rose in rank. Later, he taught in the Poland, Ohio, schools.

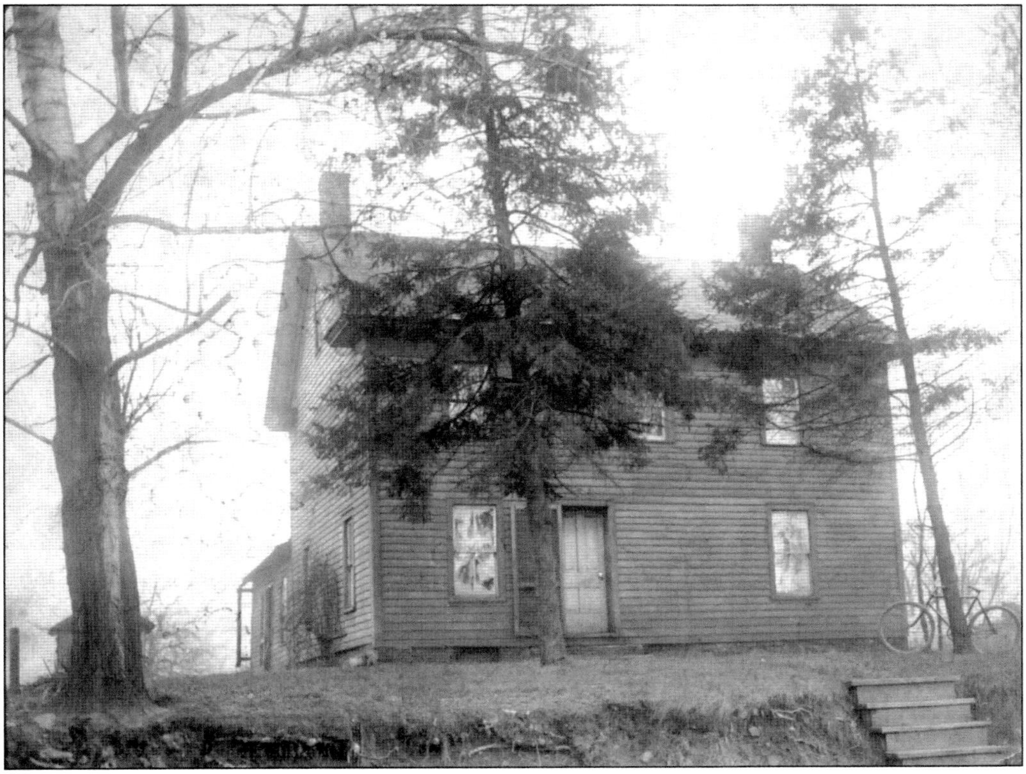

HOME OF NANCY ALLISON MCKINLEY. Although this home no longer stands, this was the residence of President McKinley's mother and grandmother. Humble in origin, McKinley's mother prayed upon his election that her son would remain humble. His attention to Lisbon in family, village, and church indicates the humility.

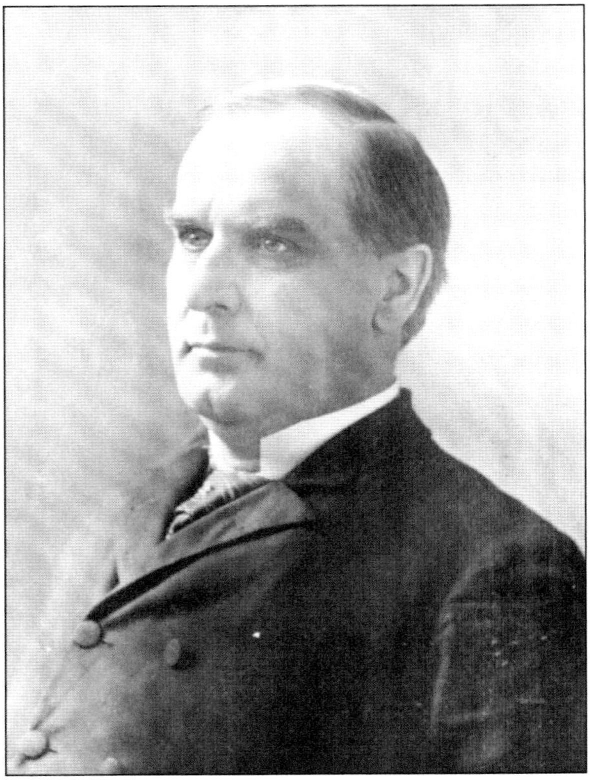

GOV. WILLIAM MCKINLEY. Having served as governor of the State of Ohio from 1893 to 1895, McKinley was then elected to the presidency of the United States. There is evidence in Lisbon of his continued association with the birthplace of both of his parents, as he participated in local events and donated a memorial window to the First Presbyterian Church.

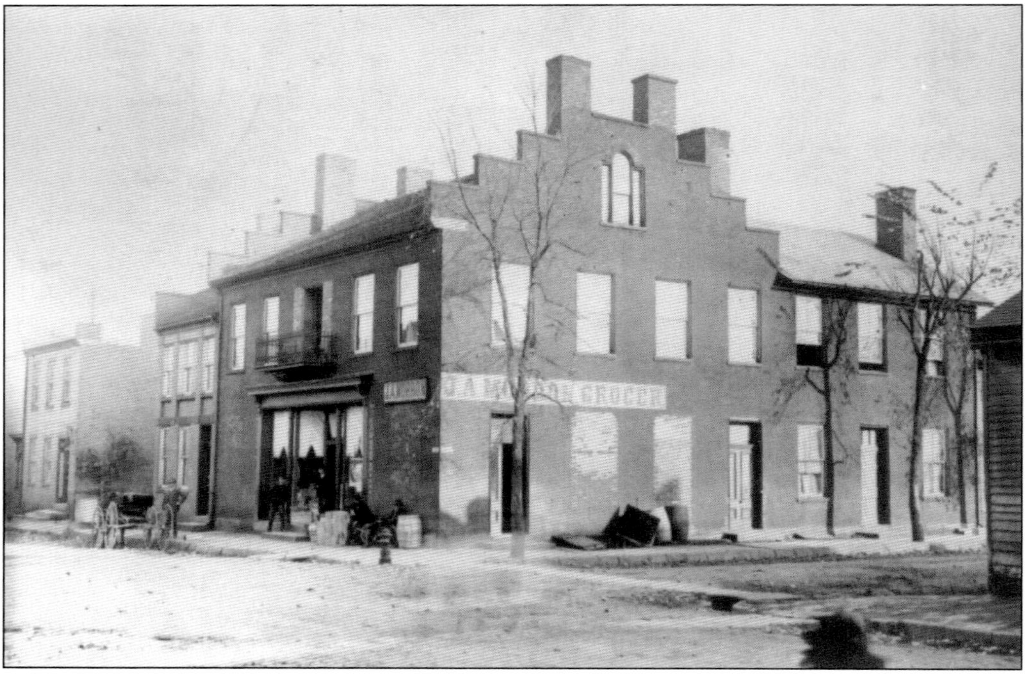

A McCook Family Home. A family called the Fighting McCooks occupied numerous residences in Lisbon. In addition, they were amazing in both their military service in the Civil War and their professions ranging from medicine to ministry. This house, no longer standing at the corner of East Lincoln Way and Jefferson Street, is the birthplace of Dr. Henry C. McCook.

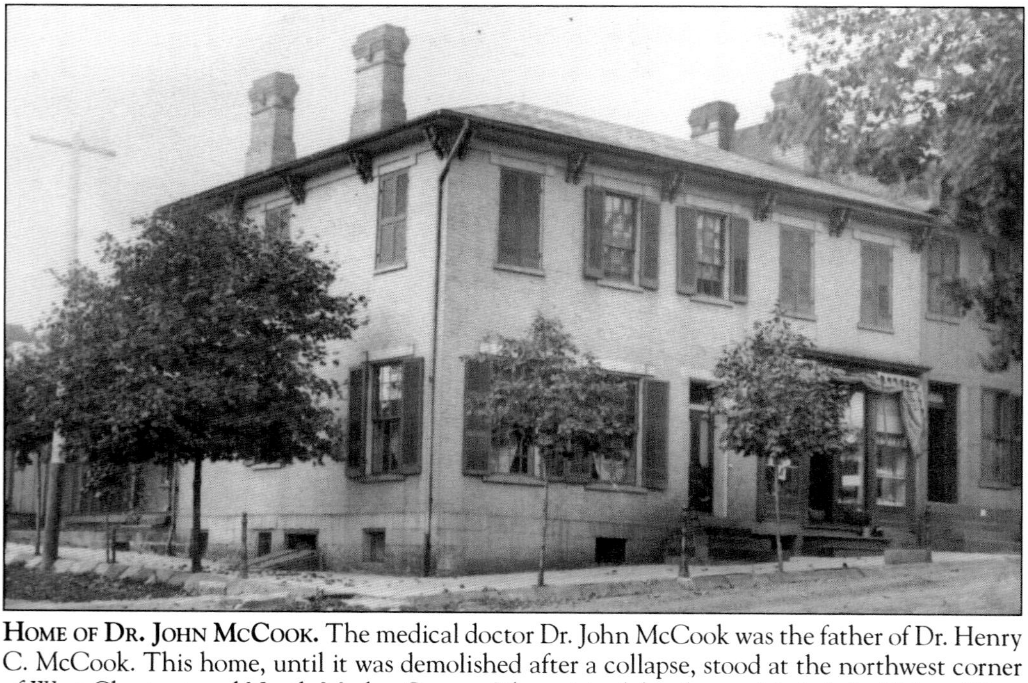

Home of Dr. John McCook. The medical doctor Dr. John McCook was the father of Dr. Henry C. McCook. This home, until it was demolished after a collapse, stood at the northwest corner of West Chestnut and North Market Streets. The original family was labeled the Tribe of Dan and the Tribe of John. Major Dan lost his life in a skirmish with Morgan's Raiders. Dr. Henry McCook became a prominent Presbyterian minister and naturalist.

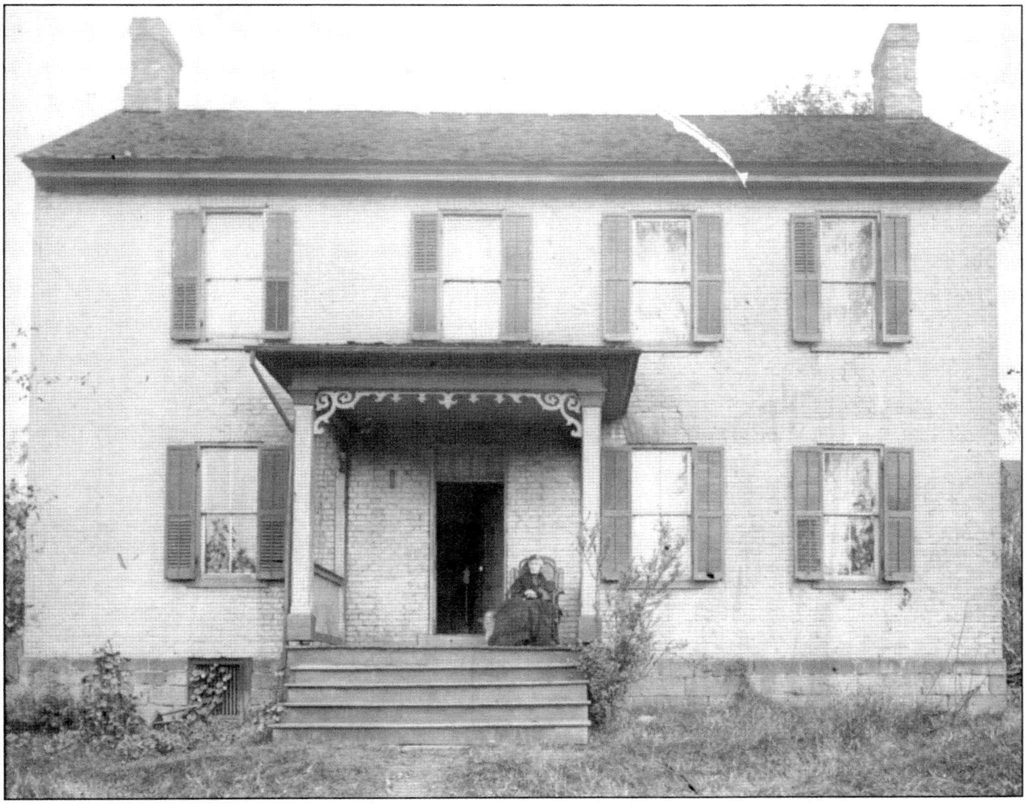

The Vallandigham Home. Although there are numerous views of the home built by Rev. Clement Vallandigham and his wife, Rebecca Laird Vallandigham, this one of the elderly widow sitting on the porch is most interesting. Having come to the community as a bride at the age of 17, she gave birth to seven children, including the well-known Clement L., and served in her role as the Presbyterian pastor's wife for 32 years.

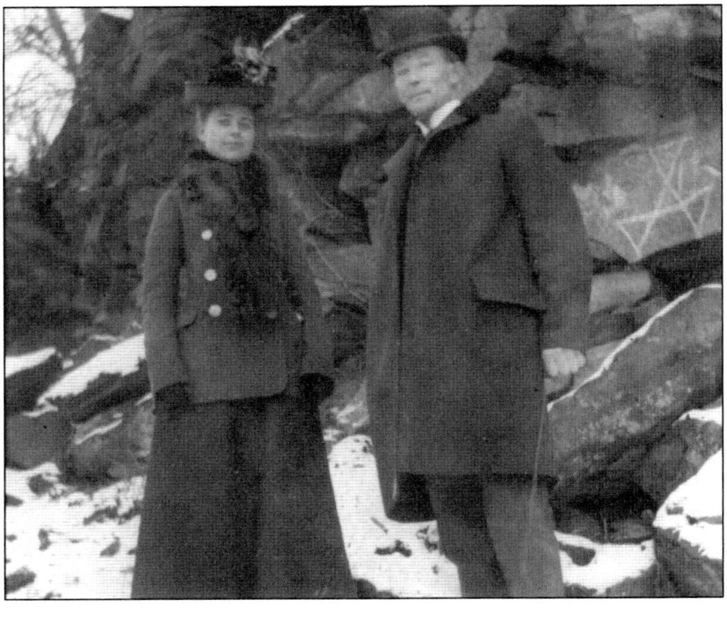

Morrows Climbing the Rocks. Another West Lincoln Way couple was H.W. and Stella Burns Morrow. Here, they are pictured in heavy attire climbing rocks in a wintry scene. Morrow is known as the inventor of a new process for the soda straw, a point of pride for the Lisbon community. Stella Morrow remained very active in the town for many years after his death.

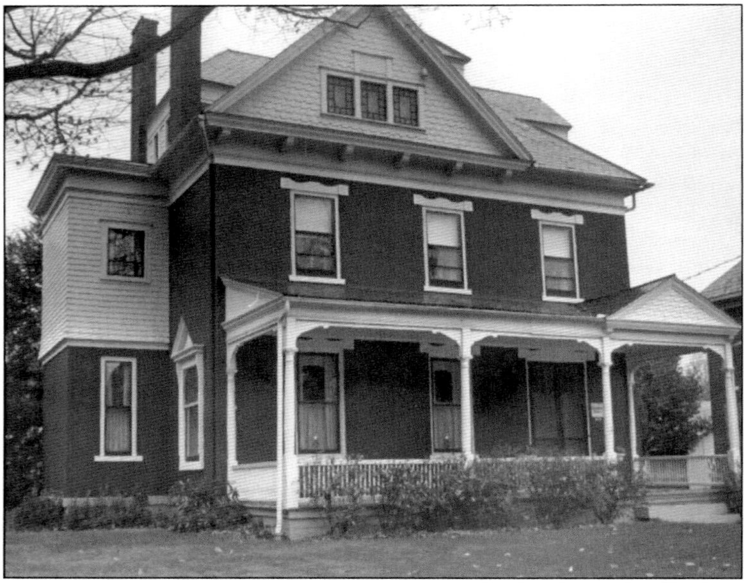

The Billingsley Home. Although known historically as the Billingsley Home, this East Lincoln Way Queen Anne–style dwelling has been occupied by the Zeppernick and Harris families. Today, it is the Bye residence. Dr. Seward Harris, much loved as the town doctor and athletic team physician, and his wife, Martha Billingsley Harris, resided here for many years.

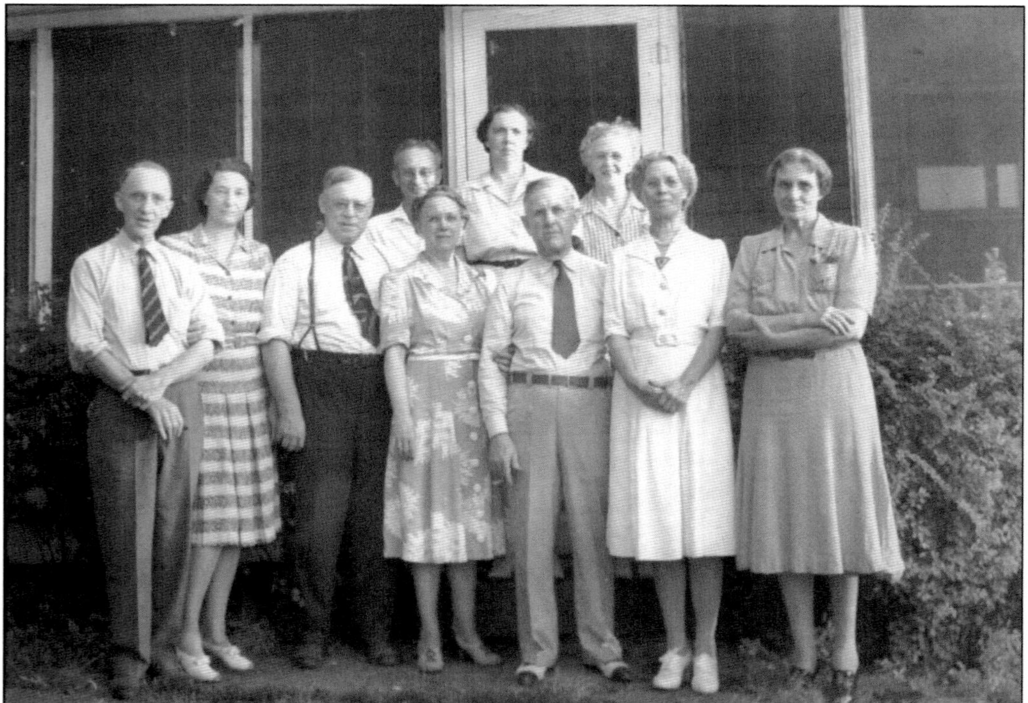

A Local Gathering. Pictured here are several individuals and couples gathered socially in August 1943. Included are, from left to right, (first row) Ed Piero, Martha Harris, Dr. Seward Harris, Abbie Moore, Jay Moore, Irva Wilson Firestone, and Nellie Firestone Vogan; (second row) Russell Hendricks, Elizabeth Hendricks, and Laura Johnson. Such social gatherings were quite in vogue at that time.

Early Physicians in the Community. Lisbon attracted three medical doctors as early as 1808. Dr. Horace Potter was the earliest in that original group. Throughout the years, several were very well known, including those bearing the names of Vallandigham and McCook. Pictured is an early physician, Dr. Tom Marquis.

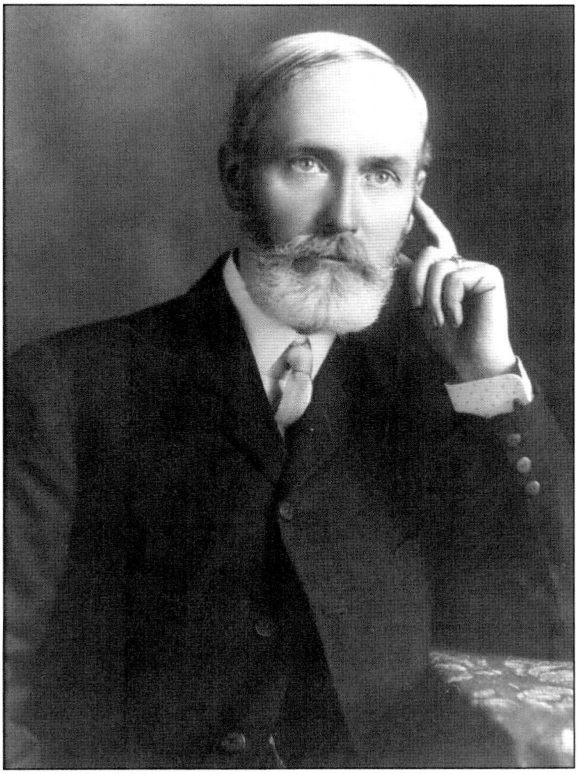

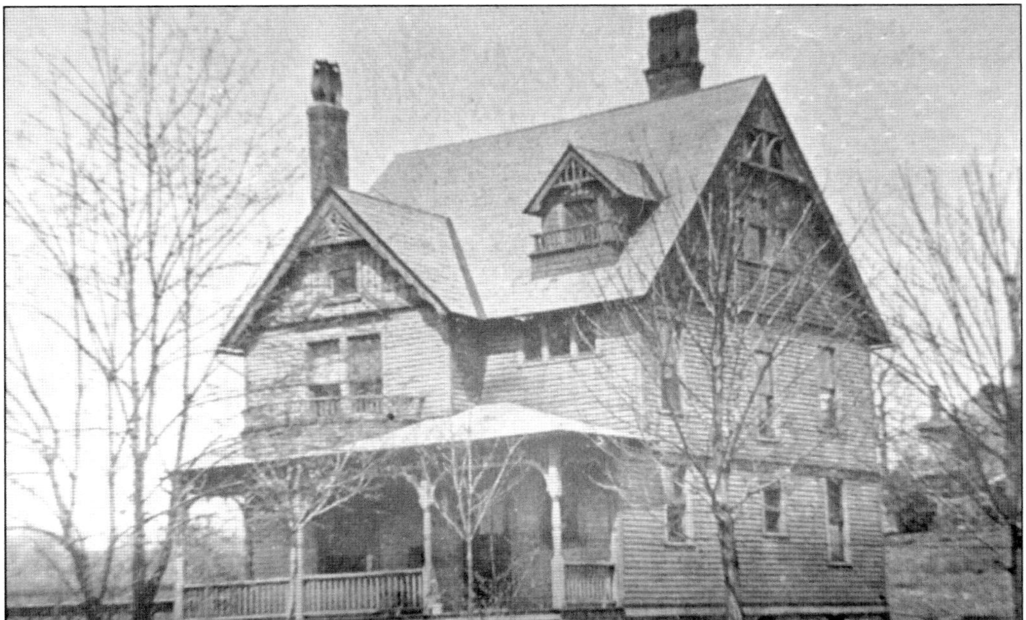

The Marquis Hospital. The early hospital established by Dr. Tom Marquis is a particular source of pride for Lisbon. This building, now a private residence, stands at the west end of West Washington Street. Little information about its patients and procedures seems to have survived, although its existence is always mentioned as an important feature of the village.

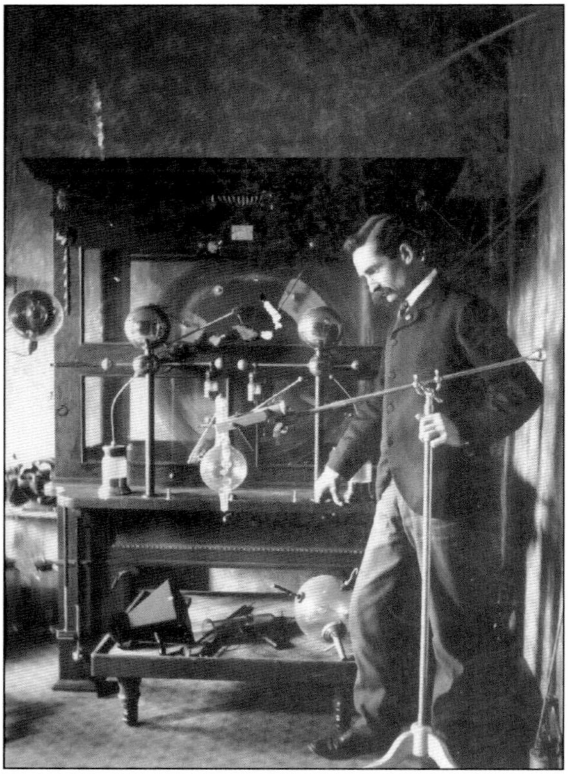

Early Medical Equipment. This photograph shows the first X-ray machine in Lisbon, around the 1890s. The doctor shown with this special equipment is Dr. William Ernest Morris. Again, there is great pride in this early achievement in the local medical community.

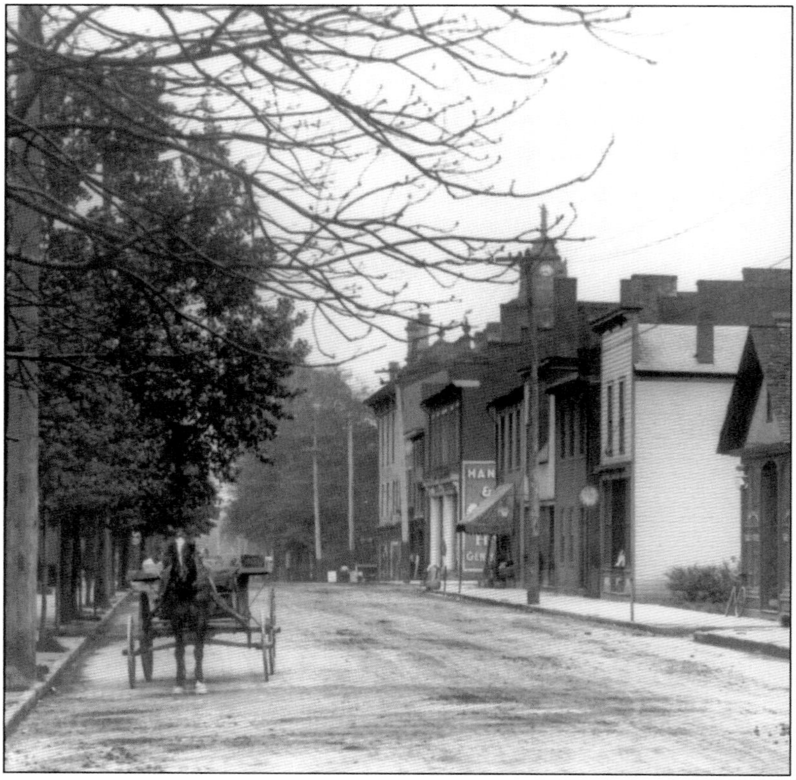

Hon. Fisher Blocksom. The earliest attorney of record in New Lisbon was Fisher A. Blocksom, who practiced law in the community from 1805 until 1852. His legal roles, as well as his community and county commitments, were numerous. The classic doorway of his home, the first building on the right, was well known throughout the community.

Associate Justice John H. Clarke. Justice John H. Clarke, son of local judge John Clarke arose from the community to take a prominent place in the national spotlight. He studied law at Case Western Reserve University for two years before moving on to Youngstown, then Cleveland. Considered an outstanding trial lawyer, he was appointed by Pres. Woodrow Wilson to the Supreme Court of the United States.

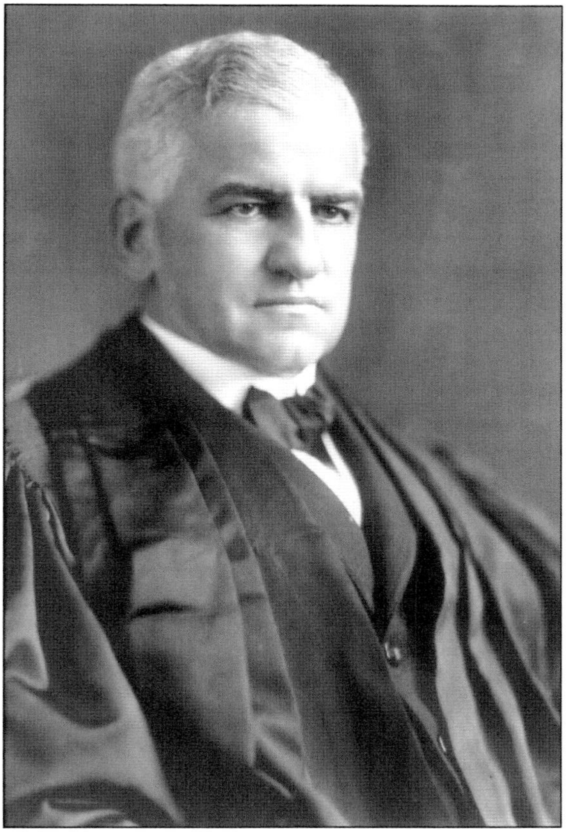

J.W. Clarke House. This house, built in 1898, was the boyhood home of Associate Justice Clarke. He was most distinguished not only in his legal abilities and Supreme Court appointment, but also in his passion for promoting President Wilson's League of Nations. So great was his devotion to that cause that he resigned from the Supreme Court to pursue the establishment of that hope. (Courtesy of Kenneth Everett.)

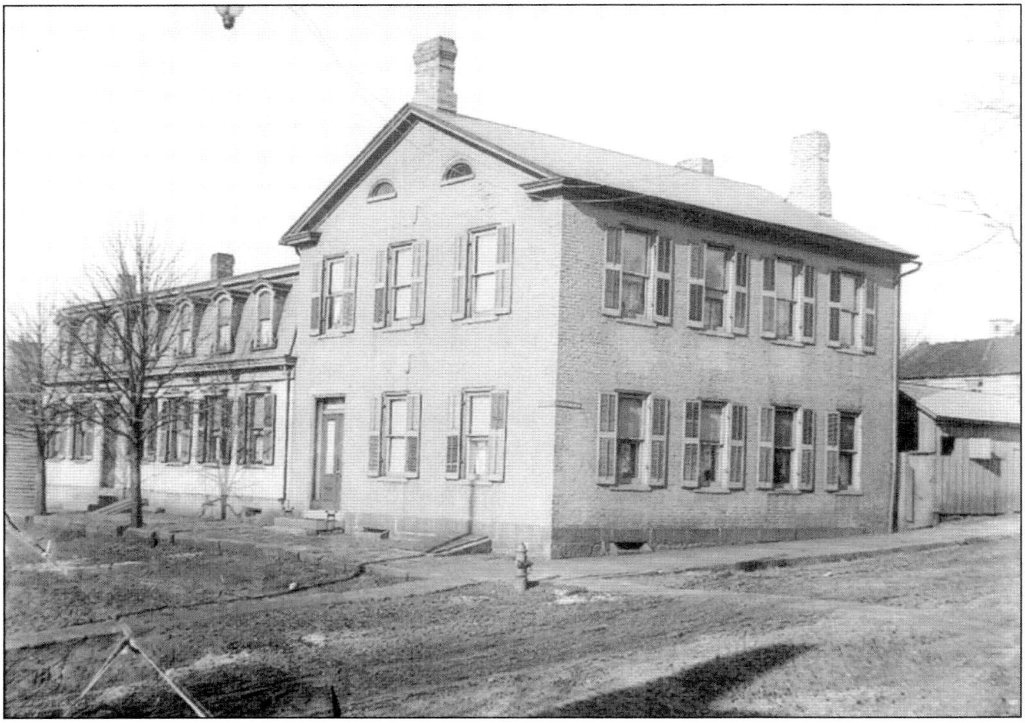

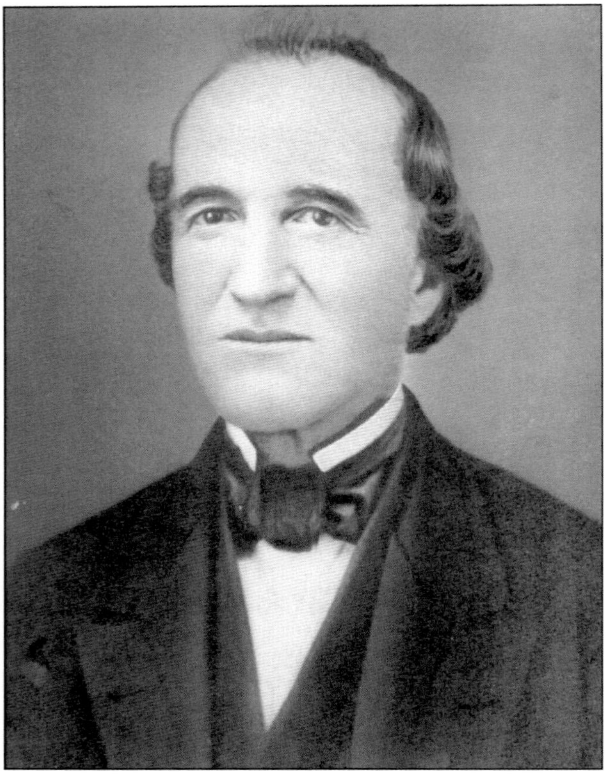

Erastus Eells I. A native of Connecticut, Erastus Eells came to the area in 1817. He began building caskets as an apprentice cabinetmaker and started a funeral business in 1828. His record for service was outstanding, as he never missed an appointment while he traveled 50,000 miles during his career by horse and buggy. With his family he founded the business that lasted under the Eells name for 119 years.

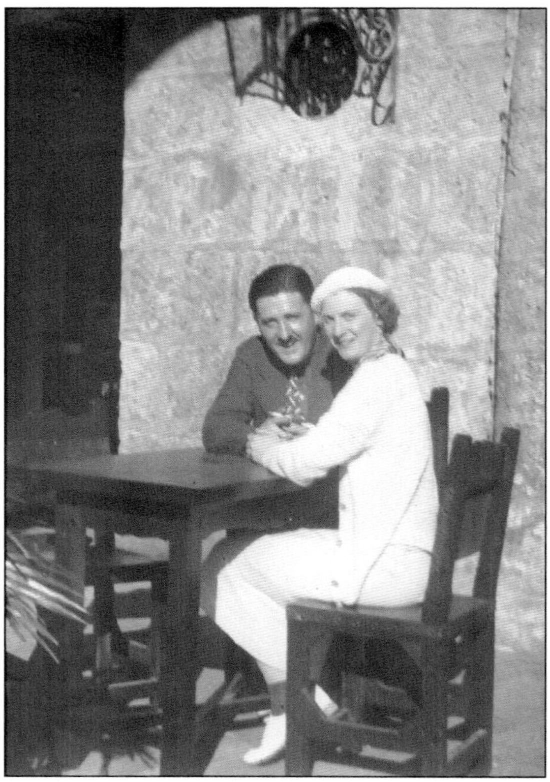

Gerald and Doris Eells. Gerald Eells, son of Erastus Eells II, and his wife, Doris Mefort Eells, daughter of Gus Mefort, the president of Lisbon Salesbook, are seen in Havana, Cuba, on vacation. Doris possessed a magnificent soprano voice that led her to New York City and great acclaim for her abilities and personality. She managed the funeral home for some time after the early death of her husband.

JOSEPH AND ERNESTINE BENNETT. Pictured here on their wedding day, the Bennetts were a leading couple in Lisbon. He was the owner of Bennett Printing and held patents for a cash register he invented. They were the parents of Josephine and Lucille Bennett, the latter a longtime teacher in Lisbon schools.

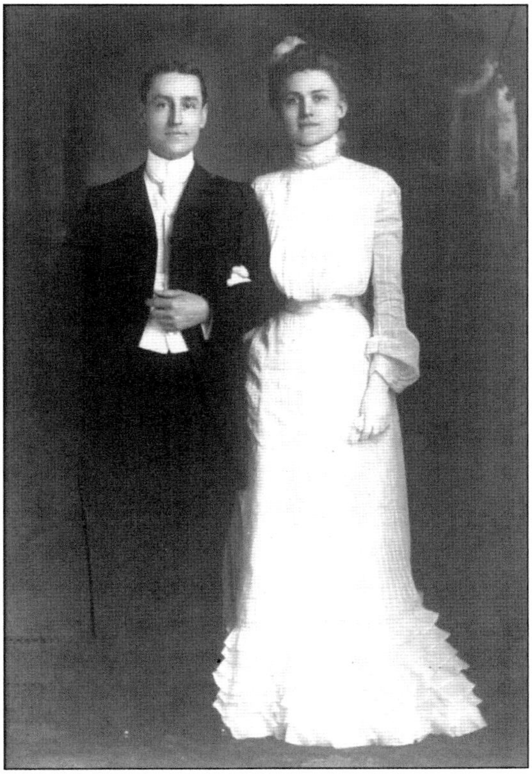

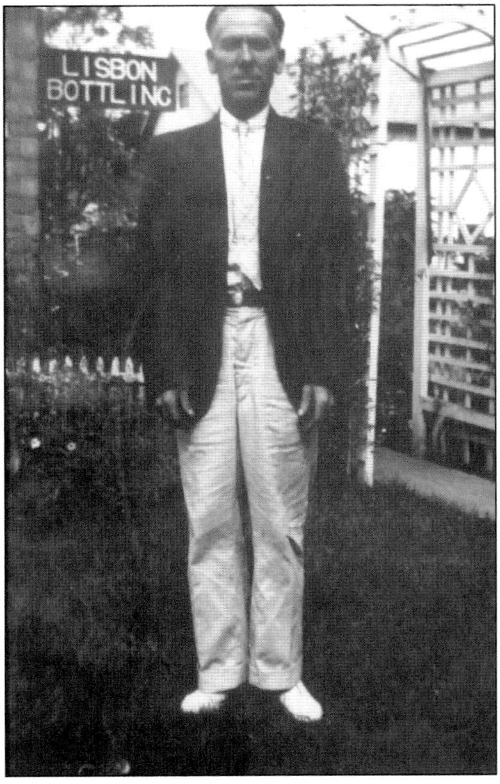

LOCAL ENTREPRENEUR. Russell Peppel, World War I veteran and entrepreneur, and his wife, Rachel, founded and operated the Lisbon Bottling Company on East Washington Street. For nearly 20 years, he and his wife made and bottled fruit drinks and soda pop; a case of pop sold for 64¢. In addition, he was very active in church and community.

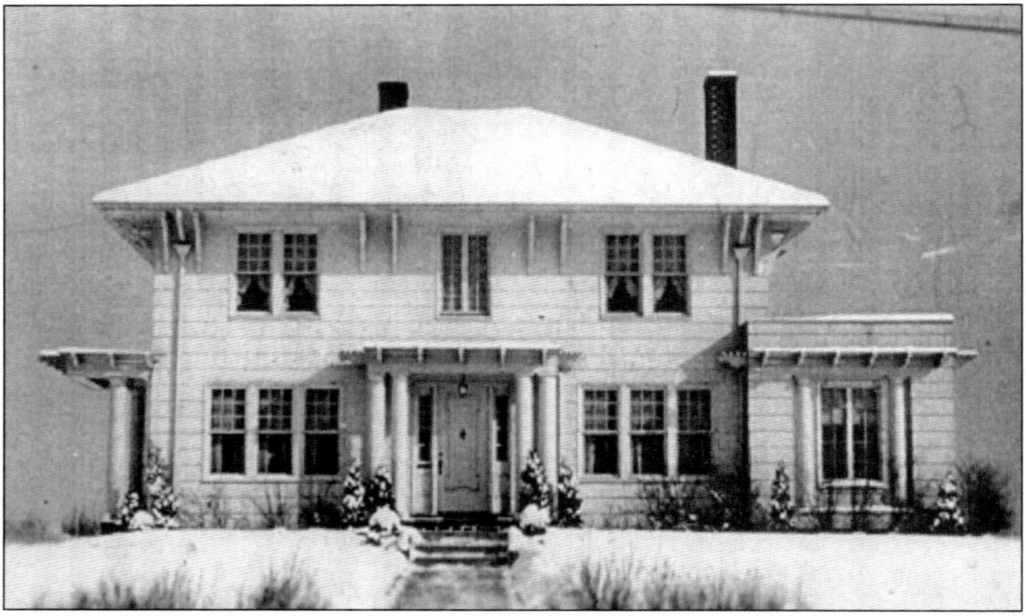

North Market Street Home. This home, the present-day residence of Lee and Diane Dull, was built by Harry Neigh, owner of the Lisbon Lumber Company. The Neighs and their children first built and occupied the home in 1925. Their son Kenneth became a prominent Presbyterian minister with administrative and executive positions beyond the pastorate in that denomination.

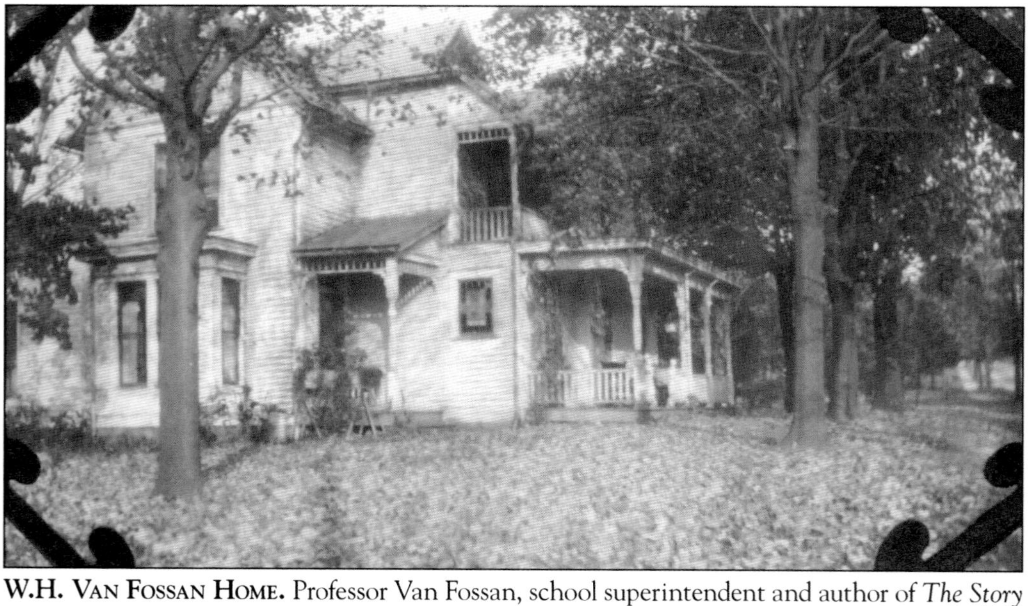

W.H. Van Fossan Home. Professor Van Fossan, school superintendent and author of *The Story of Ohio*, lived in this home at the juncture of North Beaver and North Market Streets. He and his wife were the parents of six children, including World War I nurse Elaine Van Fossan Hurd, and US district tax court judge Ernest Van Fossan.

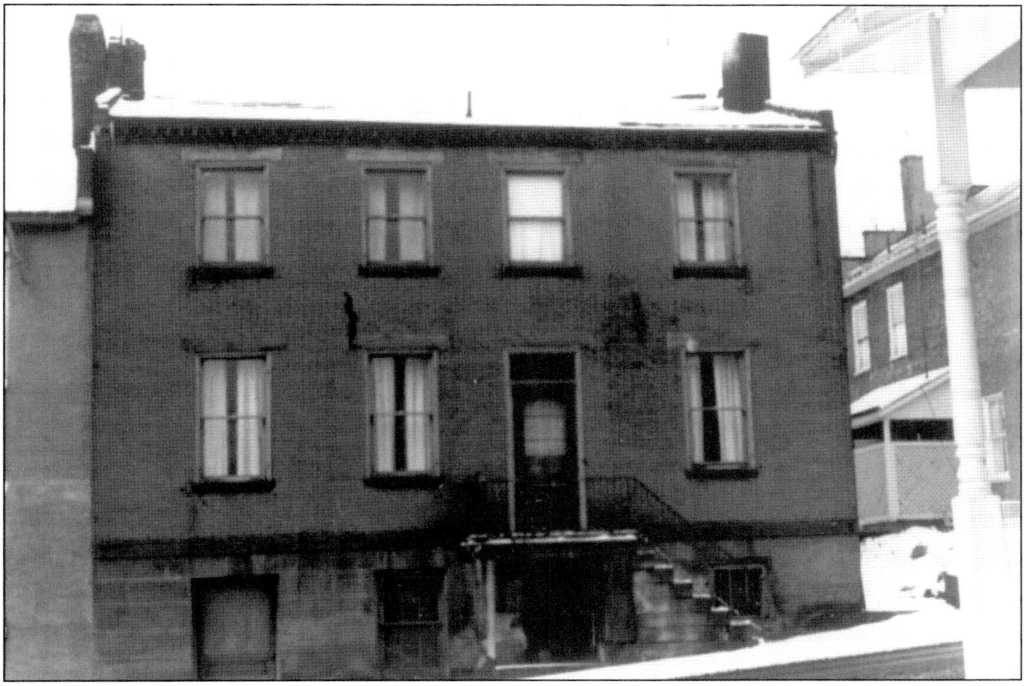

A Classic Brick Home. This was one of the early homes on North Market Street, two houses above the McCook House on Chestnut and Market Streets. Like that house, it no longer stands, but in its many years of service, it illustrated Lisbon's wealth of brick houses—freestanding or in rows.

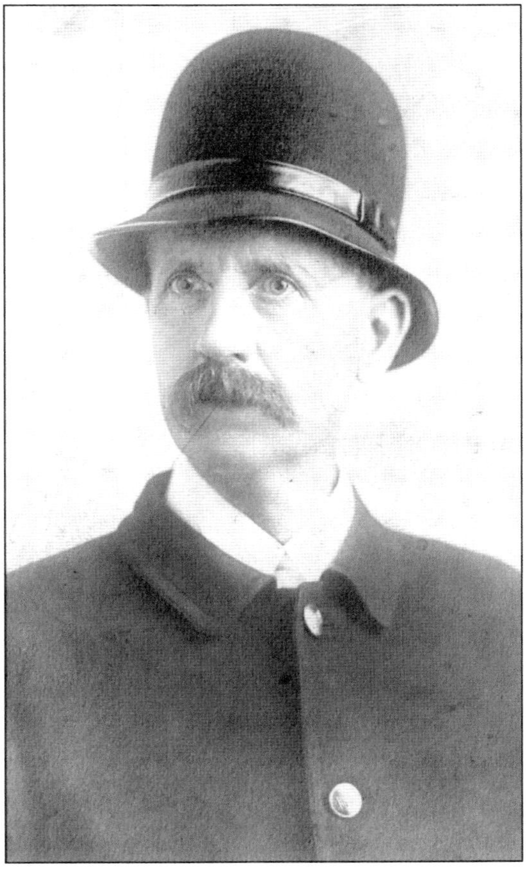

Lisbon's Police Force. This member of the police department of Lisbon was not only an officer, but also the father of Paul Webber, a local plumber, and grandfather of Charles Webber. Lisbon still maintains strong police and fire departments with responsibility and care for the residents.

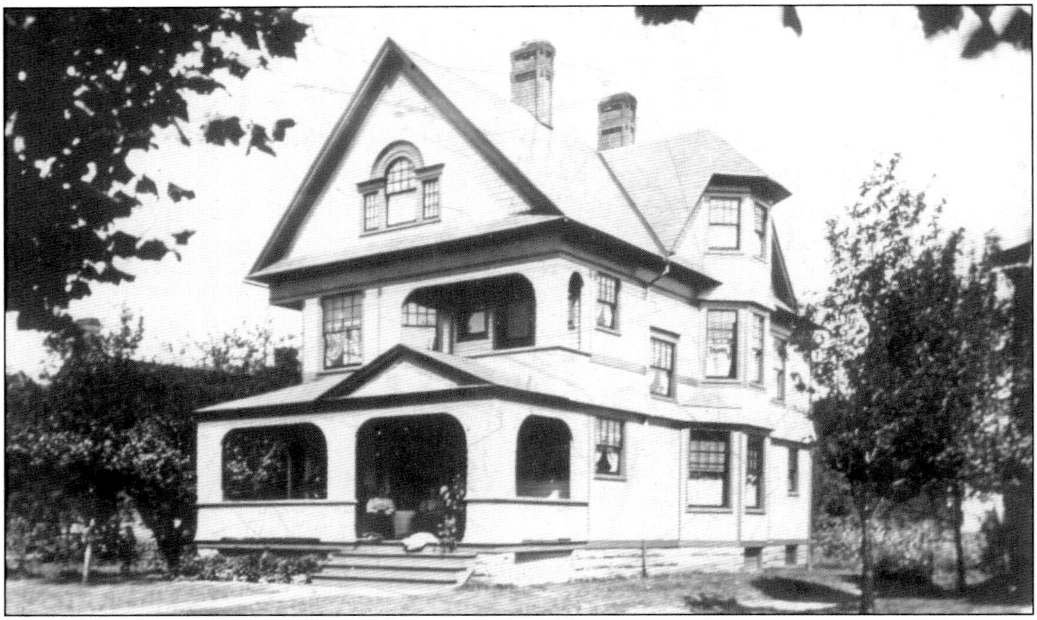

The Home of the Frews. This 1892 photograph of the Frew residence shows a typical Victorian family home. Built of wood, it housed the Frews, of newspaper prominence. Because the United Presbyterian Church was so full for its morning classes, Jospehine Frew, the church organist, brought the choir to her home across the street for Sunday morning rehearsals.

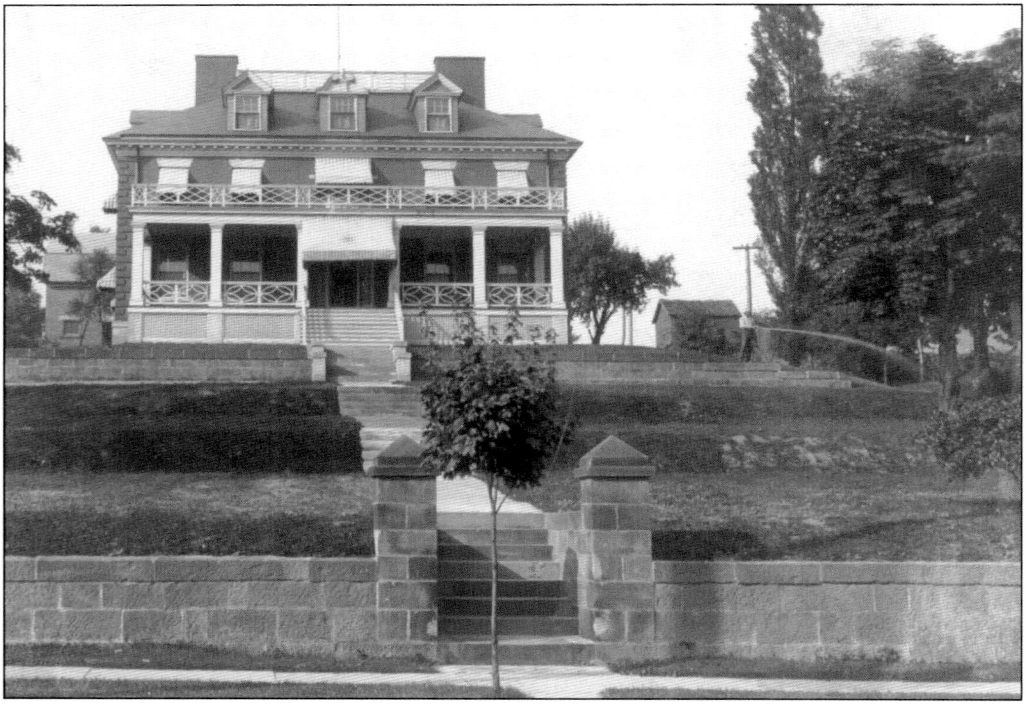

A Stately Home. This home is still a local residence on the northwest corner of West Lincoln Way and Thomas Road, known locally as Firestone Hill. Called a mansion and complete with a carriage house, it has been the home over past years of former congressman R.W. Taylor, Judge U.C. De Ford, Dr. Julian Jones, Charles Webber, and their families.

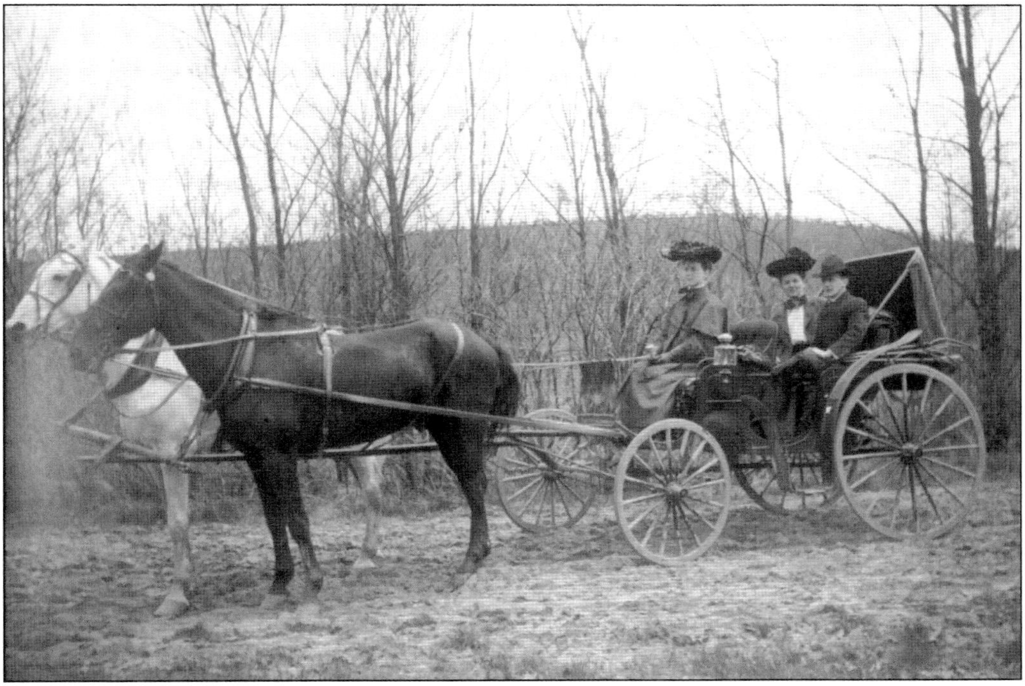

The Carriage Ride. Carriage rides with friends were typical in the days before automobiles. In the front seat is Ollie Rogers, known for her work with the historical society, the furniture store, and the Lincoln Theater. In the second seat are Margaret Griffith Thomas and Ralph Rogers.

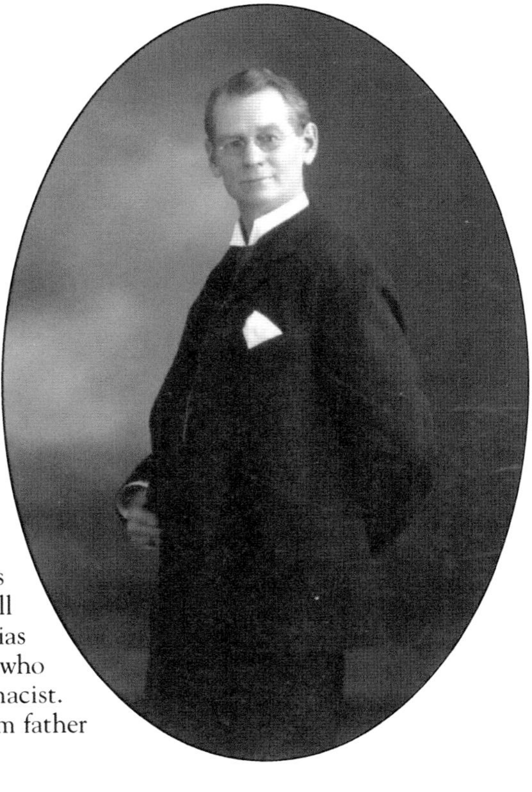

Matthias T. Nace. The Nace family members were prominent pharmacists in New Lisbon well into the 20th century. Pictured here is Matthias T. Nace, born in 1850, father of Charles Nace, who followed his father professionally as a pharmacist. The photograph was a 55th birthday gift from father Matthias to son Charles in 1905.

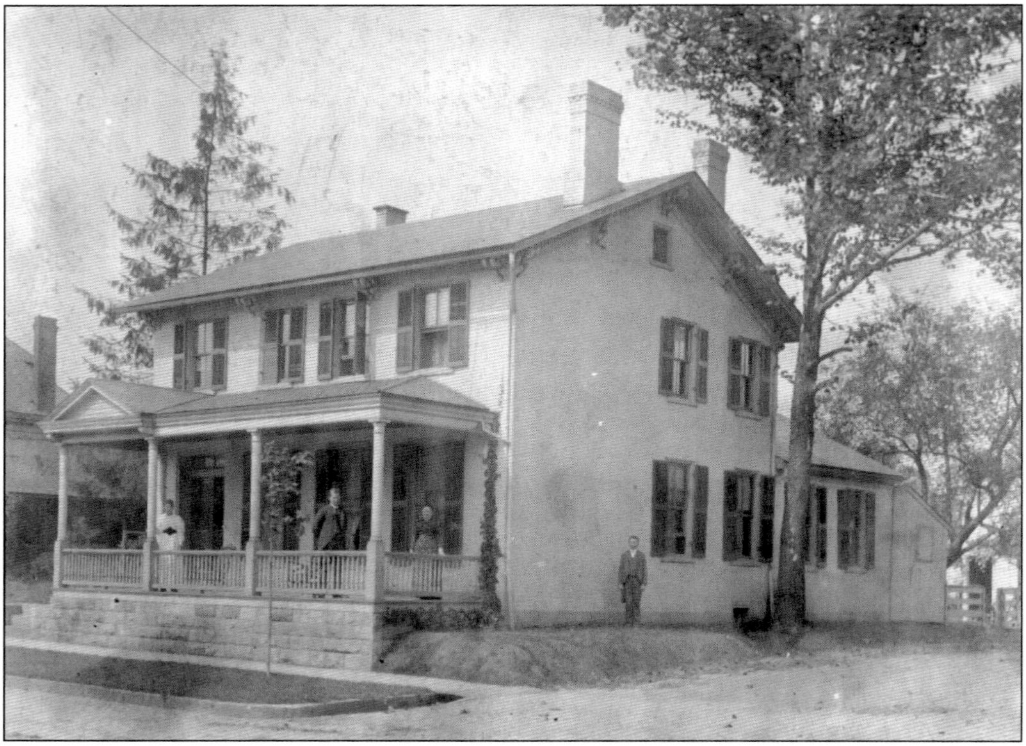

The Nace Family Home. Situated on the northwest corner of East Lincoln Way and Harrison Street, this residential photograph was taken about 1893 or 1894. Family members are pictured on the front porch, although it is prior to the birth of George Nace, later principal of David Anderson High School, where the gymnasium is named in his honor. The home has remained in the family through the generations.

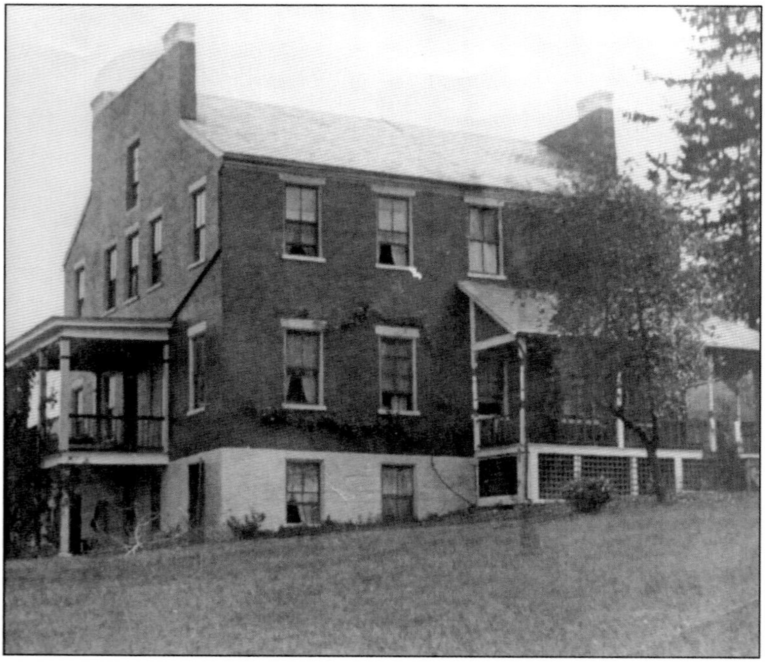

The Spirit Fruit Farm. This large brick home stood on the farm acreage that became the Columbiana County Fairgrounds. Although it is no longer there, at one time it was named Spirit Fruit Farm and housed a utopian society founded by Jacob Beilhart. Their history is quite interesting in terms of the 19th-century trend of separatist, idealistic societies.

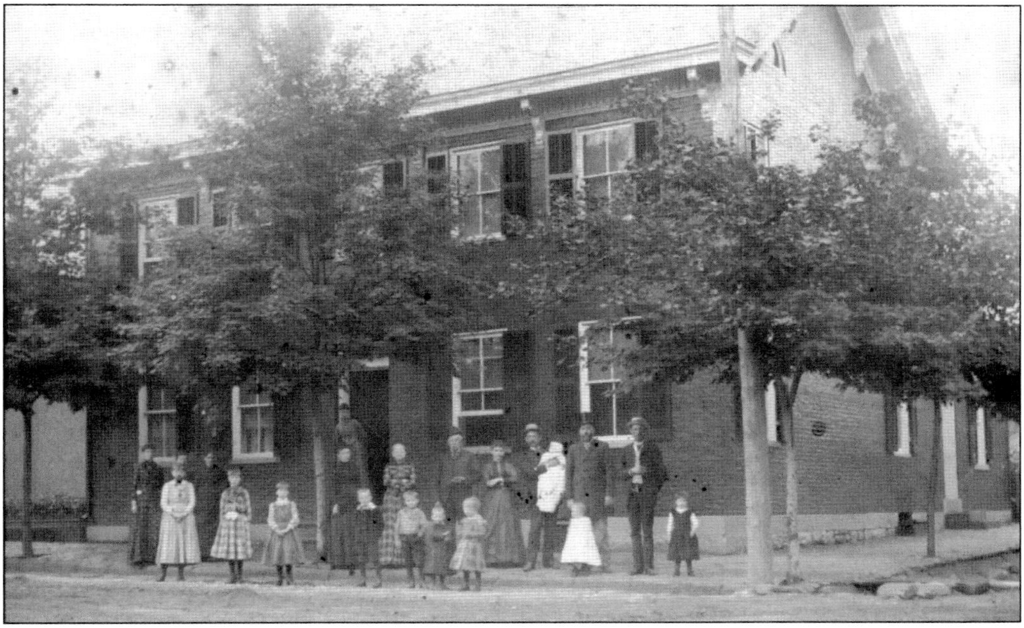

WILCOXEN HOUSE IN 1895. Originally the Wilcoxen House, this building still stands and is in use as the local Montessori school at the northwest corner of East Washington and South Vine Streets. At another time it was owned by the Glenn sisters, Alice and Gertrude, whose home was around the corner. The extended family is gathered around the front of the large building that stands close to the sidewalk and street corner.

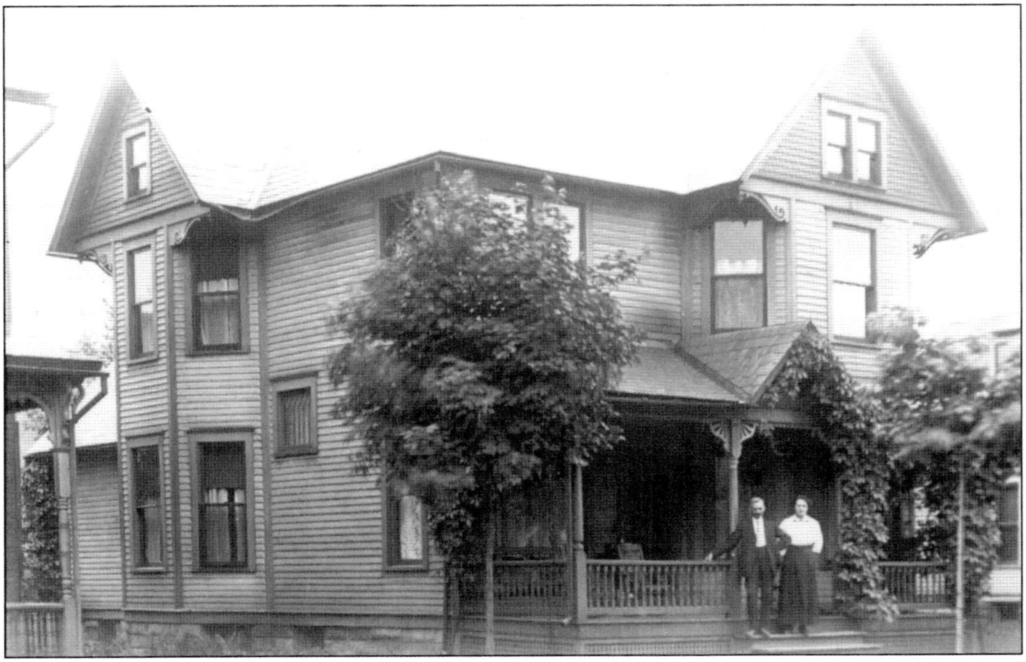

WEST LINCOLN WAY VICTORIAN. This traditional Victorian is representative of the times—typical characteristics are evident. Many of these Victorians stand on East and West Lincoln Way, still occupied and maintained, some quite large, giving a charm to the village as motorists drive the Lincoln Highway today.

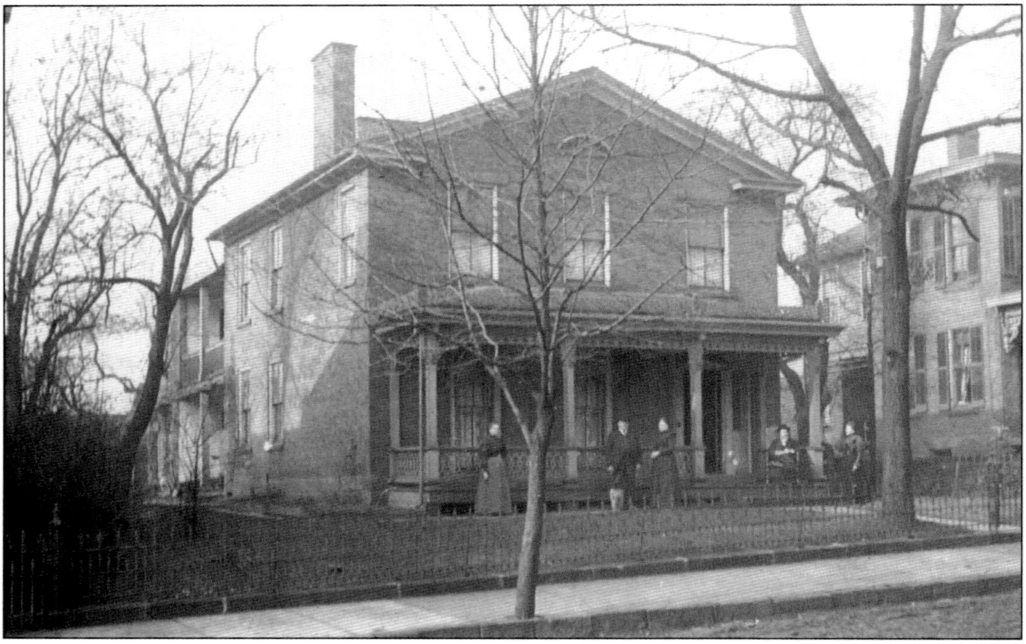

Traditional North Market Street. While this home no longer stands, it was typical of the procession of houses going north on Market Street hill. Today, it has been razed, and a commercial enterprise is on the site.

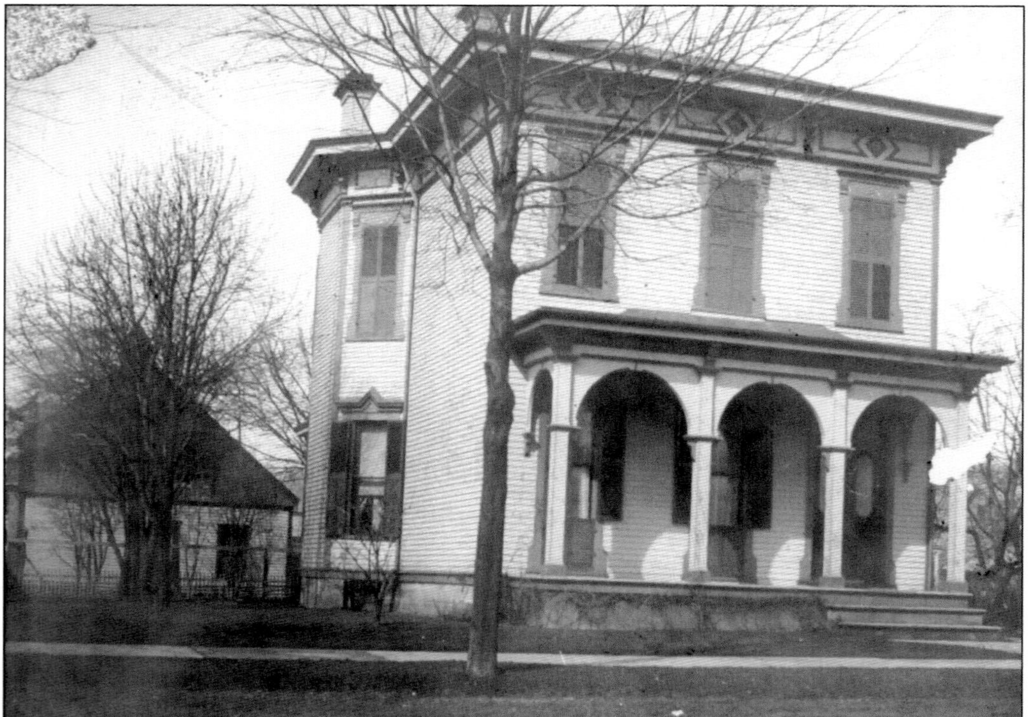

East Washington Street Classic. This home, still a residence today, shows the architectural bend toward Italianate lines. This dwelling and the house immediately next to it create interesting images in their great similarities, particularly the rooflines and porches.

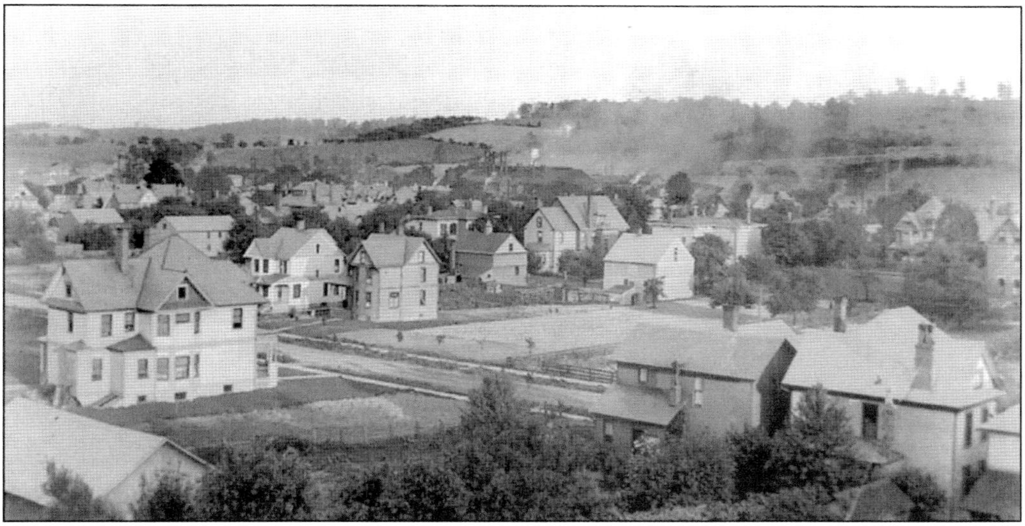

EAST END OF LISBON. This view of the East End of Lisbon was taken in 1899. The prominent house in the foreground was the home of the Farmer-Wright family, well-known local industrialists. The home remained in the family until the death of W.F. Wright in 1957, but it continues to serve as a residence along a tree-lined street now filled with fairly large family homes. (Courtesy of Kenneth Everett.)

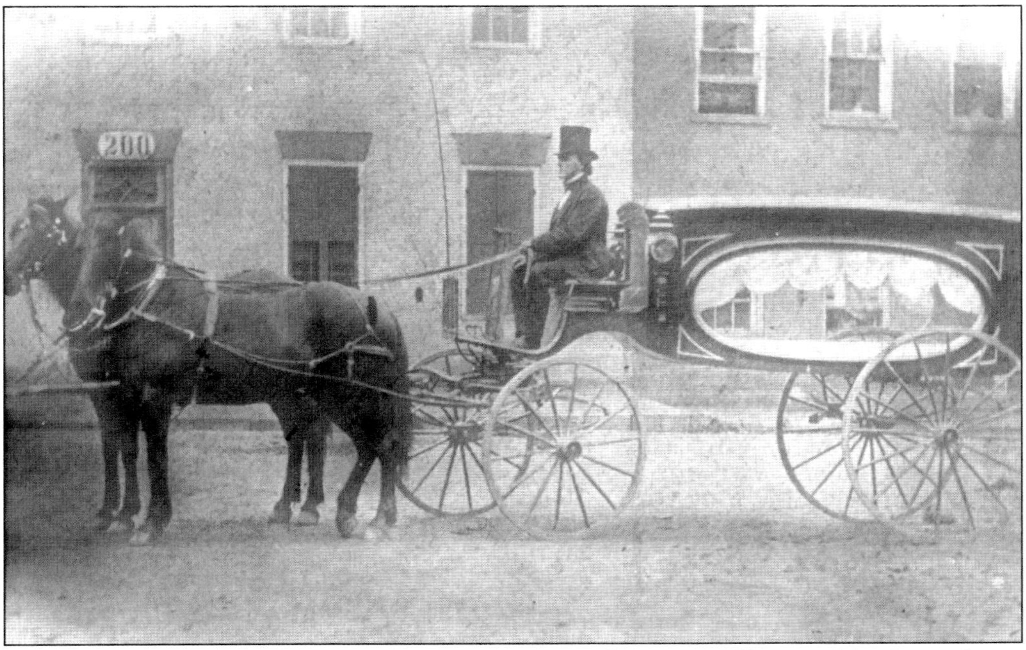

ERASTUS EELLS WITH HORSE-DRAWN HEARSE. Erastus Eells is pictured here with his horse-drawn hearse. This particular photograph is a great favorite and is often displayed in the historical society's Train Station Museum. As was so typical in those days, Eells progressed from cabinetmaker to coffins to funeral director in his lifetime.

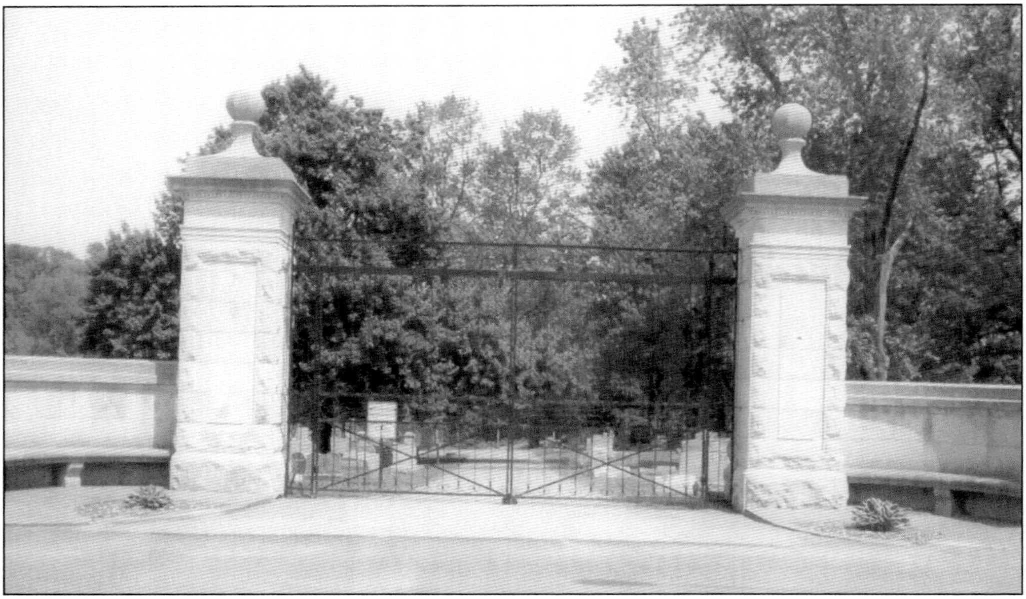

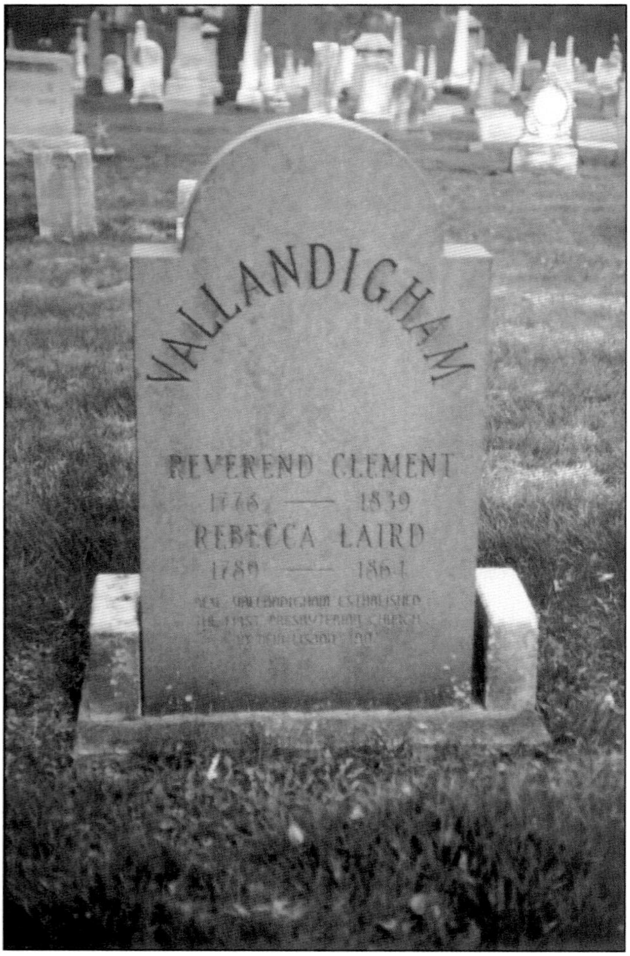

LISBON CEMETERY GATES. Continuing family tradition within the community, associate justice of the US Supreme Court John H. Clarke gave these gates as well as an endowment to the Lisbon Cemetery. Standing at the main entrance, they are majestic in size as they usher visitors to services and gravesites. Justice Clarke is buried in this cemetery with his family.

REV. CLEMENT VALLANDIGHAM GRAVE. Reverend Vallandigham, founding pastor of Lisbon's First Presbyterian Church in 1807, lies within this cemetery. His tombstone is a tribute not only to him, but also to all who founded the community and its institutions. In recent years, the church he founded, now named New Lisbon Presbyterian, has tended to his monument and gravesite. (Courtesy of Wendell Cole.)

Four

Gathering in Community

With its size, age, and traditions, Lisbon is definitely a community that maintains its gathering opportunities. Over the years, these have evolved into a spirit of expectations that certain institutions and events will result in people from the town and surrounding area coming together. The broad outlines are those centering upon the schools, the churches, the events staged by the town, and the organizations.

The schools have their calendar of musical, sporting, and academic events. Lisbon has always been a community where sports are very important. Teams have won championships over the years, including a state football title in 1995 and a state track championship in the same decade. Friday night football games are memorable as well as the growth of sports for girls. Naturally, the band, also winning championships, has played a large part. Plays and musicals draw good audiences while dances and proms are still special in school life and memories. In the academic realm, there is an emphasis upon National Honor Society, the Academic Banquet, the traditional Senior Awards Day, and the naming of honor students.

From the beginning, churches have maintained individual identities, yet they have always gathered together for special services. During the mid-20th century, a series of union services was held each year, bringing prominent clergy from a variety of denominations. The churches still maintain a council of clergy called the Ministerial Association, although various churches have their own annual meals and special services. The Banquet is a new community unifier, a meal for anyone and everyone.

And there are the traditional events. Each spring, the town gathers for a pre–Memorial Day service in the village square followed the next morning by a parade to the Lisbon Cemetery with a service complete with speakers and salutes to the veterans. The midsummer Columbiana County Fair brings great crowds not only from the village, but also the surrounding areas. In years past there were minstrels, the yuletide ball, and still occurring are the very special Alumni Association and Athletic Halls of Fame events honoring notable former students each year.

Community togetherness has reigned for over 200 years. Seasonal in nature, there is a certain ambience for all concerned.

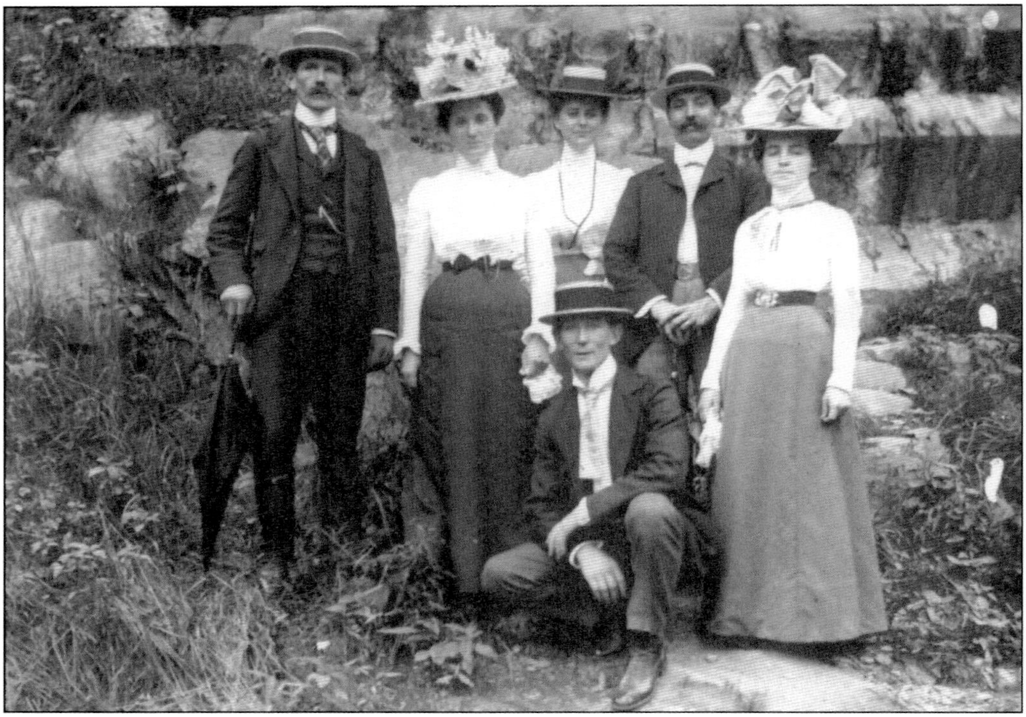

Turn-of-the-Century Grouping. This unnamed group of couples is gathered at Cabin John Bridge in this photograph dated July 29, 1900. Illustrative of the companionship among younger couples in the community that has always been and continues to be a local hallmark, they are also an excellent representation of the fashions in clothing of that day.

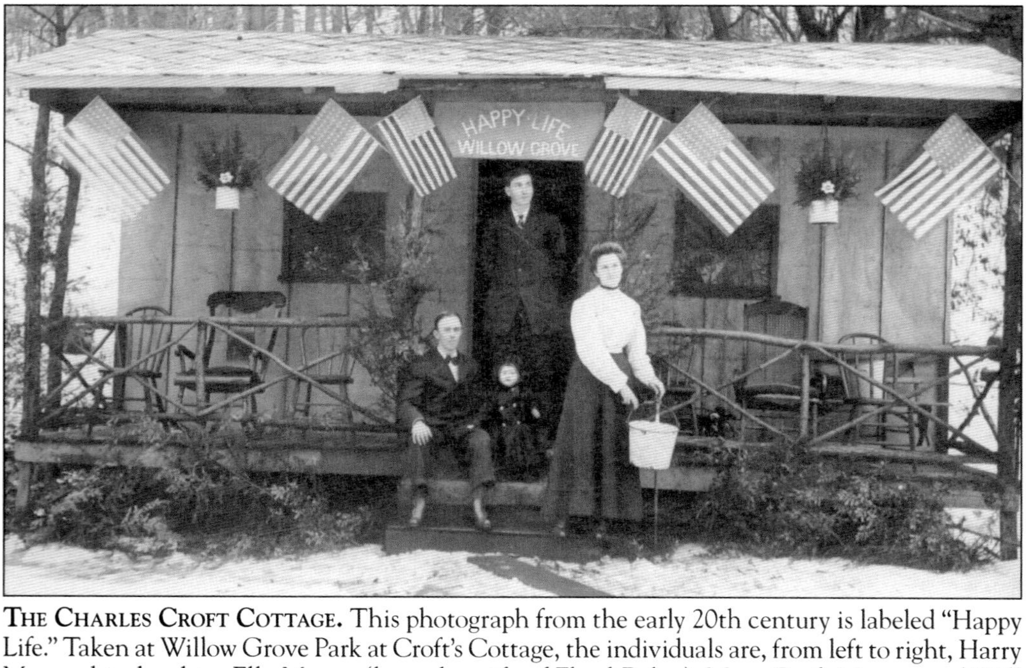

The Charles Croft Cottage. This photograph from the early 20th century is labeled "Happy Life." Taken at Willow Grove Park at Croft's Cottage, the individuals are, from left to right, Harry Mason, his daughter Ella Mason (later the wife of Floyd Baker), Mary Croft Mason, and Will Croft (standing in back). Willow Grove still exists today as a village park.

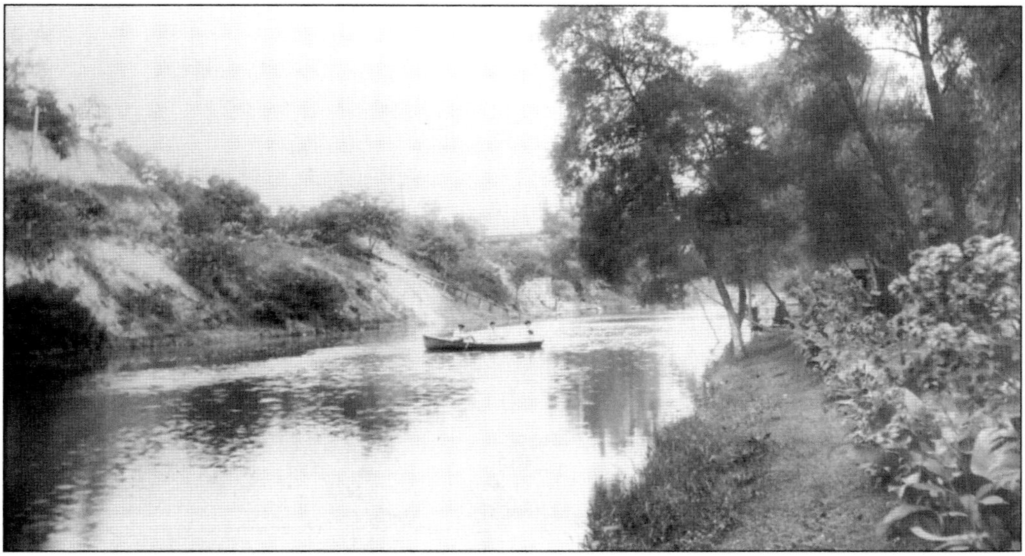

Boating in Willow Grove Park. Willow Grove Park, on the western edge of the town, stretches under the Canton Bridge northward. A natural setting, it has been in existence for a long time. Along the shores of the creek was the building of the Lisbon Lions Club, a popular gathering spot until it was lost to fire. The swinging bridge over the creek was destroyed by a flood.

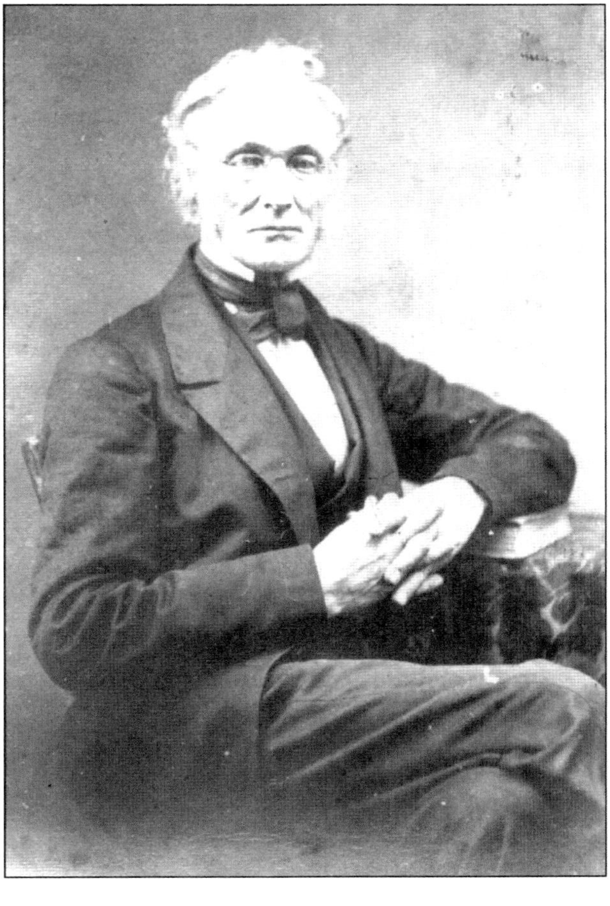

David Anderson. The story of David Anderson is a fascinating one. He literally walked to the community only to become the longtime educator of the generations. His influence was so great that the high school built in the 20th century was named for him, retaining that name today after a move to another facility.

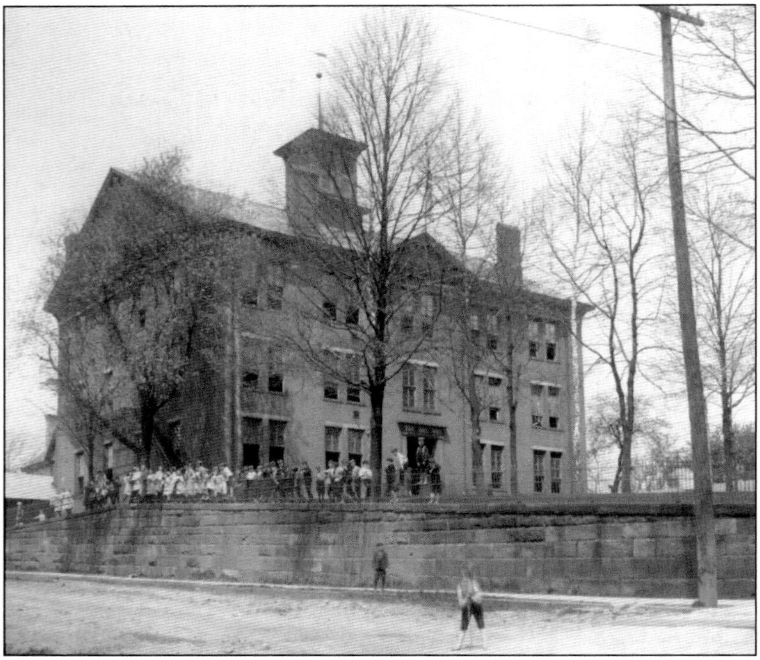

The Landmark School. Built in 1856 and serving as a schoolhouse until 1952, the North Market Street School, later renamed the Lincoln School, is indelibly associated with education in Lisbon. Housing all grades in its early years, it eventually became an elementary and junior high school in the 1920s. The schoolyard surrounded by the stone wall on two sides was the regular scene of daily recess.

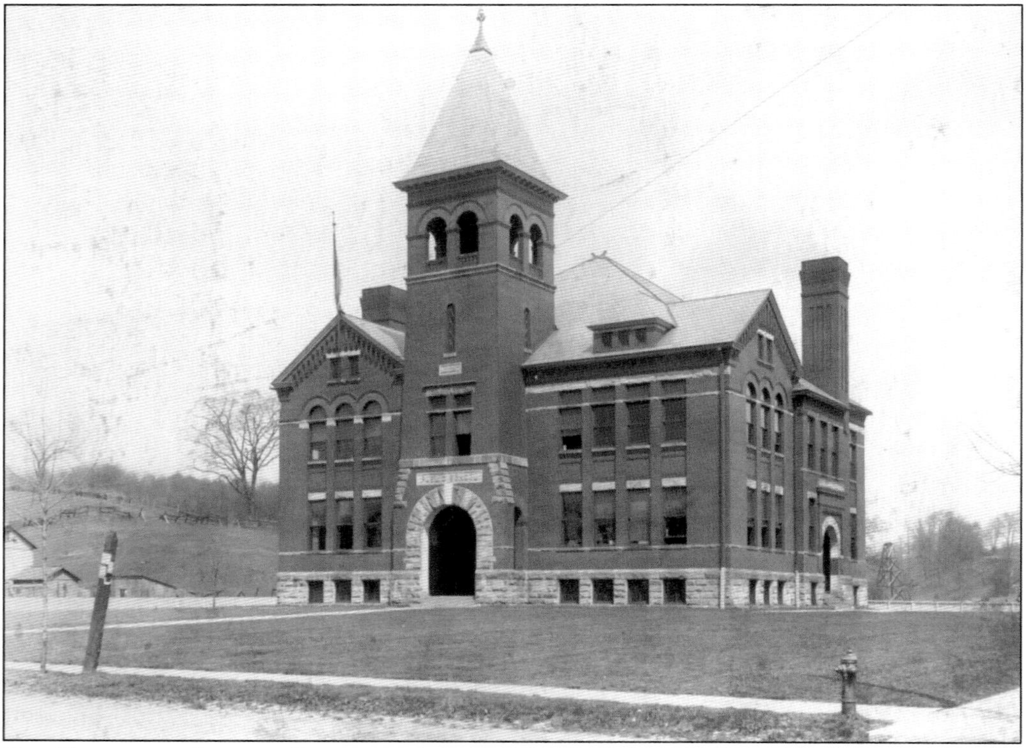

The Companion School. Constructed in 1879, the East Chestnut Street School, later renamed the McKinley School, is a well-remembered sturdy structure that housed grades one through six. In a catastrophic fire on a cold March night in 1950, the building burned completely, and the village's eastern-half students in classrooms of grades one through four and all of the town's fifth and sixth graders were scattered throughout the town in churches and public structures.

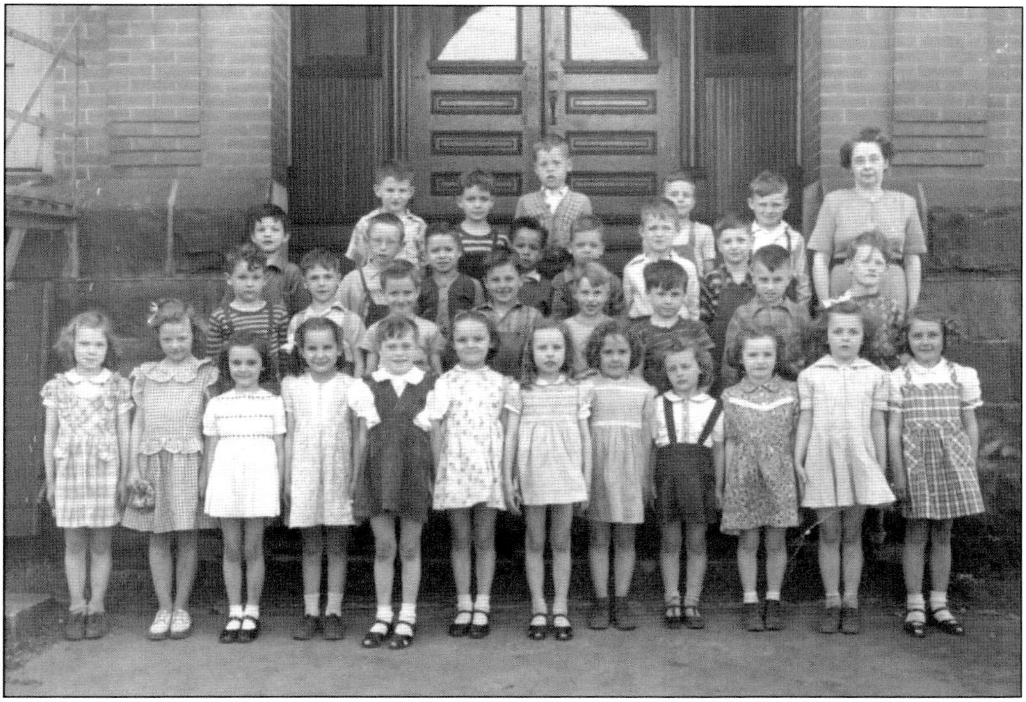

McKinley First Graders, 1946–1947. With the loved Nettie McPherson, first grade teacher for more than half a century, these first graders pose for the annual portrait. They are, from left to right, (first row) unidentified, Martha Wells, Karen Prasco, Joanne Parrish, Judy Knight, Shirley Bailey, Elizabeth Duke, Betty Moore, Ida ?, unidentified, Patricia Kelch, and Martha Boone; (second row) John Hinchcliffe, Paul Butream, Otis Lohr, Raymond Perrino, Wendell Cole, Lynn Brown, William B. Moore III, and William Garwood; (third row) Frank Chamberlain, Cecil Flory, Darrell Dillard, unidentified, Billy Conn, and Billy Brownfield; (fourth row) Raymond Dixon, Willis Bowman, Curtis Nicholson, Gary Neel, and John Coie. (Courtesy of Wendell Cole.)

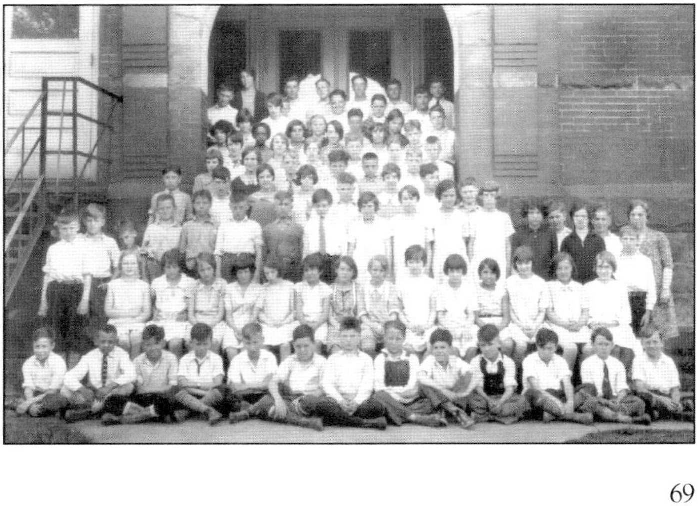

McKinley Third and Fourth Grades, 1927. With two unidentified teachers, this group of 75 students represents the third and fourth grade classes that would have occupied the two large classrooms on the east side of the school. The archways were the main entrances to the building, but the fire escapes were used for regular drills and daily recess entry and exit.

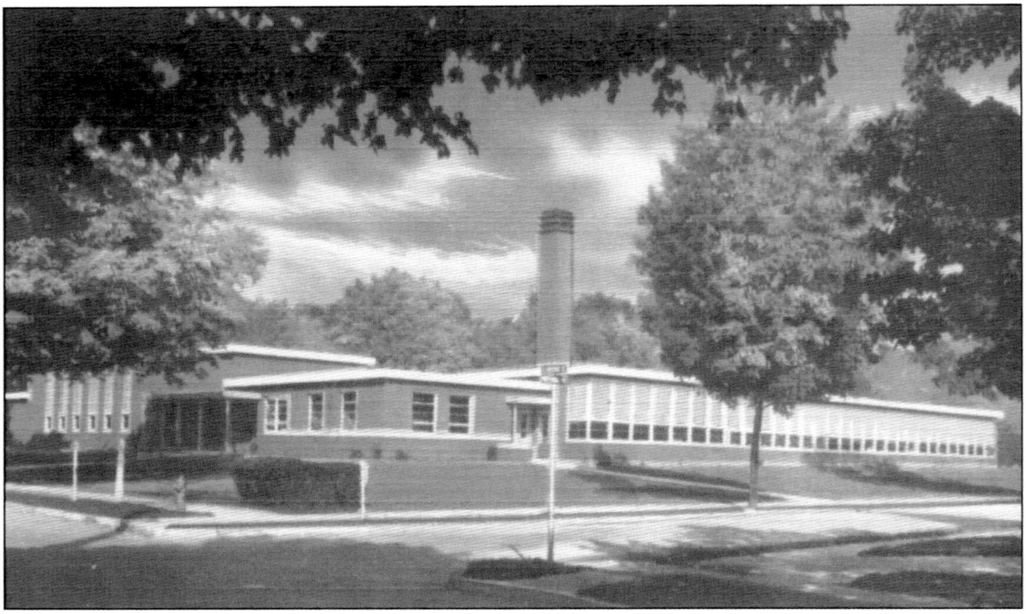

The New McKinley School. This building replaced the fire-ravaged McKinley School on the corner of East Chestnut Street and Pritchard Avenue. Very modern in its inaugural year, 1951—just a year after the fire—it has shown much progress in educational opportunities. Today, it is home to kindergarten through fifth grade. The school is definitely part of a neighborhood. (Author's collection.)

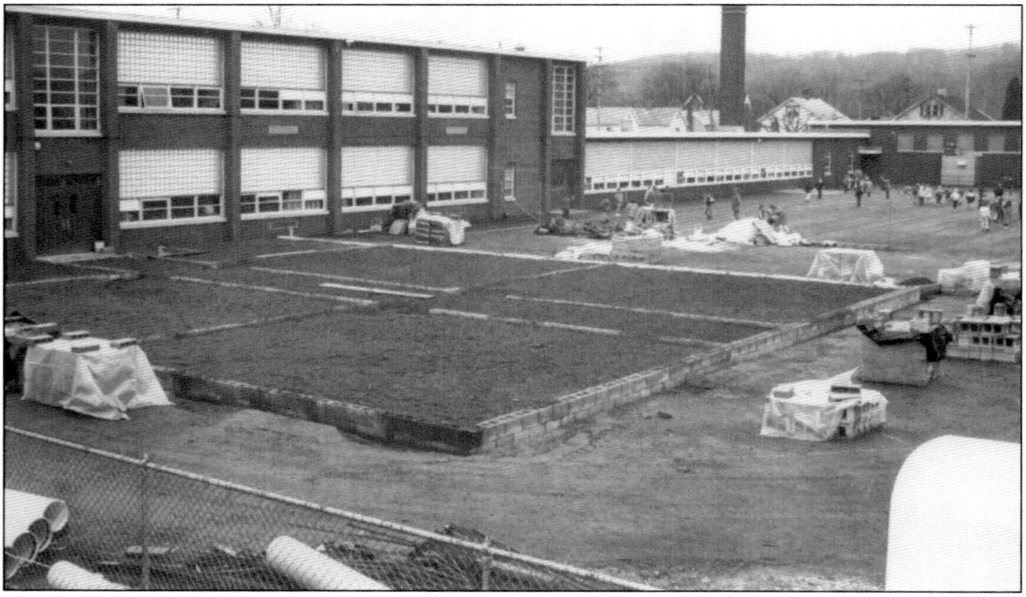

McKinley School Expansion. The McKinley School is seen here as it undergoes yet another expansion. From the basic school shown above, it has seen numerous additions as it works its way west on East Chestnut Street, replacing houses with buildings, a parking lot, and a playground.

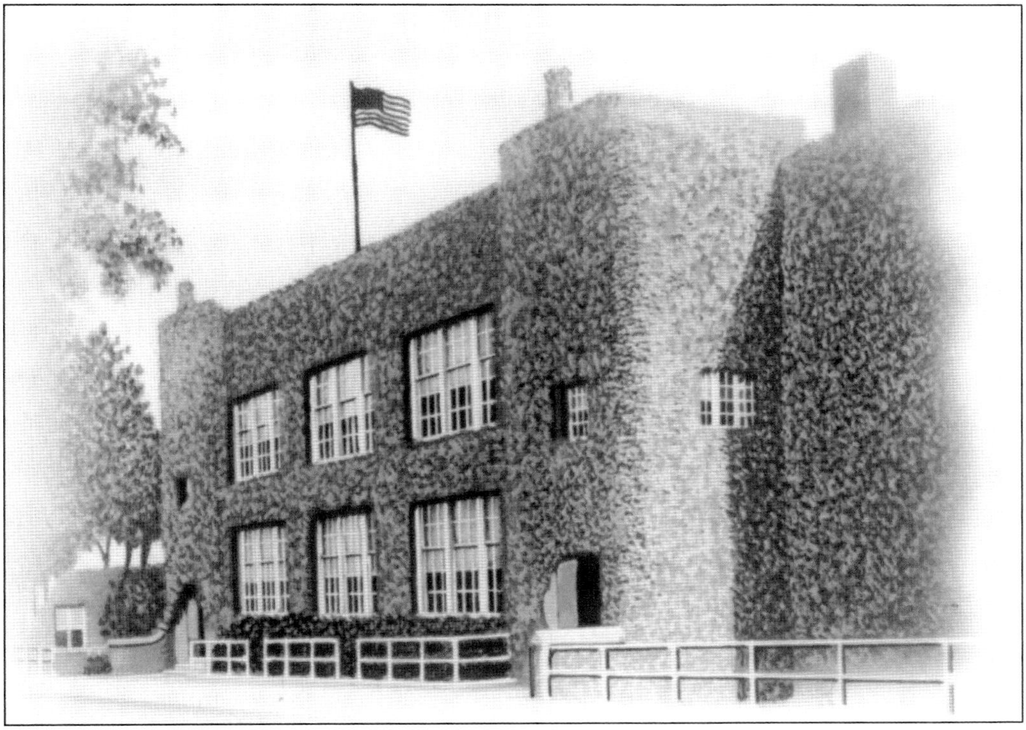

DAVID ANDERSON HIGH SCHOOL. The high school constructed in the late 1910s holds many memories for generations of students until high schoolers were moved to the new Lincoln, assuming the name David Anderson Junior/Senior High School. This building that eventually spawned multiple additions stood proudly on West Lincoln Way with its name for the venerable Lisbon educator, David Anderson. Today, it is the Judge Charles A. Pike Juvenile Justice Center.

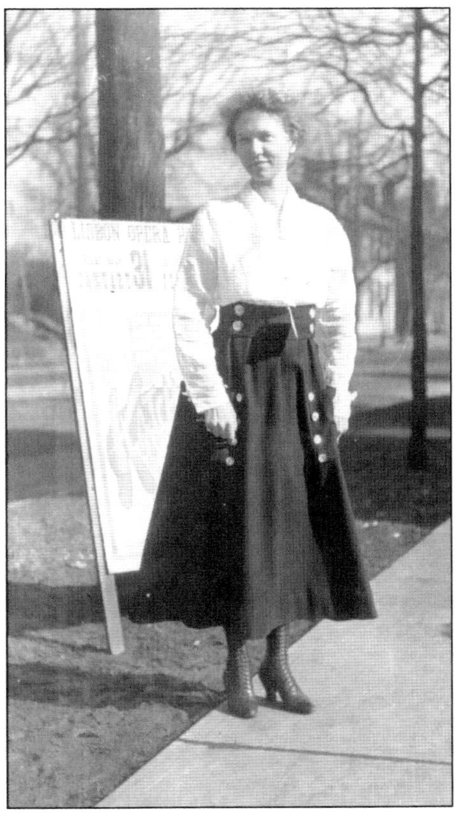

SADIE VAN FOSSAN. In this 1915 photograph, "Miss Sadie" Van Fossan is seen as a young teacher in the Lisbon Schools prior to her long tenure as the high school principal. Not only is she remembered for her excellence in that role, but also for the gift she willed to the community in initiating the town's swimming pool that bears her name.

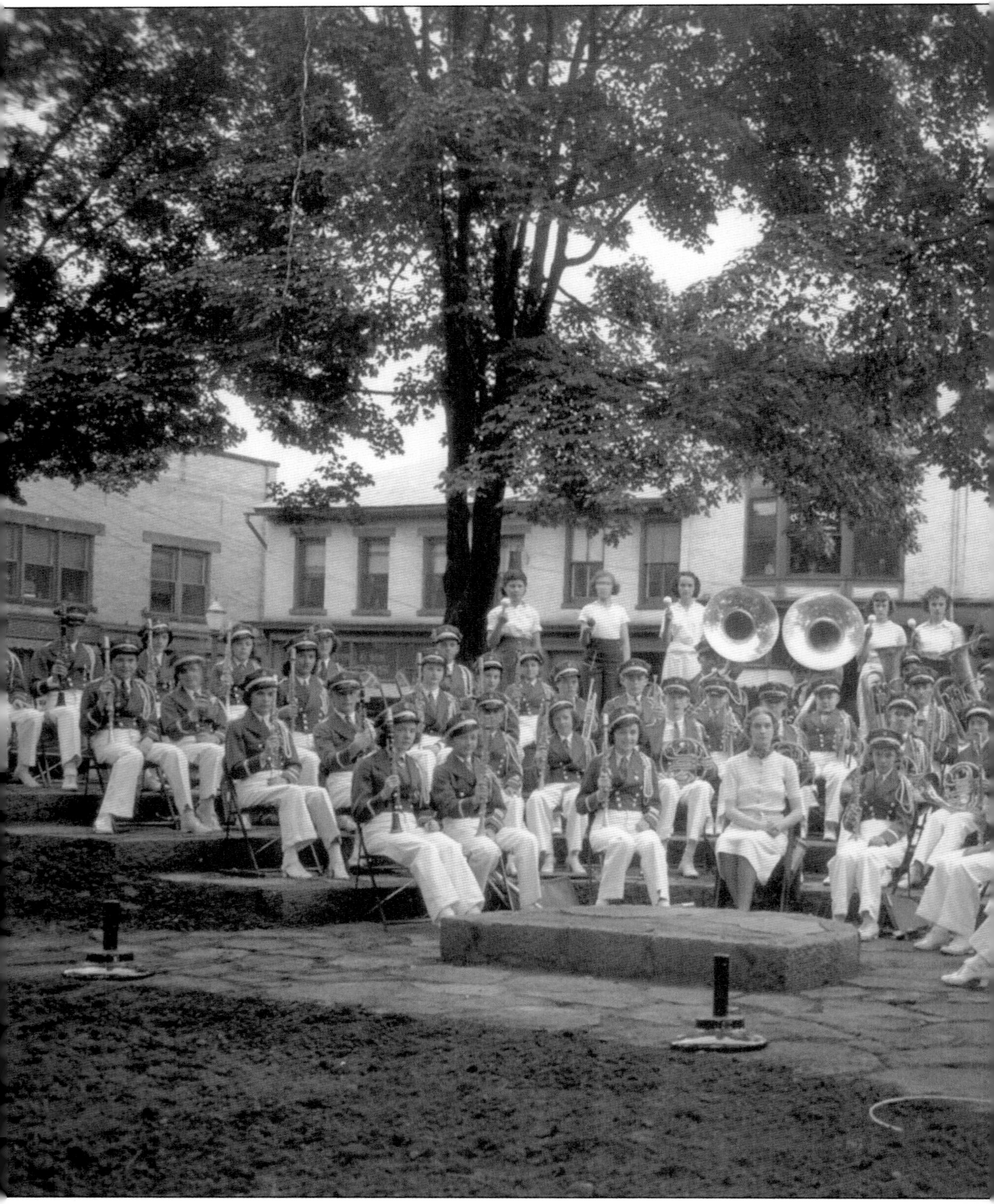

David Anderson Band. David Anderson High School has been very well known for its award-winning bands. By training students early, the instruction is continued with intensity through junior and senior high school years. Shown here is the 1935 band grouped on the south portion of the village square. Prof. Arthur Wise was the well-known conductor of these bands, which drew

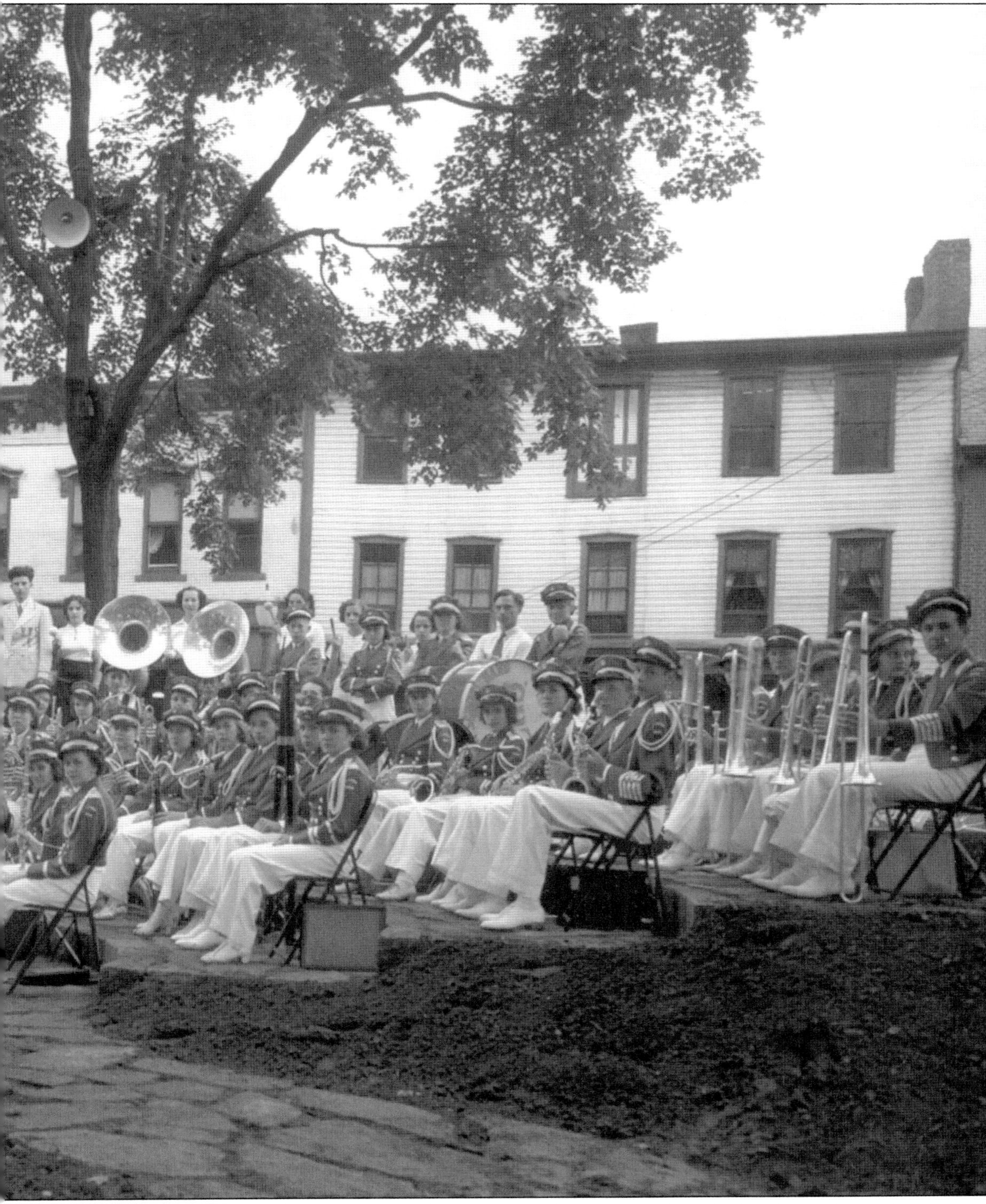

attention with their performances, awards, and travels. Here, not only is the band prominent, but also the buildings of the village square; all of them stand today except the far left one. Housing a five-and-dime store as well as Lafferty-Lewis Law Offices, it was destroyed in a huge fire in 1976 that also ruined the adjacent O.S. Hill Building.

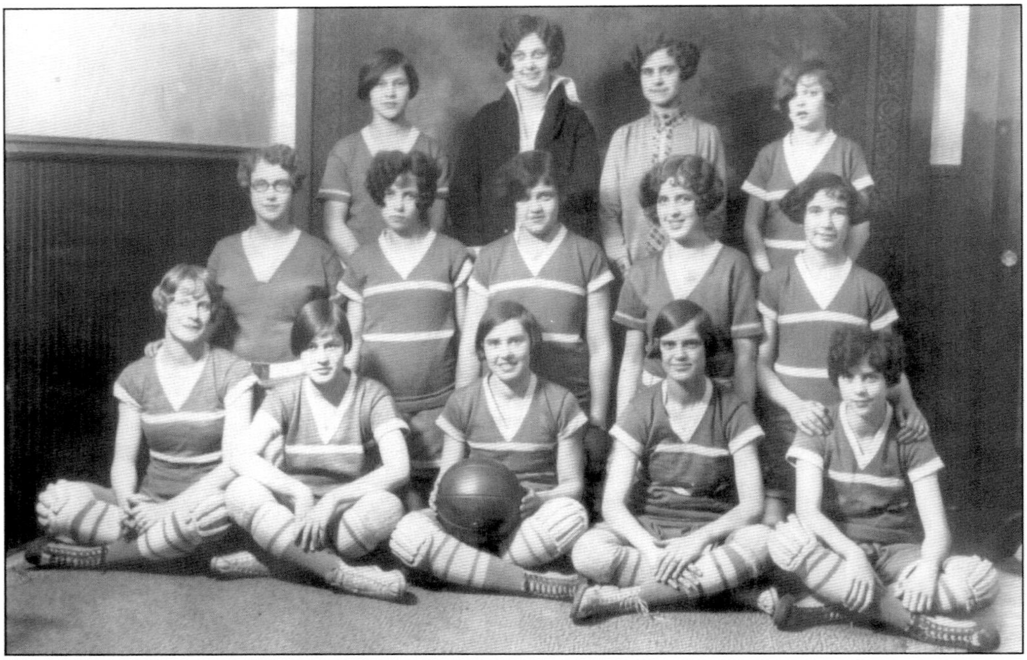

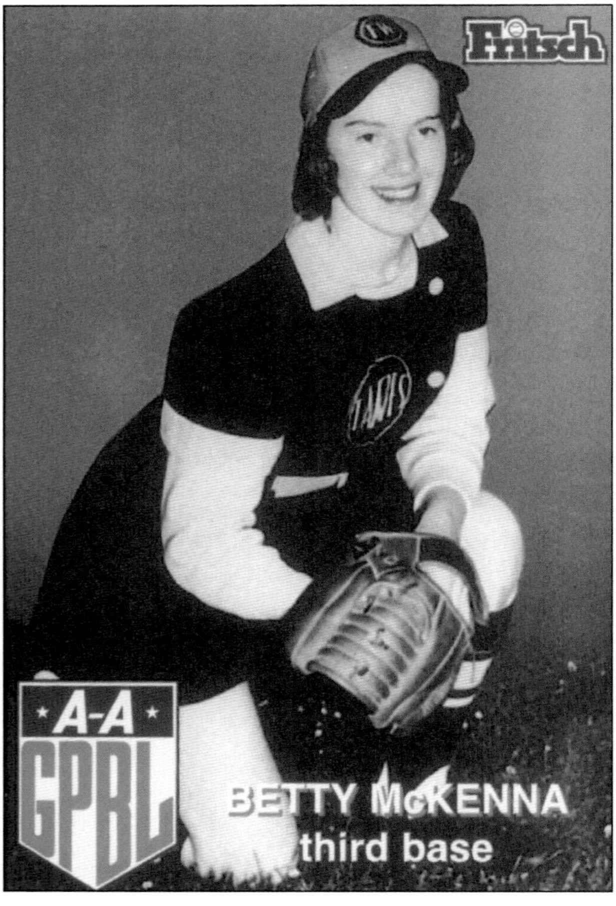

Early Sports for Women. This shows an early women's basketball team, a base for the growth of women's sports in Lisbon schools. Although no names are given, Alice "Tommy" Armstrong, longtime physical education teacher in the school system is identifiable, first row, fourth from left.

Baseball's Betty McKenna. Lisbon native Betty McKenna achieved early prominence in her athletic abilities. She played for three different teams in her initial 1951 season in the All-American Girls Professional Baseball League. They were represented in the Tom Hanks movie *A League of Their Own*. At age 22, she held the permanent third-base position until the closing of the league.

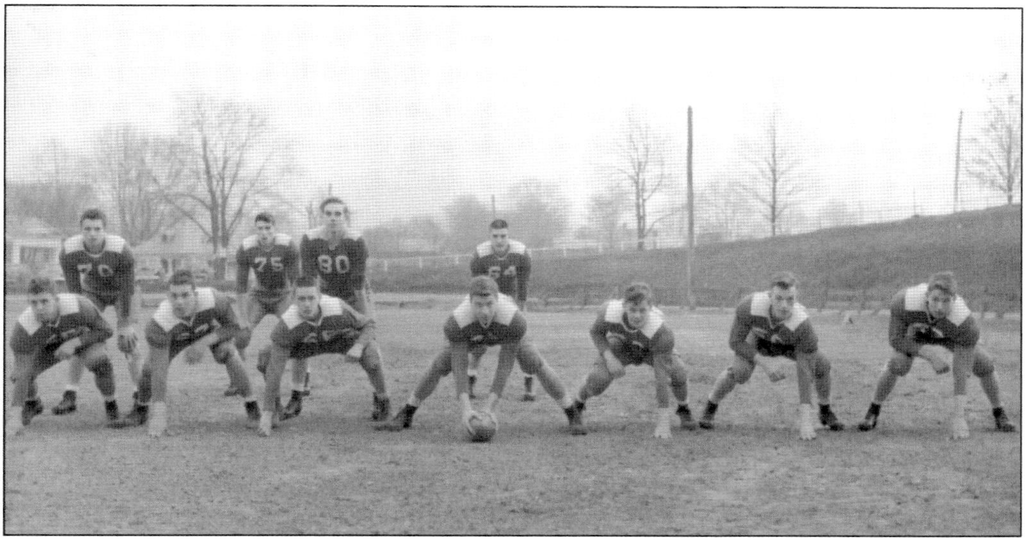

LISBON FOOTBALL CHAMPS, 1946. Through the years, Lisbon has produced many strong football teams. This championship team included, from left to right, (line) Felix Rutecki, T. Gilmore, Dave Borrow, Ken Robinson, Roger James, W. McDevitt, and Bud Woods; (backfield) D. Stark, Alan Webber, Tom McKenna, and Ray Davies.

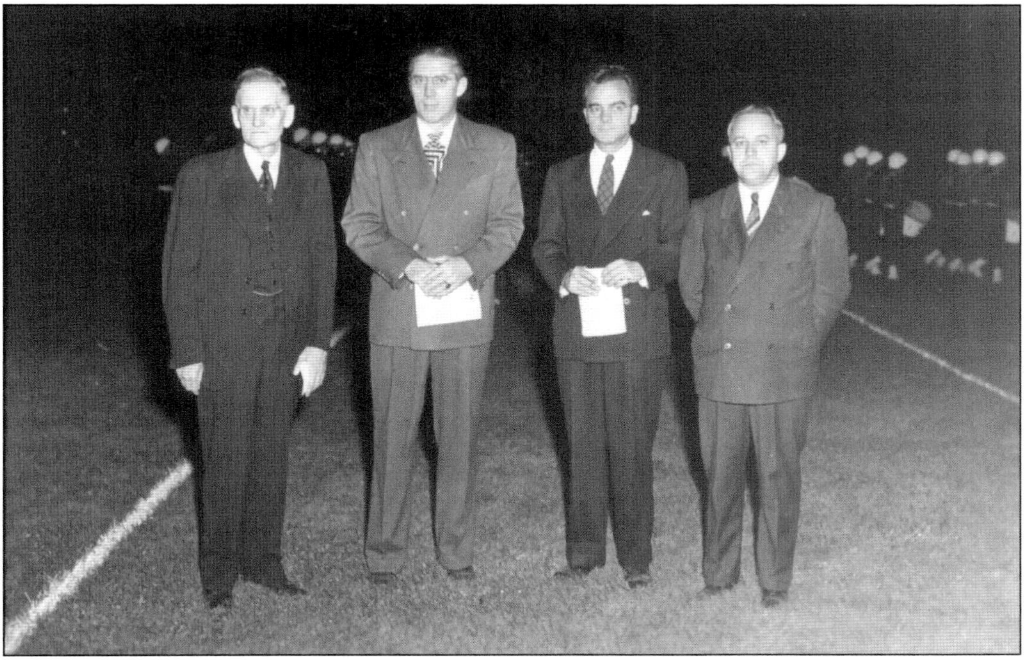

STADIUM DEDICATION, 1948. In 1948, the new stadium was dedicated; originally called War Memorial Stadium, the playing field is now named Bucher Field in honor of the longtime football coach. From left to right are Supt. H.C. Leonard, Mayor Kenneth Hiscox, Rev. Christian Kenneweg of United Presbyterian Church, and Rev. Paul Gerrard of First Presbyterian Church, all participating in the dedication.

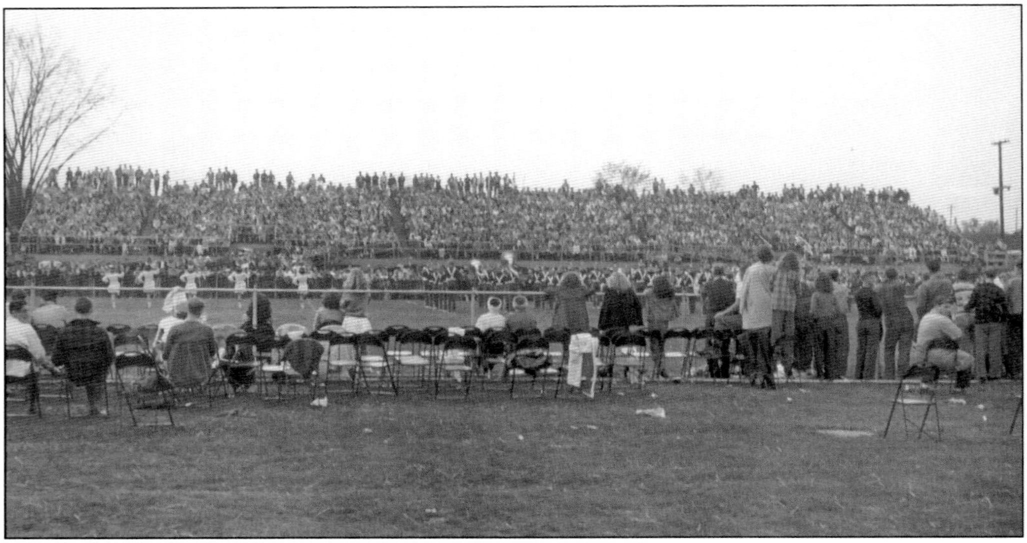

Stadium at Its Dedication. The stadium is filled to capacity at its dedication, still a familiar sight of many fans more than one night per week in season. While some new facilities have been built, the stadium retains its original look and many memories over the years for players, coaches, band members, and local fans.

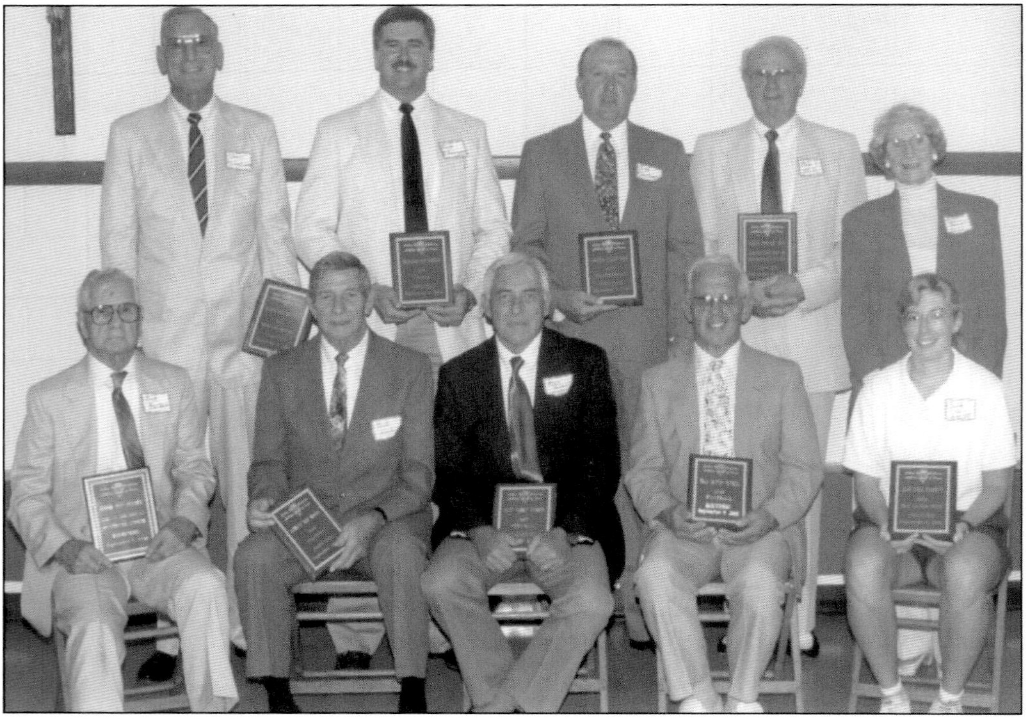

First Athletic Hall of Fame. Begun in 1992, the Athletic Hall of Fame inducted these athletes, who participated in various sports throughout the years, in its first induction ceremony. They are, from left to right, (first row) Bud Bucher (football coach), Bud Woods (football), Alan Webber (football), Felix Rutecki (football), and Julie Cole (track); (second row) Dean Nicholson (basketball), Rick Pittenger (track and field), Jim Courtney (basketball), Jack Mills (basketball coach), and Doris Eells (accepting posthumously for her brother Sky Mefort).

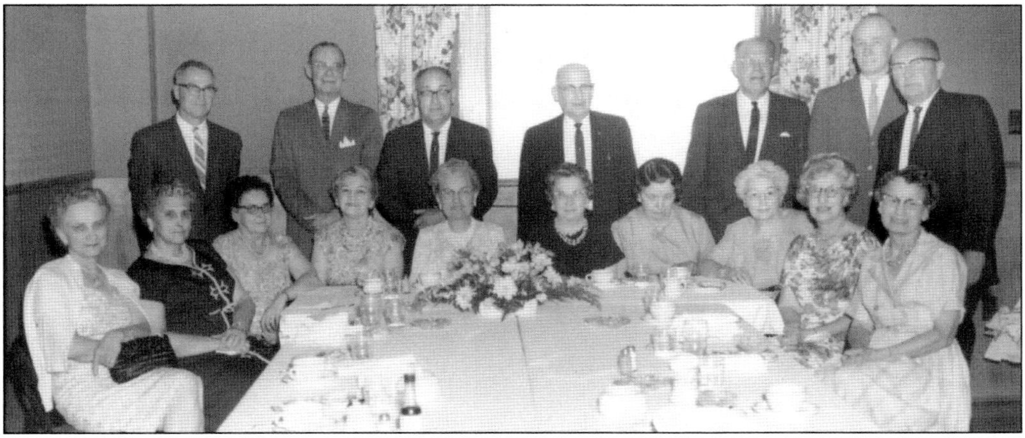

CLASS OF 1919 REUNION. While the names are not available, this class enjoyed reunions for many years. This one, occurring at the then popular Timberlanes Restaurant in Salem, was, undoubtedly, an evening of reminiscing about stories of long ago. Many local friendships are maintained through these gatherings. Some meet monthly, some annually, and most every five years.

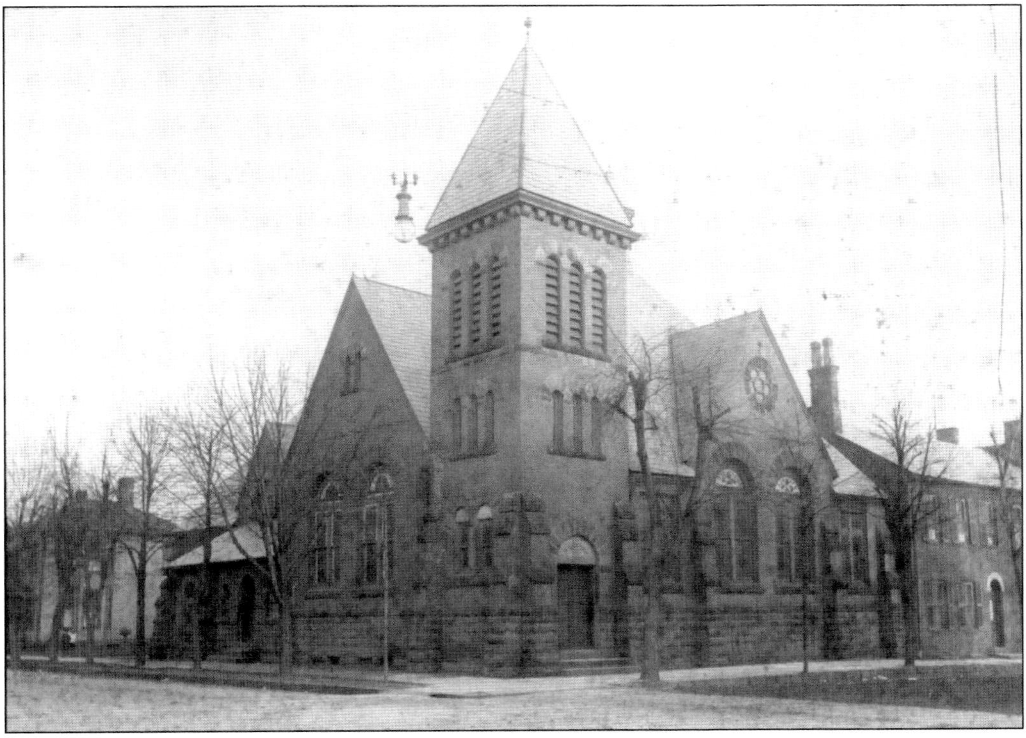

METHODIST EPISCOPAL CHURCH. This Methodist church at the corner of South Market and East Washington Streets served the congregation from 1888 until it was destroyed by fire on February 28, 1944. After the fire, the members held services in David Anderson High School until the new church was built on the same site.

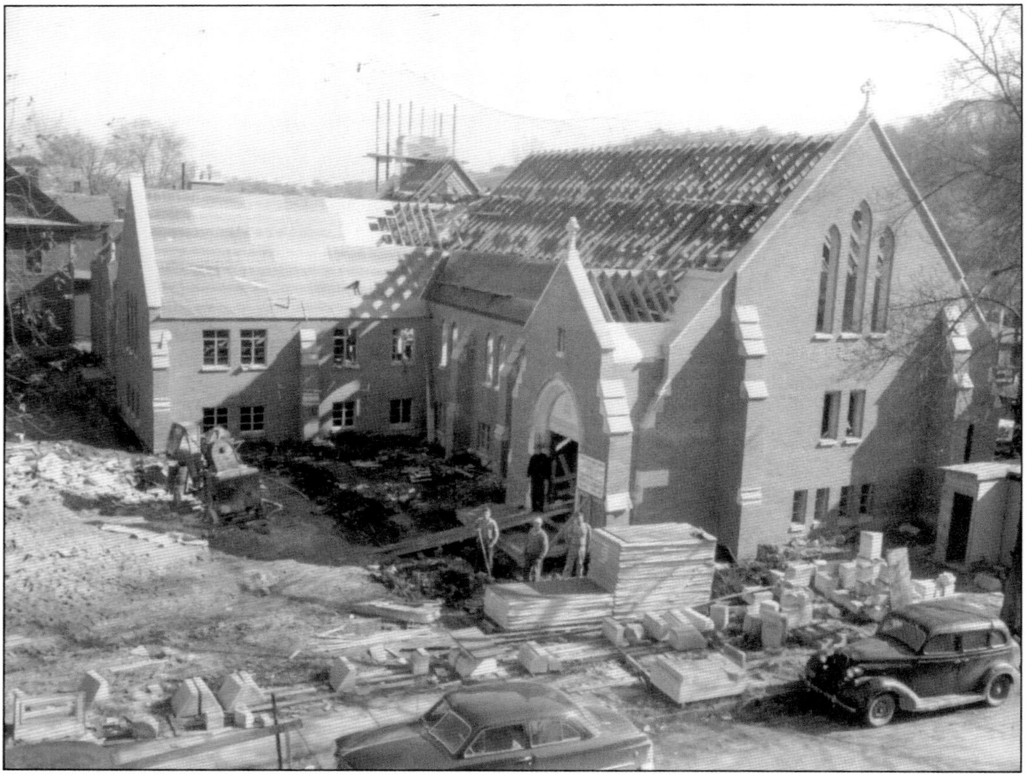

First United Methodist Church. This photograph shows the new Methodist church under construction. The cornerstone was laid in 1949; while the building was being finished, a fourth grade McKinley School class displaced by that fire was already meeting there. Since the original building was completed, other additions have been made to this well-used church.

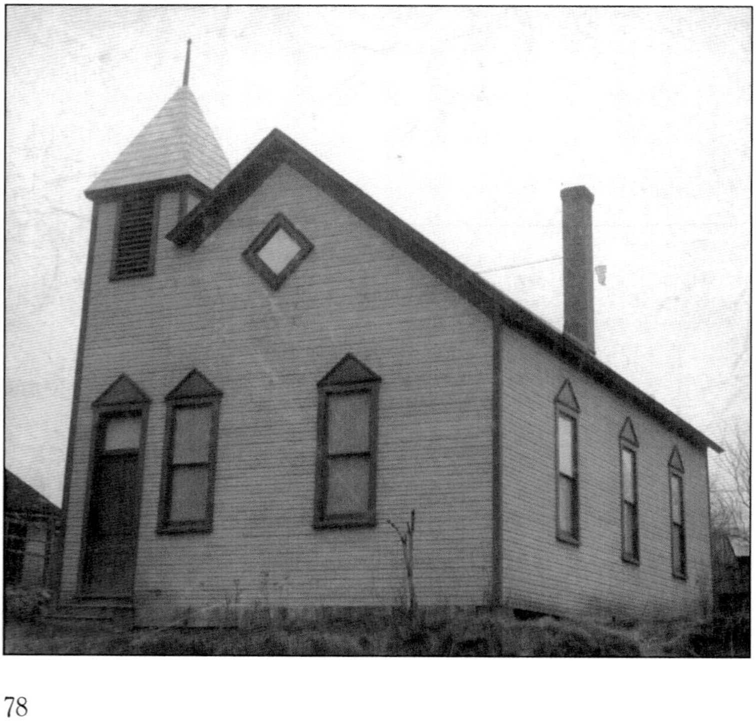

A.M.E. Zion Church. This African American church was built on North Beaver Street in 1886. It served as a church from that date until the congregation was dissolved in 2015. The building has changed somewhat in appearance since this 1900 photograph.

DISCIPLES OF CHRIST CHURCH. This building was erected in 1841. Its early Baptist background and the evangelistic movement conducted by Walter Scott, a Steubenville Academy instructor, are important aspects of the church's history. Alexander Campbell, frequently called the founder of the Disciples of Christ, is said to have preached here.

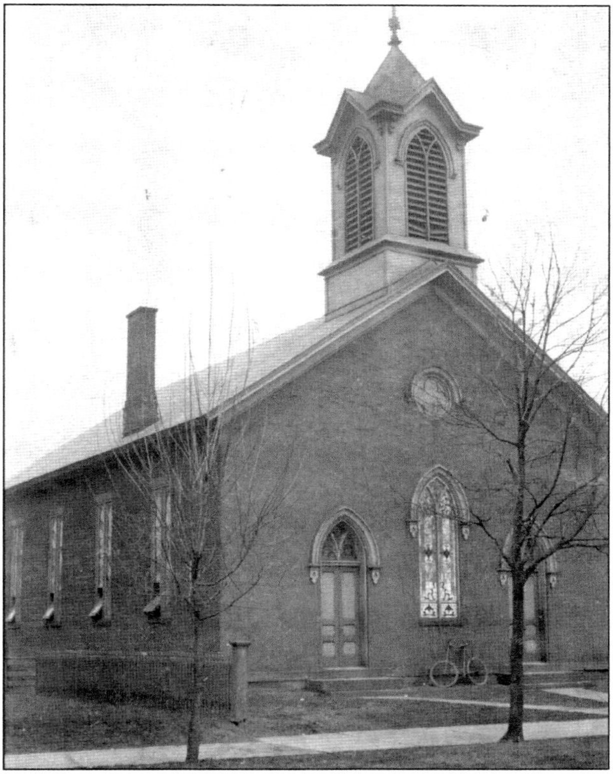

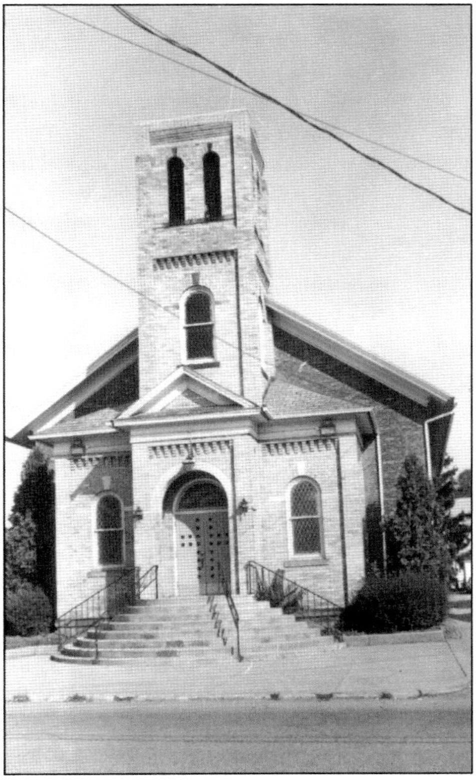

LISBON'S CHRISTIAN CHURCH. This same East Washington Street building pictured above has had extensive remodeling through the years, specifically in 1875 and 1910. While it is interesting to contemplate, this is the basic church with the addition of a front section, the tower, and the elaborate steps leading to the front door. Lisbon is also home to two similar churches, the Church of Christ and the Lisbon Church of Christ.

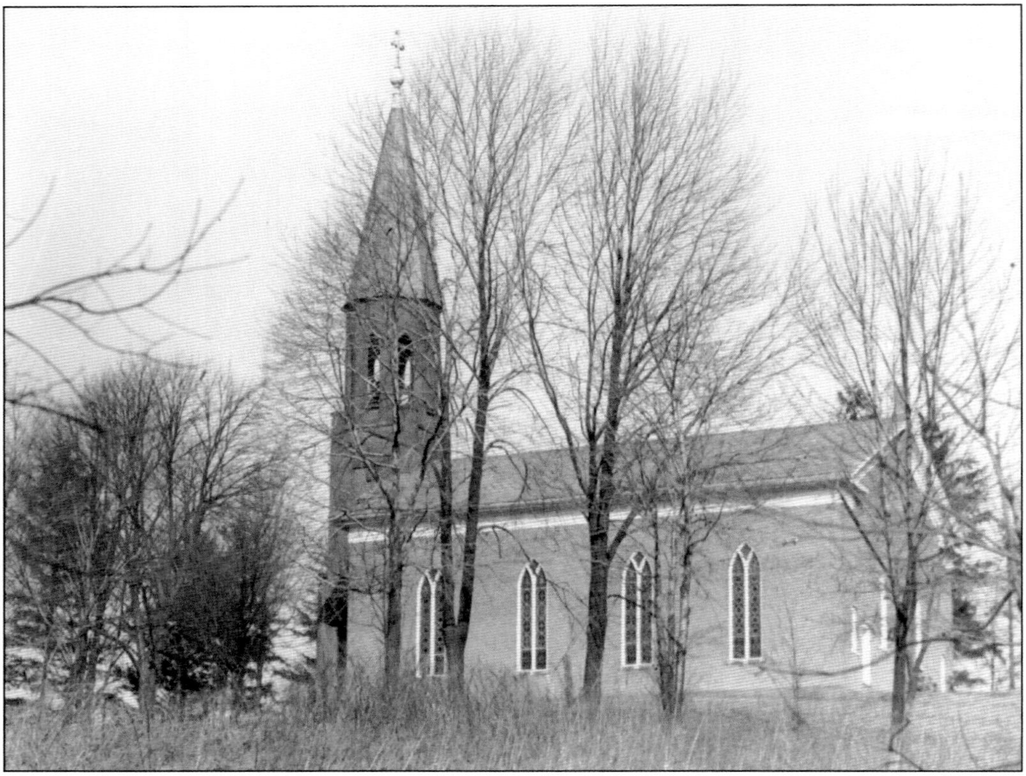

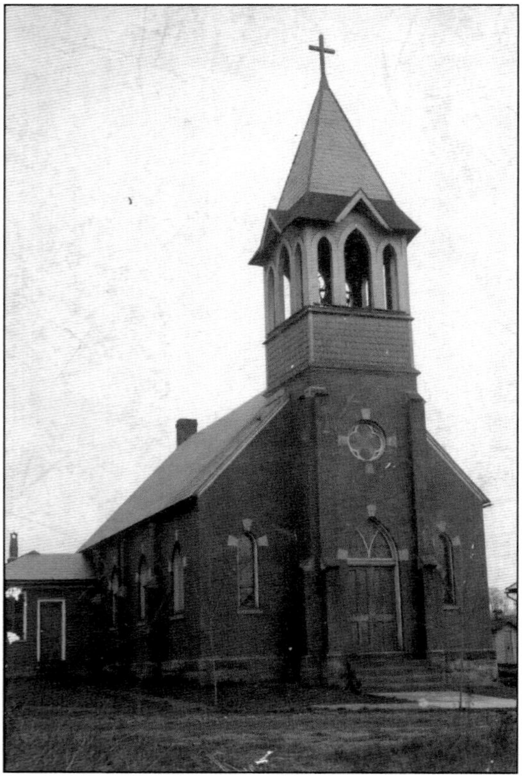

St. Phillips Neri-Dungannon. Early churches in Lisbon were often linked to other churches nearby; such was the case with the Roman Catholics and the Dominican order at Dungannon. It is remembered that during Morgan's threatened raid, the parishioners in this building literally jumped out the windows.

Old St. George's Catholic Church. Roman Catholicism has roots in Lisbon dating to 1820; this building was begun in 1888 and completed in 1894. The church has been a very stable one, as it has expanded over the years with an educational center and Knights of Columbus Hall.

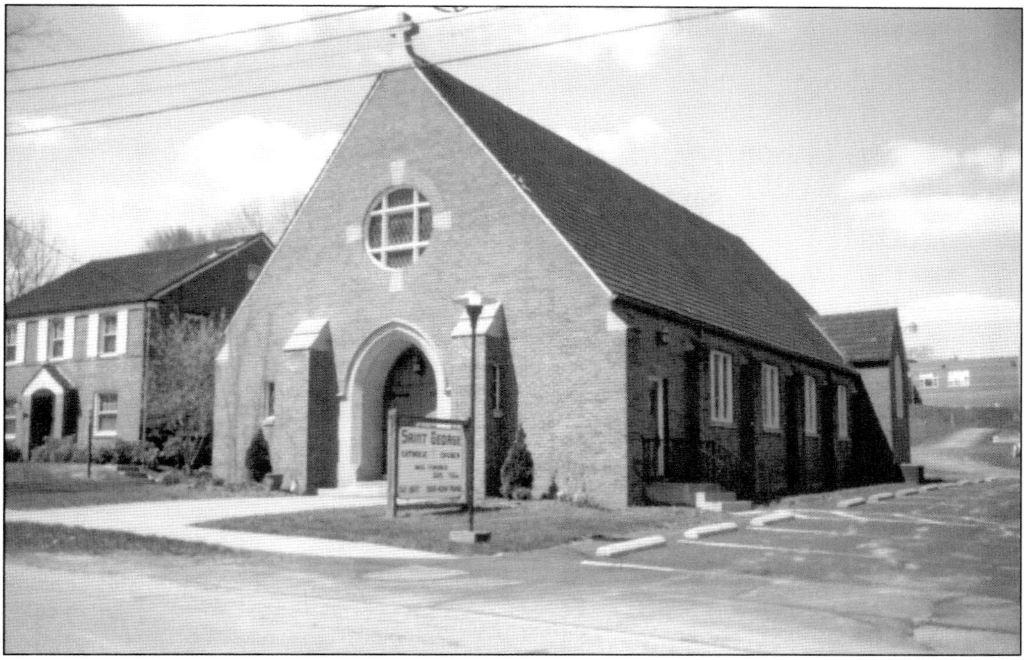

PRESENT ST. GEORGE'S CATHOLIC CHURCH. Today, the newer building, a Gothic brick with an accompanying rectory, built in 1938, stands on the same site on West Chestnut Street. James Costello was responsible for a large gift to build the church, and the members financed the rectory. Through these years, there have been many hard-working parishioners. (Photograph by Wendell Cole.)

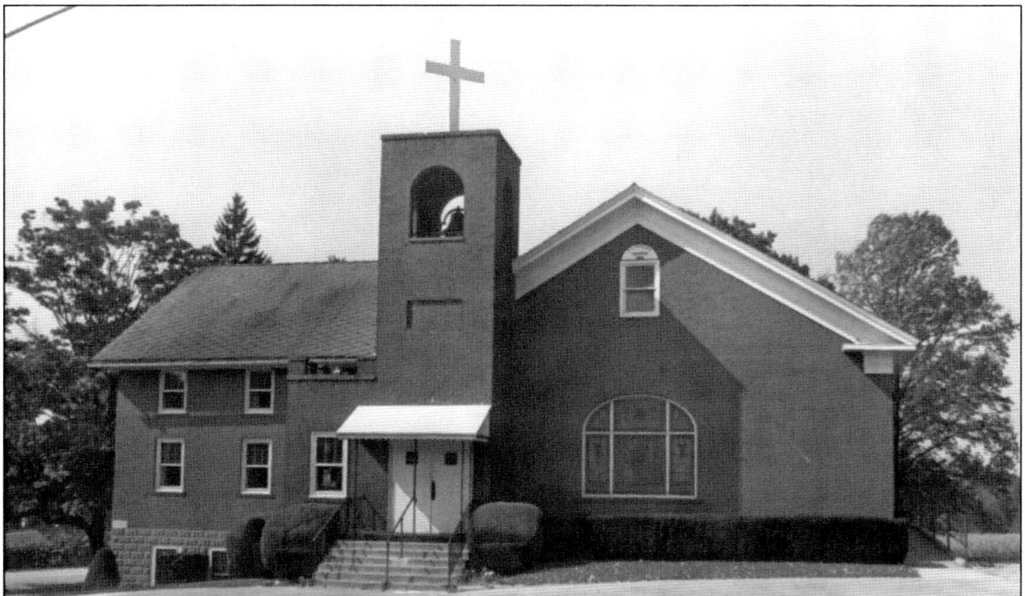

ST. JACOB'S UNITED CHURCH OF CHRIST. This congregation's church, formerly reformed, stands a few miles north of the community. In addition to the original sanctuary, substantial additions have been made to the building. It is, in its rural setting, an active participant in the Lisbon ministerial activities.

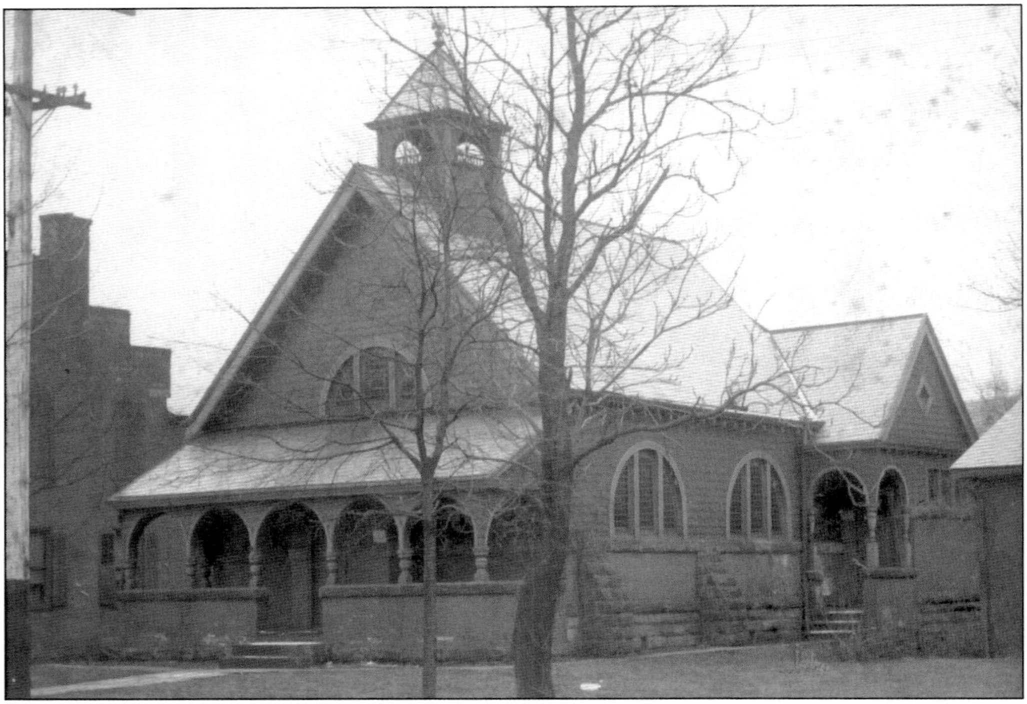

Holy Trinity Episcopal Church. This Episcopalian church stands near the heart of the community. Constructed in 1888, this building is reminiscent of English country churches and chapels. Interestingly, it is across Lincoln Way from the similar architecture of the Lepper Library.

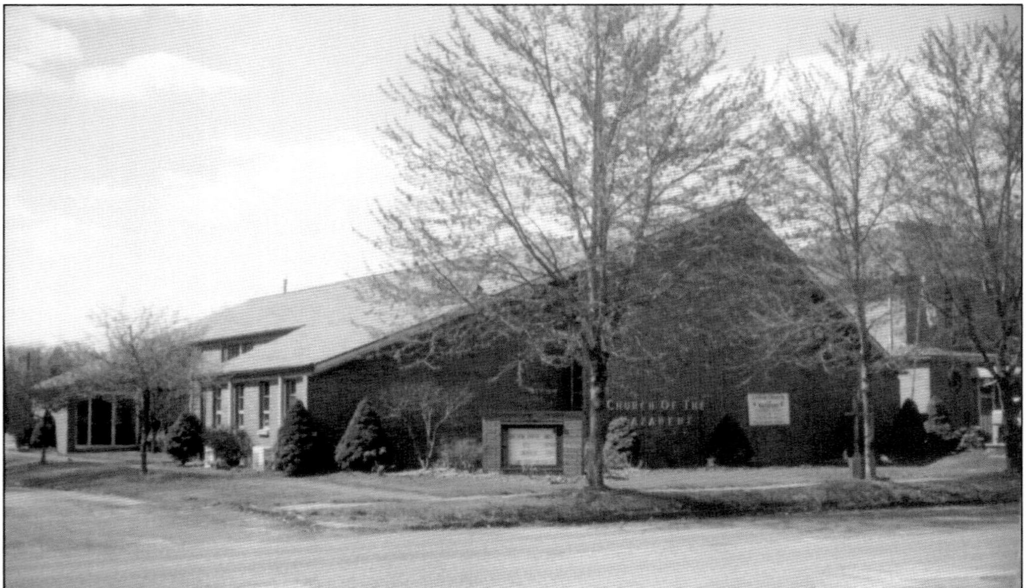

The Lisbon Nazarene Church. This congregation was begun as the Holiness Mission of Lisbon and became the Church of the Nazarene in 1909. Their original building was at the corner of East Washington and Jefferson Streets, but this new structure was constructed at the corner of North Market and Spruce Streets in more recent years to accommodate a growing congregation. (Photograph by Wendell Cole.)

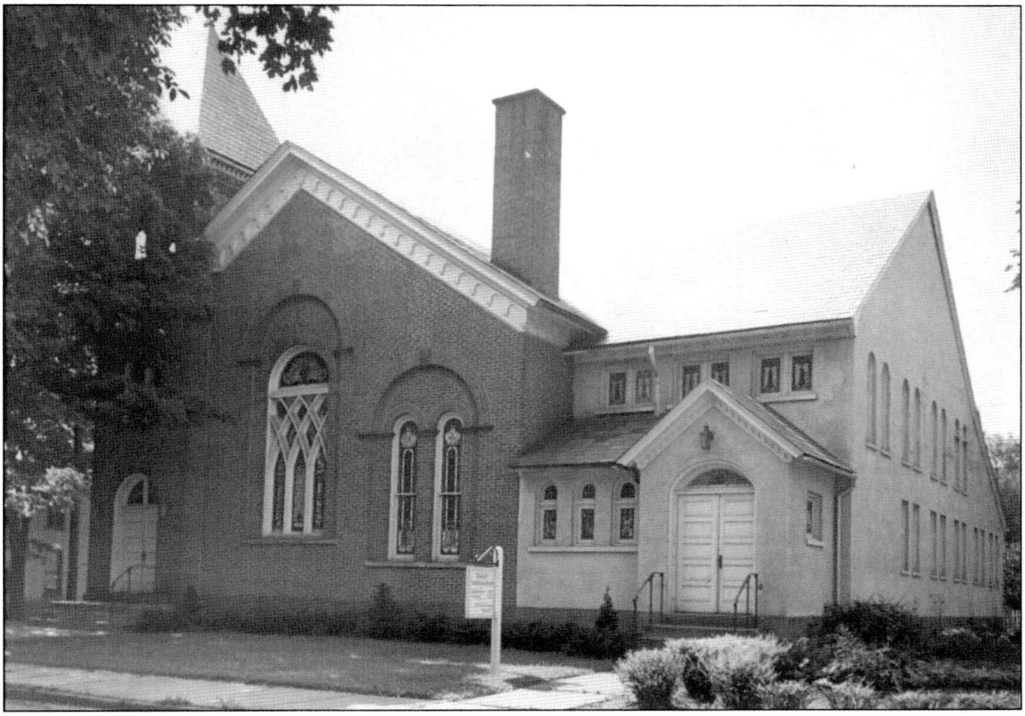

Trinity United Presbyterian Church. Originally First United Presbyterian Church, this building was constructed in 1859. During its history, the basement under the sanctuary was dug by a couples class, and the church school addition to the west was added later. The congregation merged with First Presbyterian Church; now the building is home to Stage Left Players, a local drama company. It has served the dramatists for most of their 22 years of existence.

First Presbyterian Church. The second building on this site, this church was constructed in 1895 after the previous one burned. In 1926, a large Christian education unit, built on the Akron Plan, was added. Since 1998, it has housed the merged Trinity and First Presbyterian congregations under the name of New Lisbon Presbyterian Church. Frequently, through the years, it has hosted community gatherings in its large sanctuary and fellowship areas.

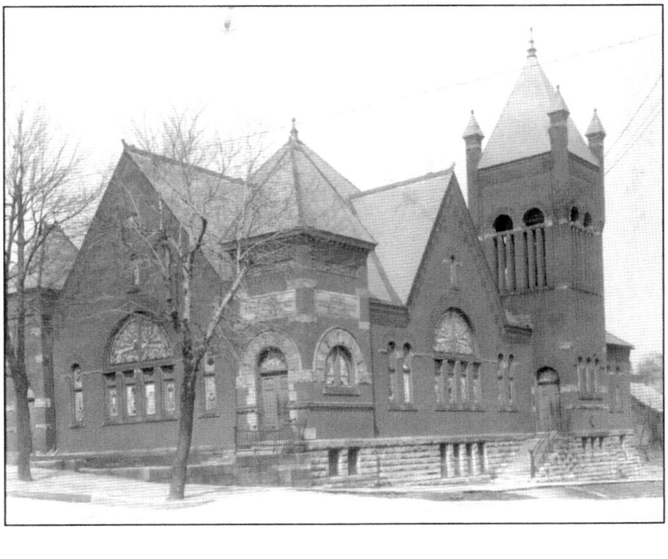

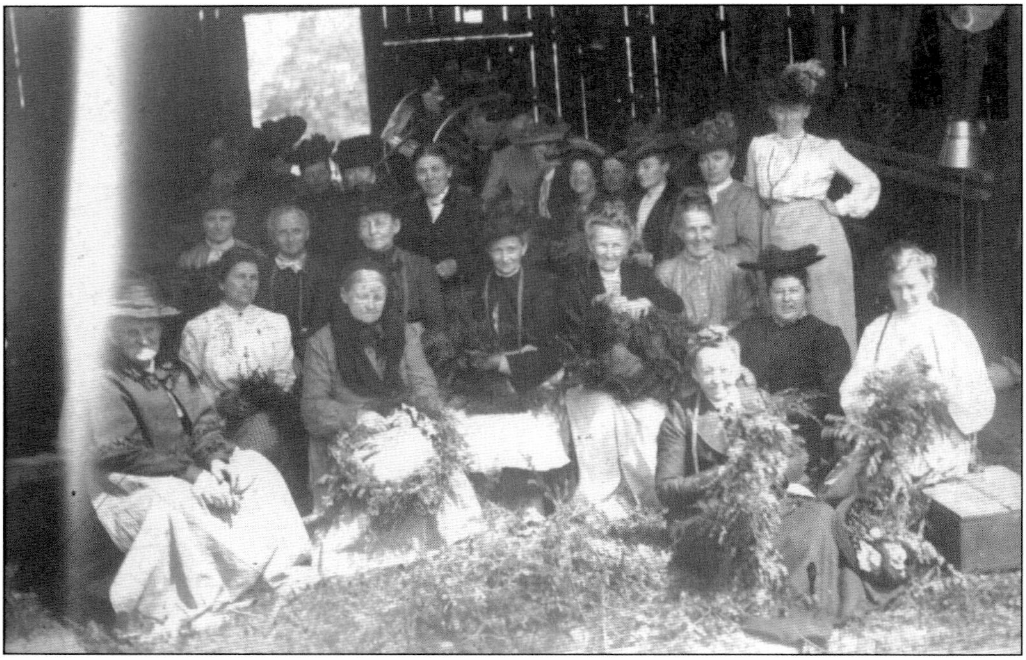

Ladies of the GAR. In this 1890 photograph, the Ladies of the Grand Army of the Republic (the Civil War Union army) are seen making wreaths to decorate graves for Decoration Day. Some of the women are Jennie Pritchard, a Mrs. McDonald, Kate Prosser, Lizzie Eells, and a Mrs. Sipe. This commemoration, called Memorial Day, was traditionally on May 30.

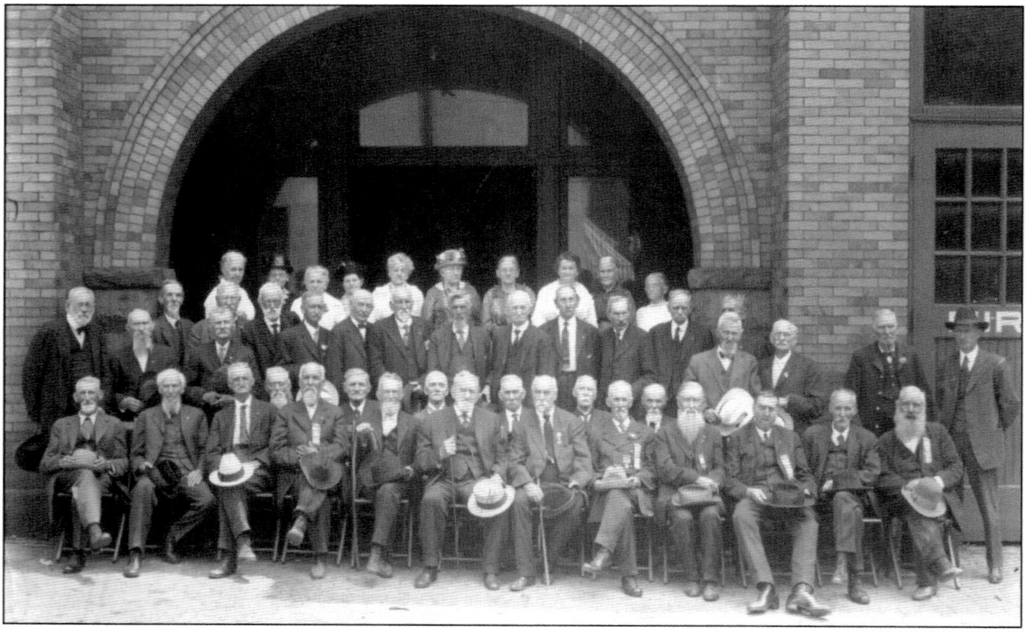

Civil War Veterans Reunion. The 143rd Ohio Volunteer Infantry Reunion prompted this photograph on the steps of the village hall on Nelson Avenue. In this image taken in the early 1900s, these men who had served approximately 40 years before in the War between the States are gathered. In the back row are women whose role is undefined, although they are probably the spouses.

Johnny Appleseed Festival. This festival began in the second half of the 20th century and has continued into the 21st. Sponsored by Lisbon's chamber of commerce, it draws upon the legend of Johnny Appleseed (John Chapman) traveling around the countryside planting apple trees. The festival has grown. Here, Fred Lutz as Johnny Appleseed visits schoolchildren.

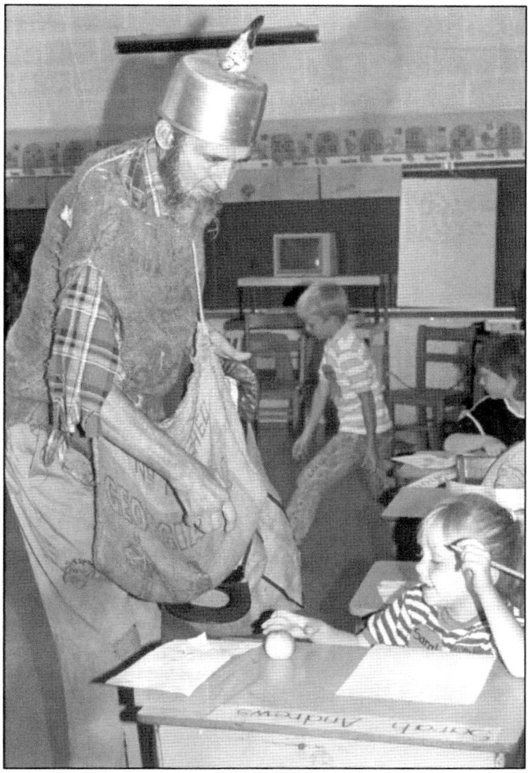

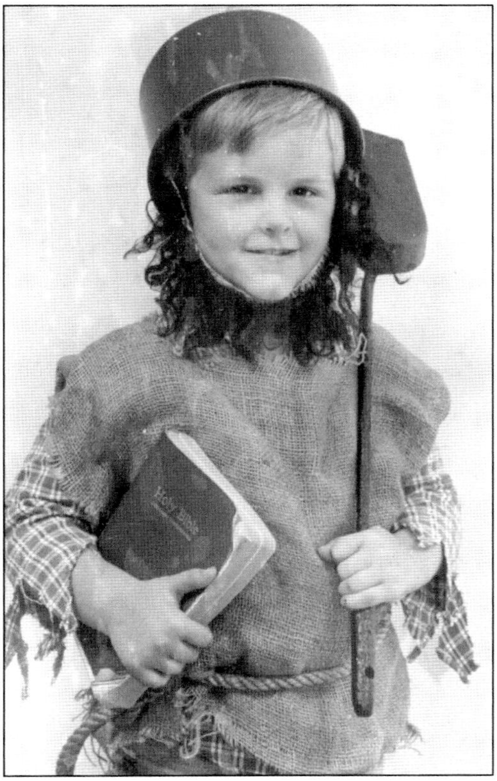

Johnny Appleseed Look-a-Like. This festival is definitely child friendly. Each year, not only is a Johnny Appleseed queen crowned, but two young children play junior roles as well. This young man, Adam Hayes, is obviously dressed to be a young Johnny Appleseed, complete with Bible and shovel.

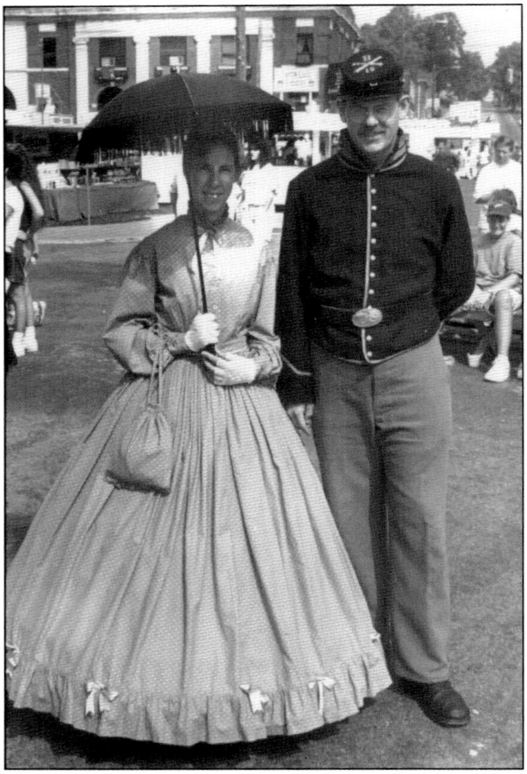

Johnny Appleseed Costume Contest. In an atmosphere of food stands and themed windows, costumes are important. This couple reflects the days of long dresses and military service in the 19th century. Every September, this festival attracts many people to the downtown area with its exhibits, food stands, rides, and parades.

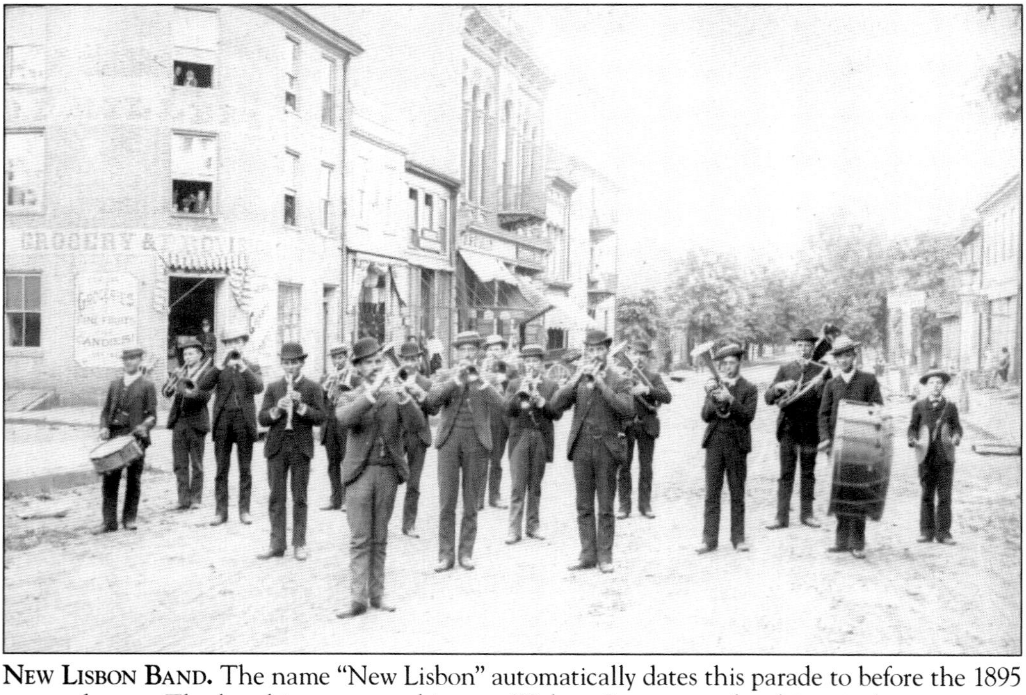

New Lisbon Band. The name "New Lisbon" automatically dates this parade to before the 1895 name change. The band is seen marching on Walnut Street, another historical name—now Lincoln Way. The structures in the background include the Round Corner and the Gailey-Firestone Building, which also housed the Masonic temple.

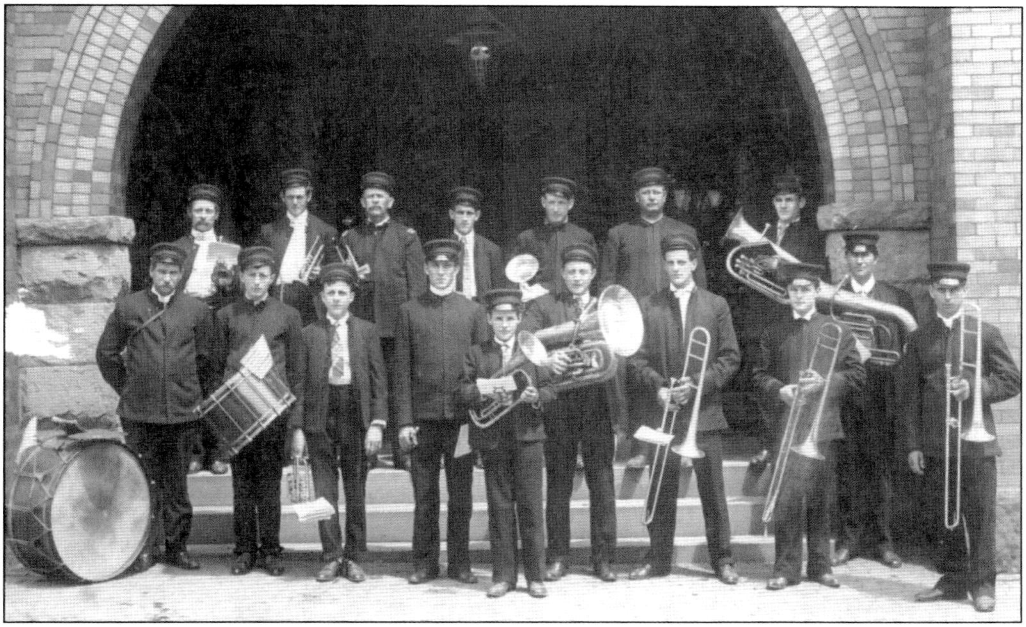

LISBON VILLAGE BAND. The name change is obvious to a band posed in 1908 in front of the 1904 village hall. Members include Ed Sexton, Jack Devan, Walter Brown, Dan Jackson, Raymond "Snap" Wilhelm, Oscar Altdoerfer, Max Crawford, Arthur Wainwright, Lauren Wainwright, Ed McKee, Harve Helman, Henry Fox, Frank Altdoerfer, Joe Wainwright, John Wainwright, Joe Devitto, and John Garrod.

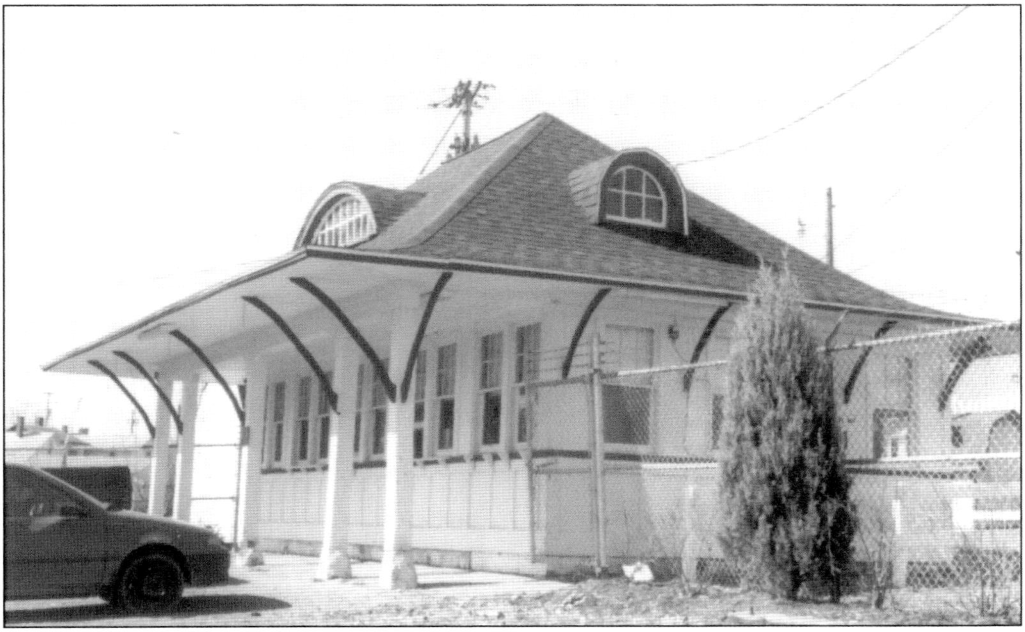

ENTRANCE TO FAIRGROUNDS. This charming building was a Youngstown & Southern Railway ticket office. Moved to the Columbiana County Fairgrounds, it has come to represent the excitement of the annual trip to the county fair, established about 1846. Once through the gate, there is always a variety of foods, programs, and animals as well as throngs of people well beyond the local citizenry.

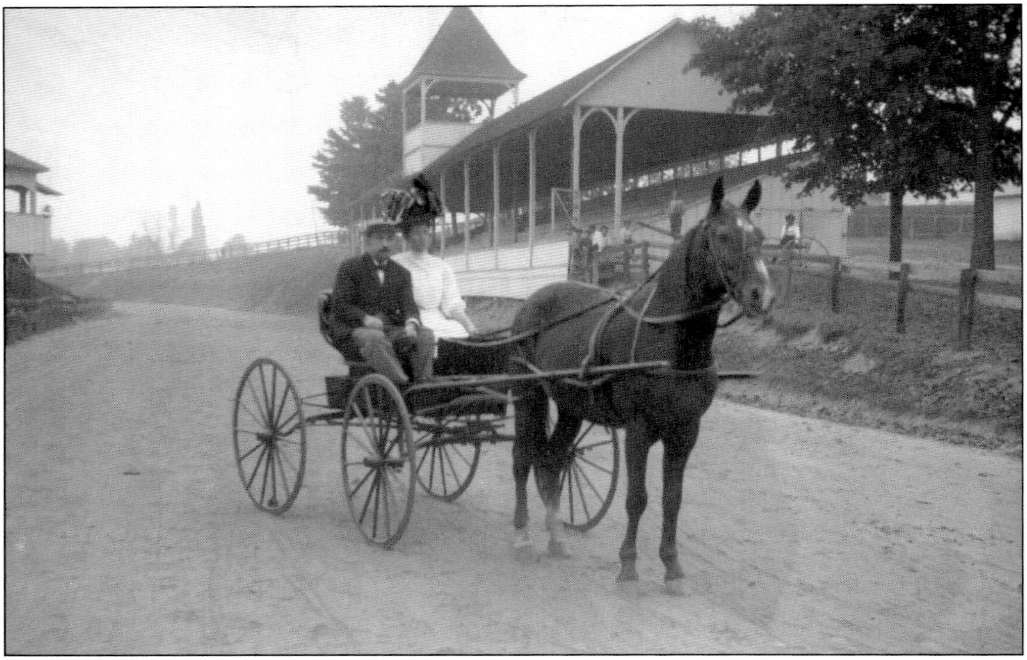

GRANDSTAND AND JUDGING. The old grandstand, recently replaced, and the judge's stand are evident in the background. In the foreground is Joe Wilkes with his lady as they ride behind a horse. Showmanship is an important part of the fair's activities in the realm of many different animals that are shown, judged, and raced.

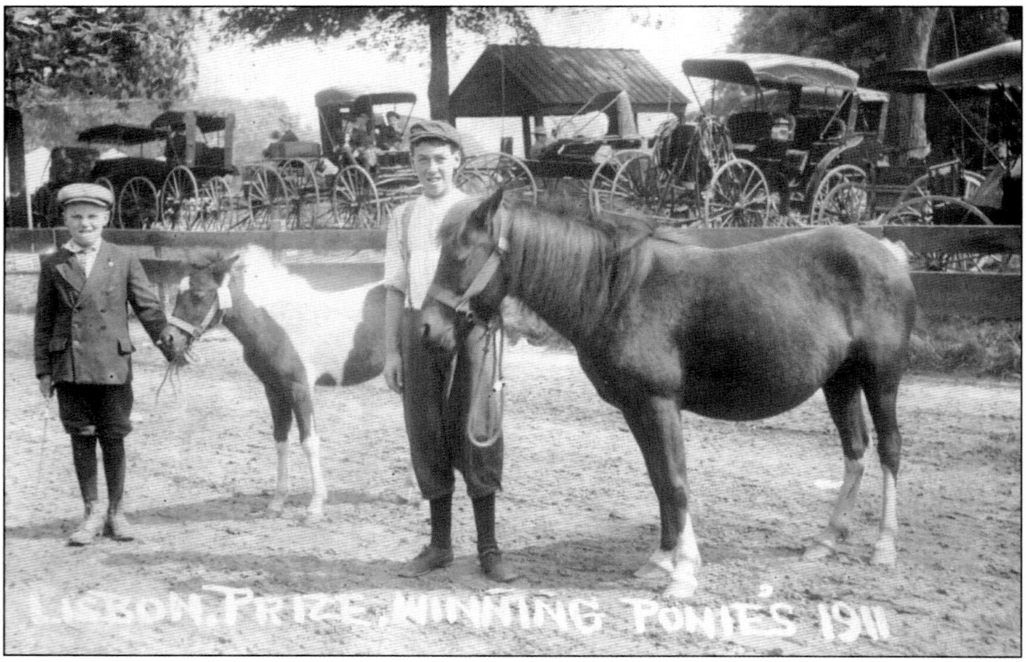

PRIZE-WINNING PONIES. These two young boys pose with their prize-winning ponies at the 1911 Columbiana County Fair. To this day, young people, especially those in 4-H, bring their carefully tended animals to the fair; they often spend days and nights in the barns tending to them. Later, the local newspaper publishes the results in a multitude of categories.

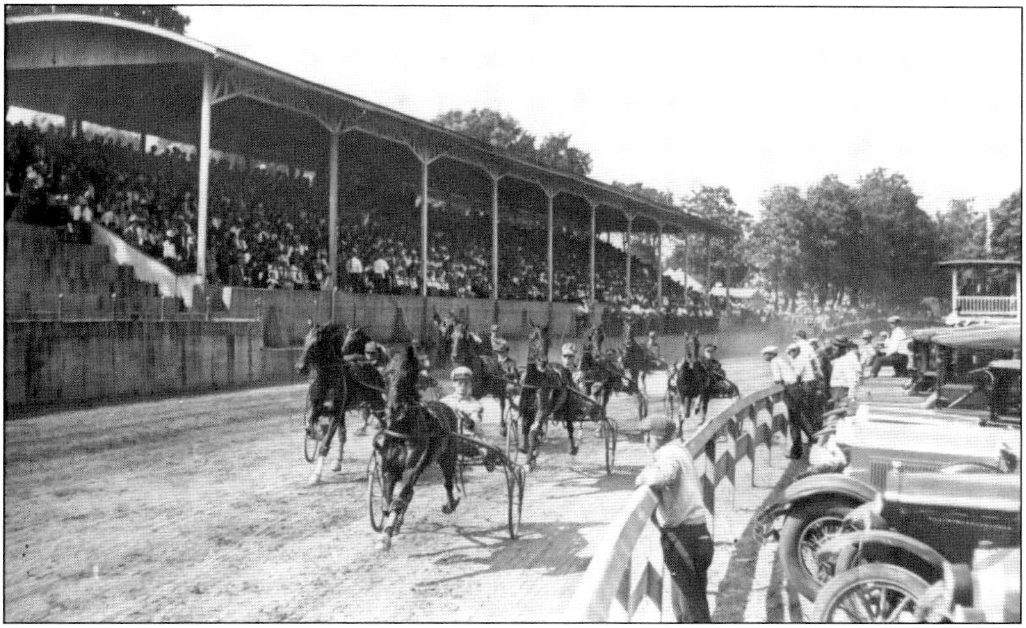

Excitement of Racing. In this 1920s photograph of the racetrack, there is so much to see. The grandstand on the left is filled with spectators, the sulky racers fly down the track in hopes of winning, and the enthusiasts stand by the fence backed by vintage automobiles. Fair week is a busy, exciting one for the fair enthusiasts.

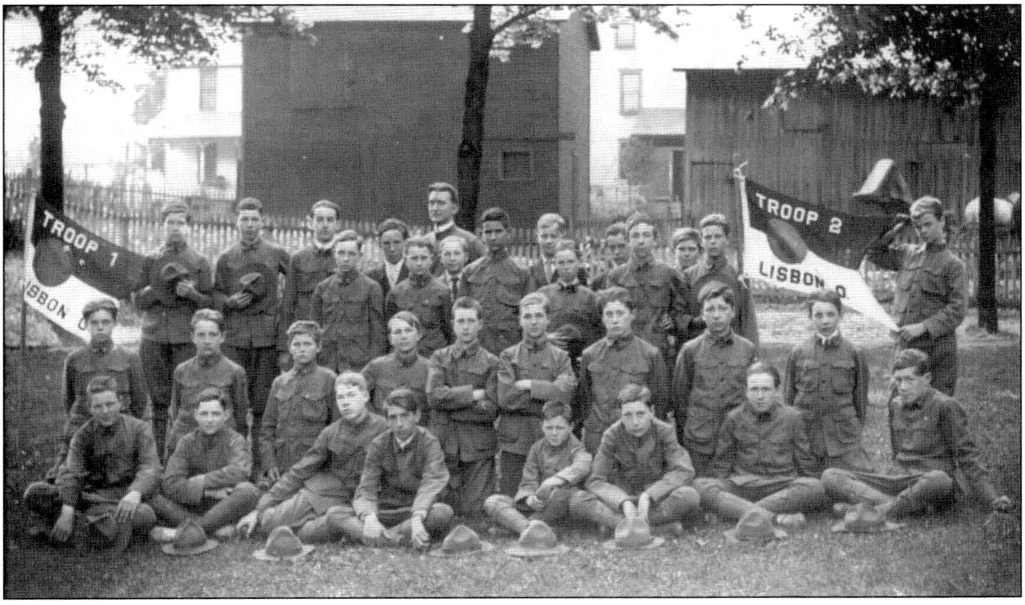

Organizations in Lisbon. Clubs and organizations have been very important in the history of the community. Pictured here are two Boy Scout troops, including, in no particular order, Rev. Herman Reichard SM, Bill Morris, Lynn Riddle, Lester Ewing, Lester Sexton, Floyd Crawford, Albert Hartman, Willis Armstrong, Roy Clunk, ? Armstrong, ? Thompson, Russell Frankfort, Clyde Frankford, Bill Armstrong, Leland Longshore, ? Snow, Graham Steele, Reginald Gorsuch, Leland Lewton, Myron Eells, James Moore, Earl Stockman, Adrian Evans, Clarence Sexton, George Burns, George Thompson, Bob Evans, Bill Bennett, Dick Mason, and Frank McGee.

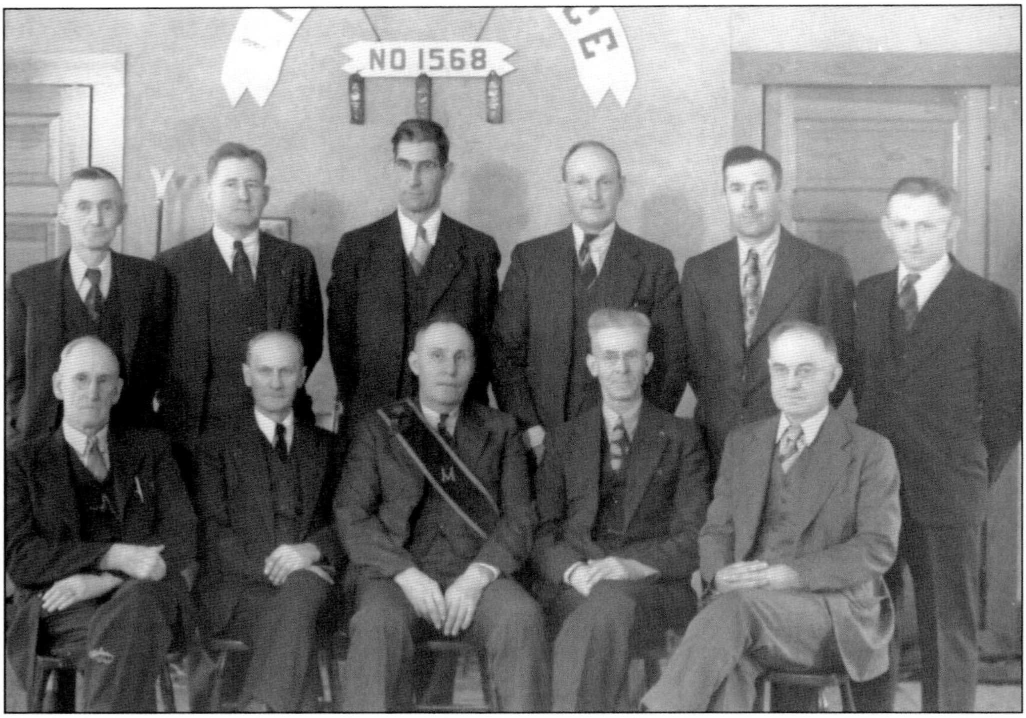

The Lisbon Grange. The Lisbon Grange represents the agricultural interests of the area. Most of these men are listed by their last names, Lindesmith, Ramsey, Thomson, Watkins, Shaw, Crosser, Hill, Crowell, Boring, Crowell, and Homer Williams. The grange is still active on Route 30, west of town.

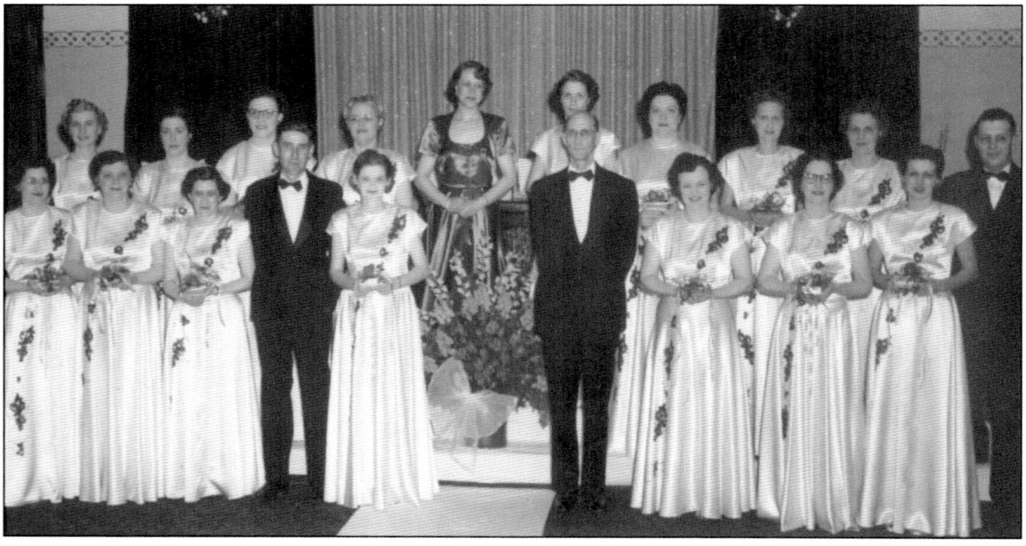

Eastern Star Installation. At the installation of Lee Jones as Worthy Matron of Iva Chapter, many were assembled. Pictured here are, from left to right (first row) Ihla Rae McGoogan, Gertrude Lewis, Sara Steele Rose, unidentified , Lee Jones, Clarence Ball, Esther Binsley Smith, Mary Lib Hiscox, and ? Hanysh; (second row) Theda Yochim Webber, Irene Frew, Evelyn Rose Burson, Lucille Rupp, Deputy ?, Lucille Porter, Elaine Griffith, Ruth Henry, Helen Morrison, and Adam Rudibaugh.

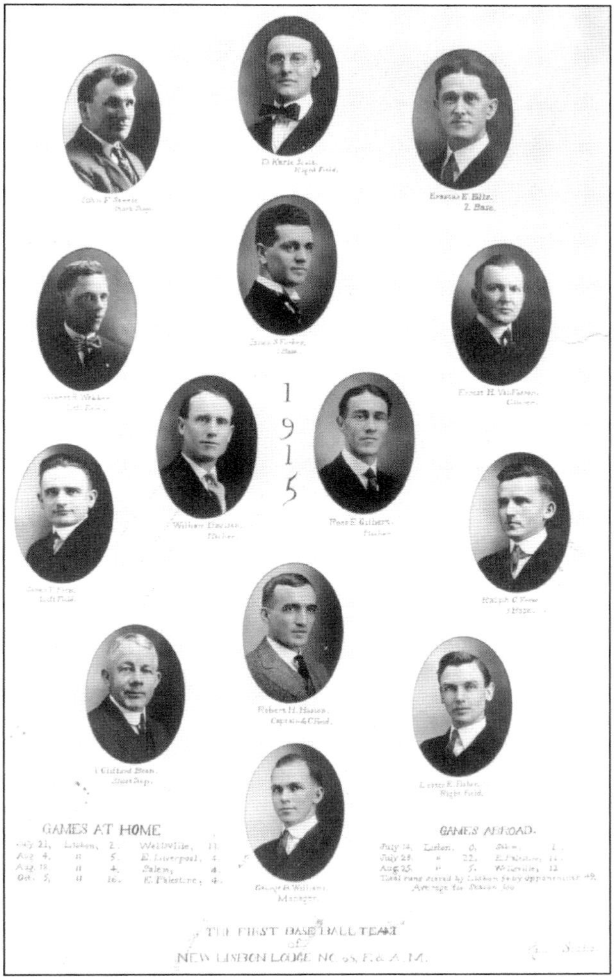

Masonic Lodge Baseball in 1915. The still-active Masonic lodge has moved to a new center in the 21st century. Their baseball team included, clockwise from top, (outer circle) Karl Scott, Erastus Eells, Ernest Van Fossan, Ralph Frew, Lester Fisher, George Williams, I.C. Bean, James Frew, Albert Webber, and Jack Steele; (inner circle) James Forbes, Ross Gilbert, Robert Huston, and William Davison.

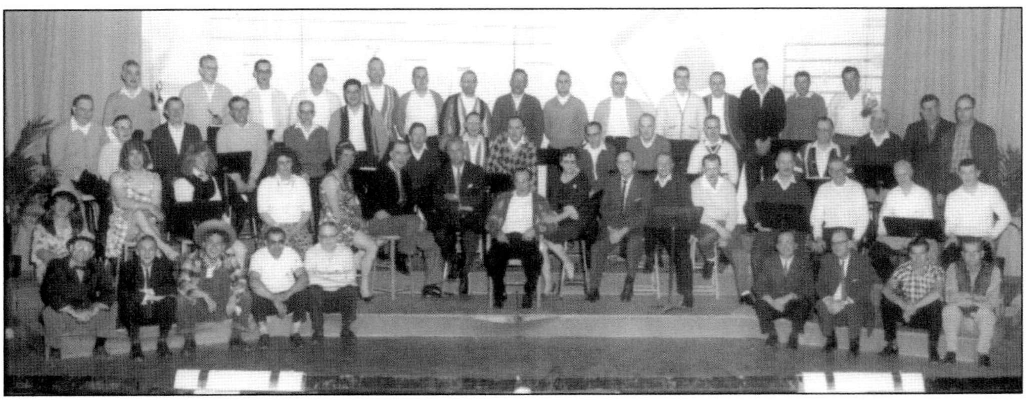

American Legion Minstrels, 1946. With the American Legion's history rooted in C.C. Connell's trip to Paris to participate in its national founding, the organization was very strong. Popular year after year were the American Legion minstrels; this one has multiple veterans included in a rehearsal: Jack Marshall, Art Black, John Tucker, Bud Bucher, Vance Brinker, Lester Robinson, Bob Fife, Bob Cameron, Chuck Lederle, Bill Morgan, Don Loch, Rich Kennedy, Byron Griffith, John Snyder, Ray Hempstead, Charles Pike, Ralph "Hoppy" Rose, David Williams, and Carl Potter.

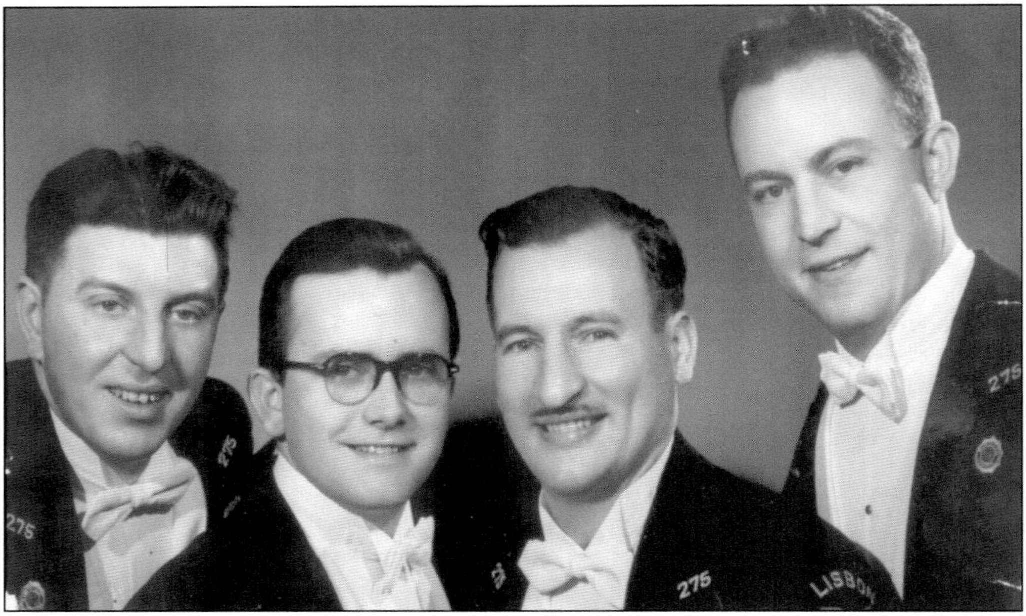

American Legion Minstrel Quartet. While the Kiwanis also presented minstrels, the American Legion performances are especially well known. Frequently, the Legion Minstrels featured special quartets. This group, the Legionnaires, was known for their excellent voices, and they were frequently asked to perform. From left to right, they are Lester Robinson, Bill Frew, Byron Griffith, and Ed Nold.

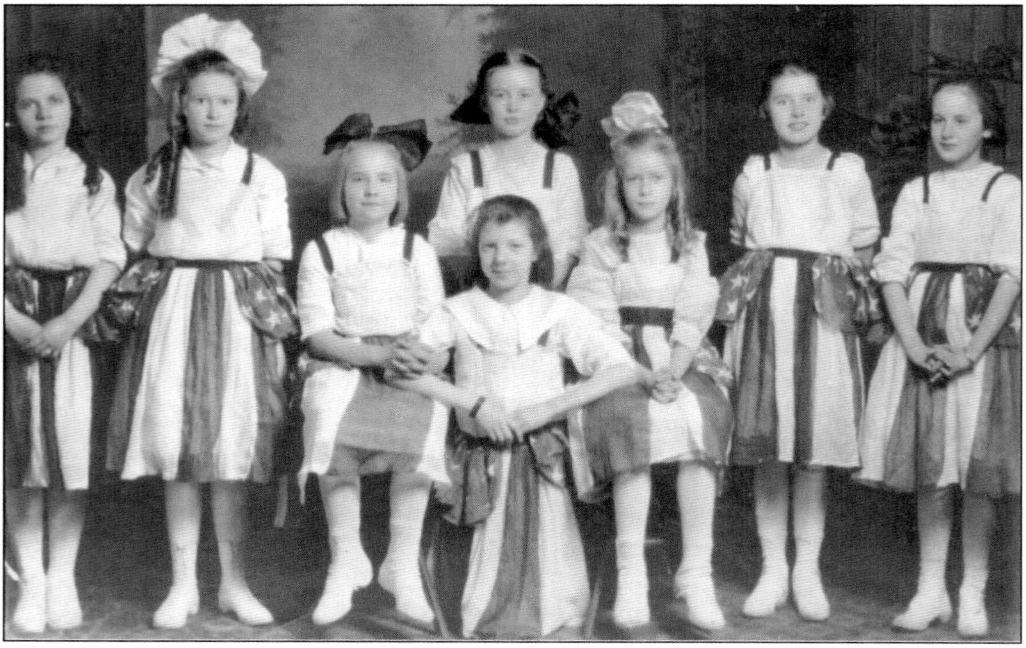

Girls Group of Entertainment. This group of girls is obviously costumed for a program. They are, from left to right, Nola McGaffick, Edna Ewing Helman, Frances Barlow Hiscox, Clara McGee (kneeling), Lucile Bennett, Phyllis Crawford, Evelyn Pike Ball, and Helen Randolph Kessler. As an adult, Clara McGee was a very valuable member of the historical society with her knowledge of the community and willingness to work.

John Oliver's Hot-Air Balloon. In the late 1950s, this hot-air balloon was prepared for jeweler John Oliver to entertain the crowds with his skill. Heat from a wood fire inflated this very large balloon for its flight. He was asked to do this dependent upon his skill in this sport from his youth.

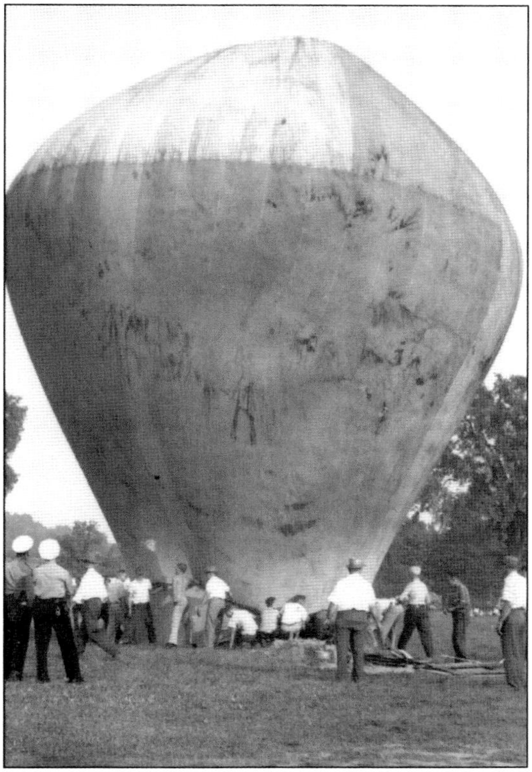

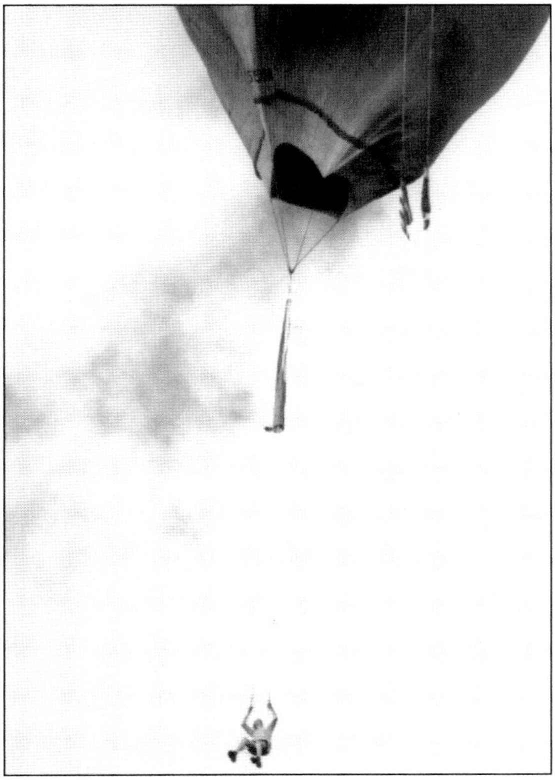

Oliver's Ride. The balloon ride proved quite successful; Oliver demonstrated that he had retained his skills for many years. After some time, he parachuted to the ground, and the balloon came to rest near East Fairfield, having traveled northeast above Route 517. The World War I veteran and local jeweler was proven still agile.

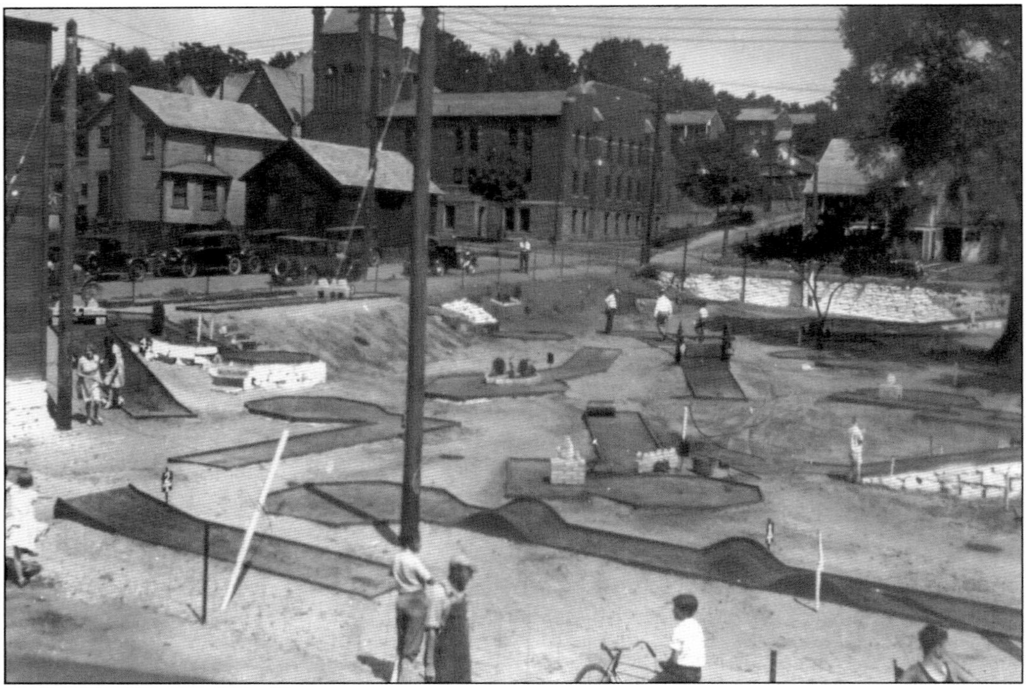

Lisbon's Miniature Golf Course. This 1925 miniature golf course was located on the corner of Nelson Avenue and East Chestnut Street. Near the Wick Hotel and the Presbyterian church, it was operated by Dave McCreary. There was an impressive list of young men with skill who enjoyed this place, including Roger Eells, Herb and Charles "Chili" Heim, Bob Madigan, Howard and Charles McCormack, Sam McVeigh, Dusty Miller, and Don Richardson.

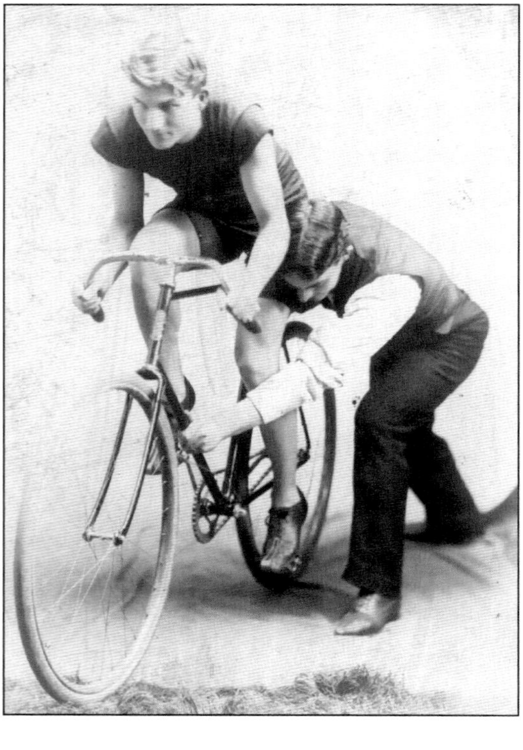

Dr. Steele, the Bicyclist. One of the noted bicyclists in the nation was Dr. J.F. Steele. He is shown here in the 1890s proving his skill as his brother Will Steele gets his race started. Dr. Steele was a well-respected local dentist for many years; his offices were over the Ewing Meat Market on South Market Street.

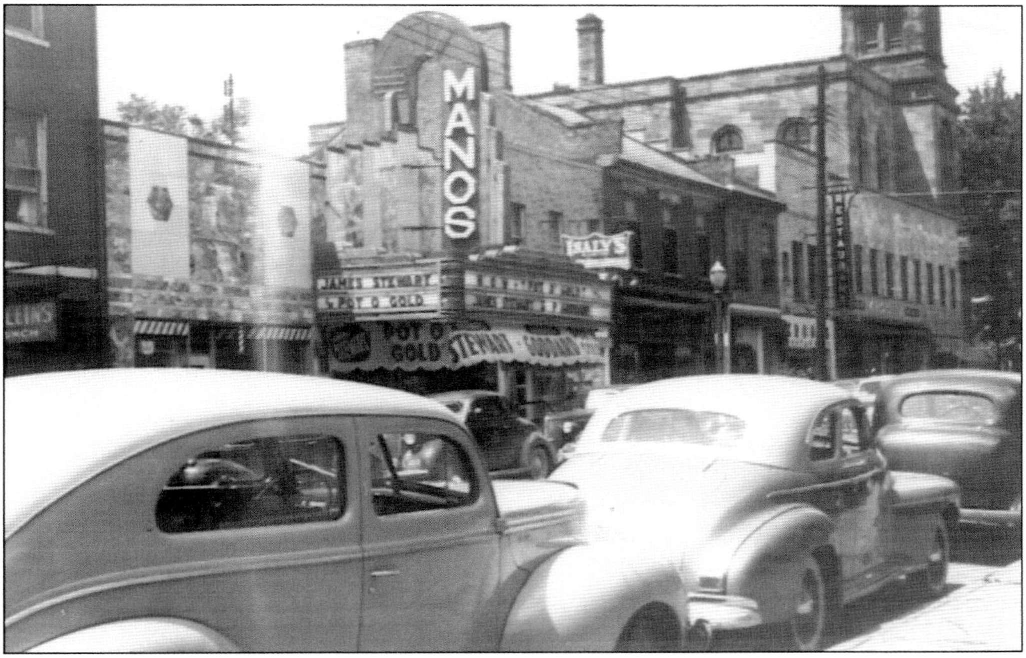

LISBON'S MANOS THEATER. This photograph from 1941 shows South Market Street with one of Lisbon's three movie theaters. The Manos was quite popular for many years with a reputation for showing first-run films in the days of extensive motion-picture entertainment.

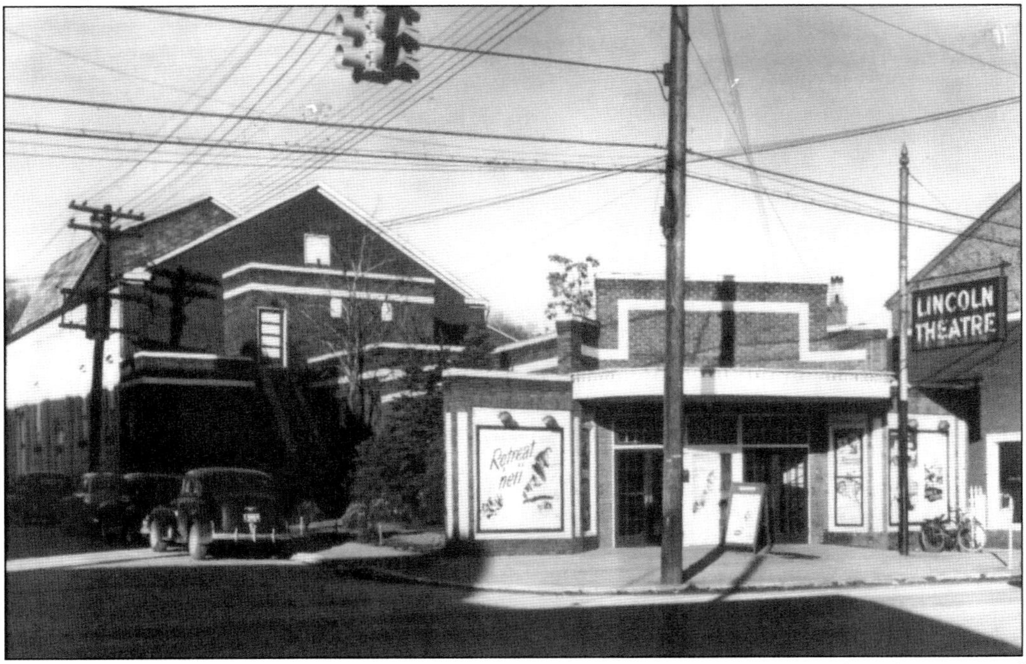

OLD LINCOLN THEATER. Pictured here in the 1940s or 1950s, this theater stood at the corner of East Lincoln Way and Jefferson Street. A large structure, it had once served as the opera house where vaudeville acts were performed. Matinees for housewives on Mondays and schoolchildren on Saturdays were quite popular in the community. The Saturday matinees cost each child 10¢ in admission.

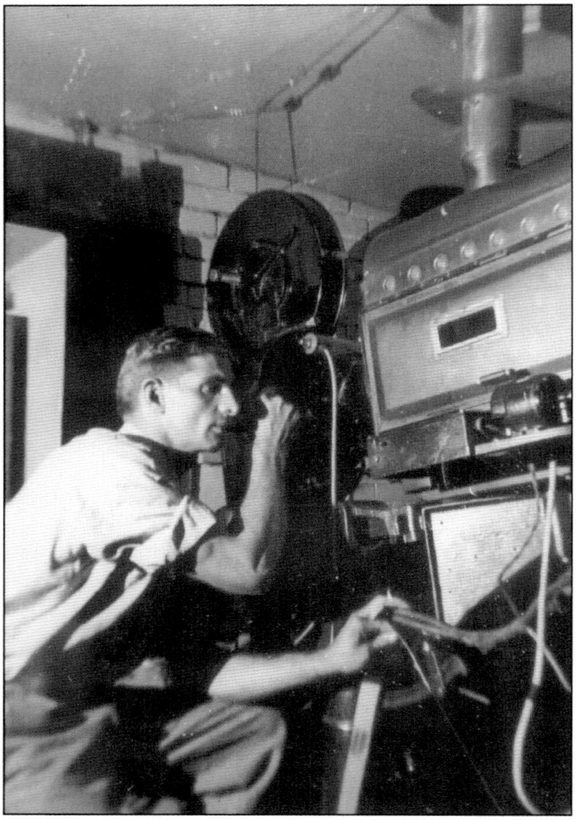

The Projectionist's Trade. One position occupied by both high school and post-secondary young adults was the projectionist in each of the local theaters. Keeping alert for signals and knowing how to run the equipment was critical. Here, Walter Horner is in charge of the screening of a movie at the Lincoln Theater.

Lisbon and Baseball. The all-American sport of baseball was part of early Lisbon. This 1905 team included, from left to right, (first row) F. Carlisle, Harry Kirk, Bert Durant, "Kittens" Albright, and Don Hasbrouck; (second row) two unidentified players, Bob Huston, Pete King, H. Henderson, Bill Gailey, "Kid" Carlisle, and "Pode" Clunk.

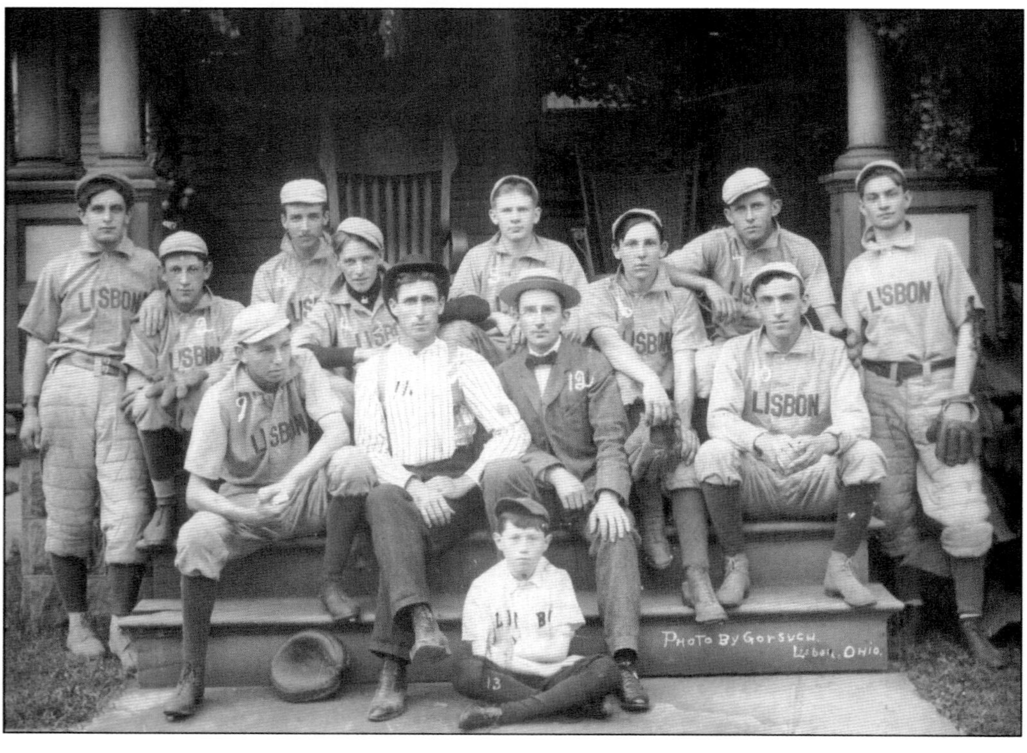

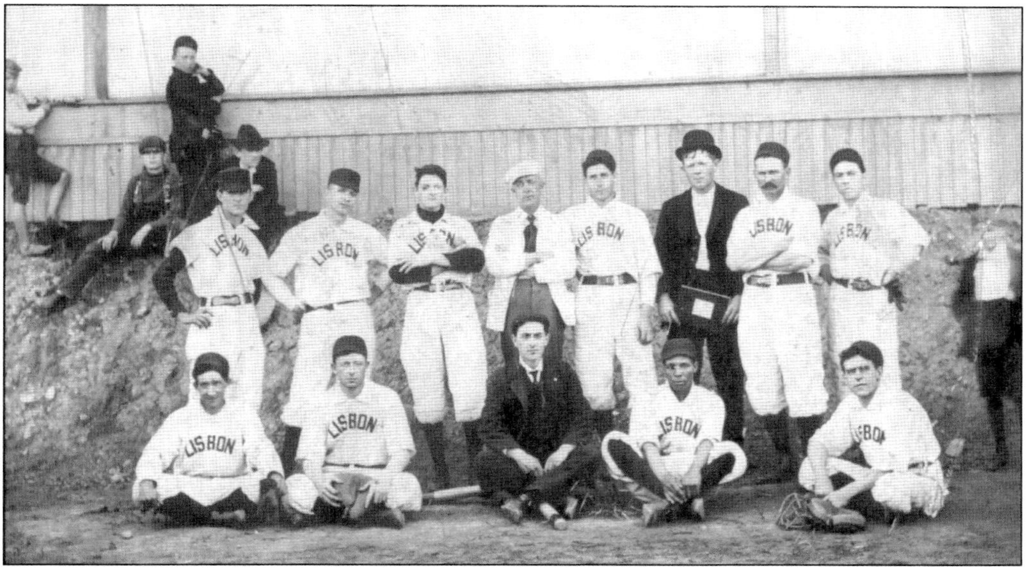

LISBON BASEBALL TEAM. This appears to be an early baseball team with some of the members identified. They are, from left to right, (first row) unidentified, Frank Heim, Will Steele, ? Dillard, and ? Allcorn; (second row) Erastus Eells, ? Eaholtz, unidentified, Pop Nicholas, Harry Kirk, ? Marquis, and two unidentified players. The names are familiar local ones.

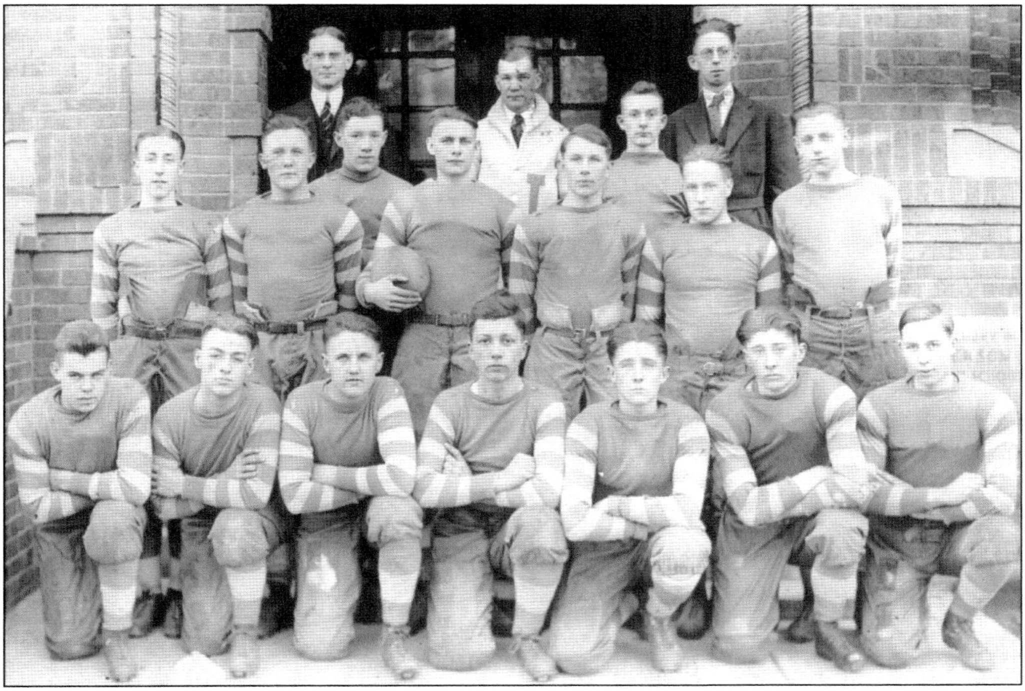

YET ANOTHER TEAM. Although no information is given, this football team is possibly school related, since the background doorway appears to be at David Anderson High School. The members are, from left to right, (first row) James Armstrong, Cliff Donnelly, John Lewis, James Moore, Gerald Eells, Myron Eells, and Lester Sexton; (second row) Edgar Kirk, Frank Lafferty, Orval Lewton, Graham Steele, Bill Pritchard, and Sky Mefort; (third row) Frank McGee and Reginald Gorsuch; (fourth row) Superintendent Geiger, Cracker Davidson, and Happy Jamison.

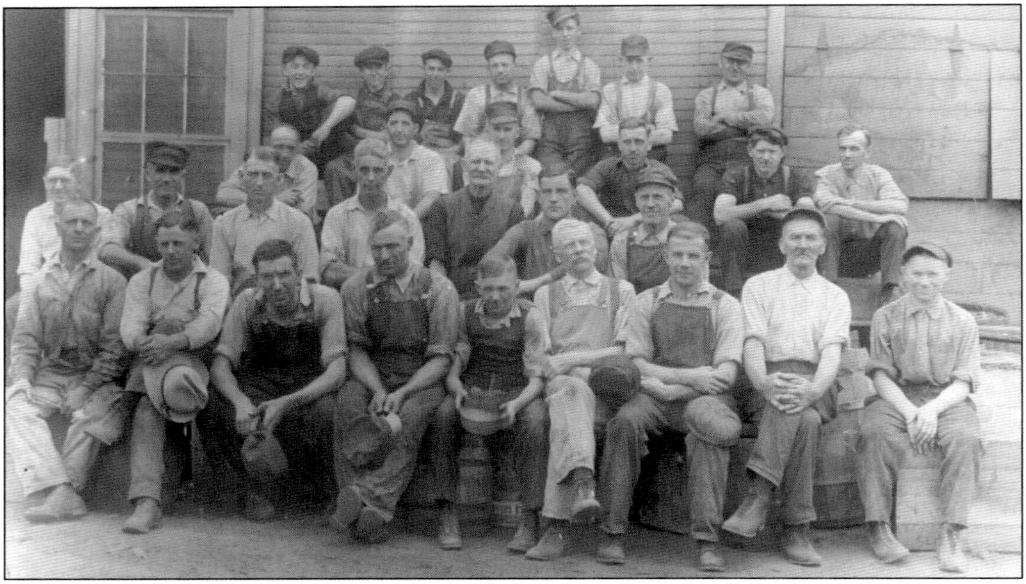

Wright's All Americans. This 1920 baseball team is part of the Wright Industries employees' sports opportunities. The players listed include Aurell Prasco, Bob Morrison, Lee Buckley, Vain Donnalley, James "Jimmy" Stockman, David McDevitt, Ed Ward, Ed Huston, James "Jimmy" Nelson, Frank Randolph, O. Welch, Clever Wilson, Arch Twiss, George Morrison, Reese Lewis, Marion Metts, William Smith, Dan McGoogan, Ed Sell, Harold "Buzz" Evans, Russ Bell, Ray Bell, Andy Kodrich, John Dallas Rupp, Raymond Clunk, and John Petrie.

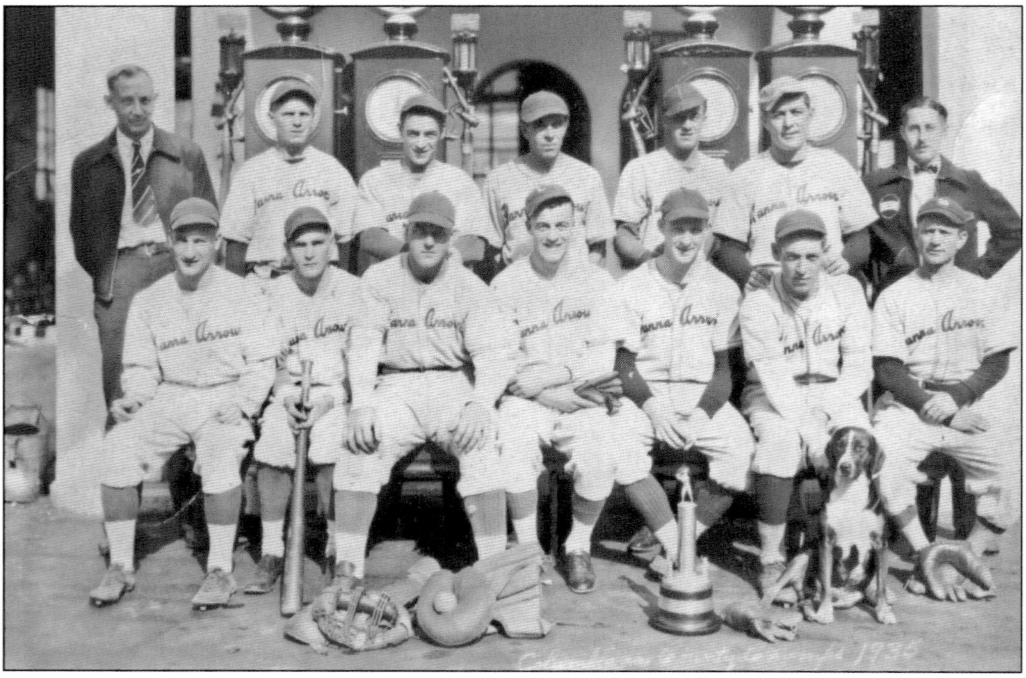

Hanna's Arrows. This baseball team is singularly noted for its link to the Hanna Gas Station on West Lincoln Way. This photograph from the 1930s includes, from left to right, (first row) Byron Griffith, ? Hough, ? Simpson, ? Hrovatic, R. Sexton, Wilbur Warren, and James Manse; (second row) Howard Crosser, James Berry, ? Hrovatic, ? Bosel, ? Hrovatic, Bus Price, and James Hanna.

Five

MAJOR MOMENTS

So often a community is defined by major moments and events. That is very true of Lisbon. In any gathering of the residents, current or former, there are always the "Remember when?" conversations. Lisbon has certainly had its share in such times and memories.

Wars have defined the history of the community. Many of the citizens served in the Union army during the Civil War; the Spanish-American War drew more. World Wars I and II saw hundreds of villagers serving in the armed forces while family members provided on the home front. As the 20th century progressed, local citizens were part of the Korean conflict, Vietnam, and Operation Desert Storm. Sadly, some did not return. To the village's credit, these veterans and their family members have not been forgotten. It has not forgotten those who were lost or those who returned home to become active in the community. Prominent markers from Morgan's Monument from the Civil War to signs in the village square and regular celebrations on Memorial Day as well as other occasions have shown the pride in those who defended the nation.

Celebrations are an important part of the community. While the Johnny Appleseed Festival and the county fair are significant annual events, the 1903 centennial, 1953 sesquicentennial, 1976 national bicentennial, and the 2003 Lisbon bicentennial have been marked in a variety of ways. And, in addition, the well-known Morgan's Raid that threatened and spared the community has been the subject of commemoration.

The reminiscences often start with the fire in 1950 that destroyed the McKinley School. That upheaval changed lives for teachers and students. Presbyterians in the past must have talked of the loss of their church building in 1894, just as some Methodists still speak of their loss in 1944. There have been major fires in businesses: Hood Chemical, Law's Feed Mill, the O.S. Hill building (then housing county records), and the Morning Journal Building. Most of the block was lost. Long ago, the opera house was lost to flames. Yet, on the exciting, frightening, and humorous side, there was the elephant that broke loose during the circus, not to be forgotten by observers. These are the moments that nourish a village.

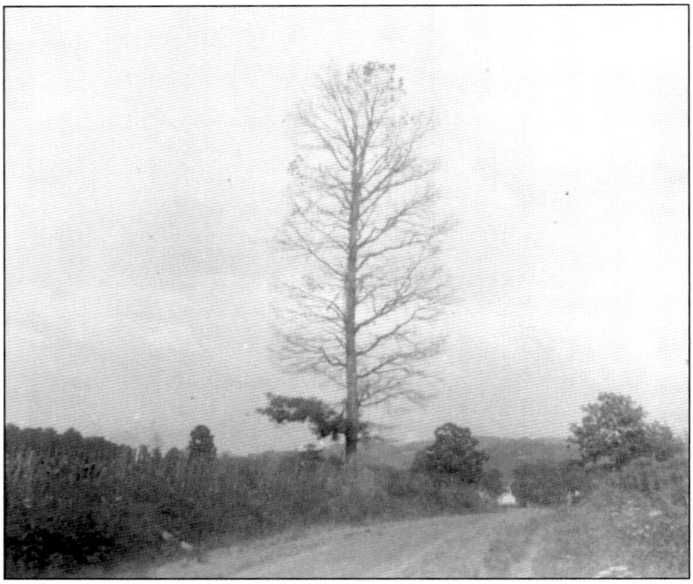

THE SURRENDER TREE. This lone tree, no longer standing, marks the spot where Gen. John Hunt Morgan and his Raiders surrendered on July 26, 1863. Their trip had been amazing, including defying the orders from the Confederacy not to invade, the death of Union major Dan McCook of New Lisbon, hasty preparations of meals and artillery, stolen horses, and disrupted church services. As his troops dwindled, Morgan ultimately had to surrender.

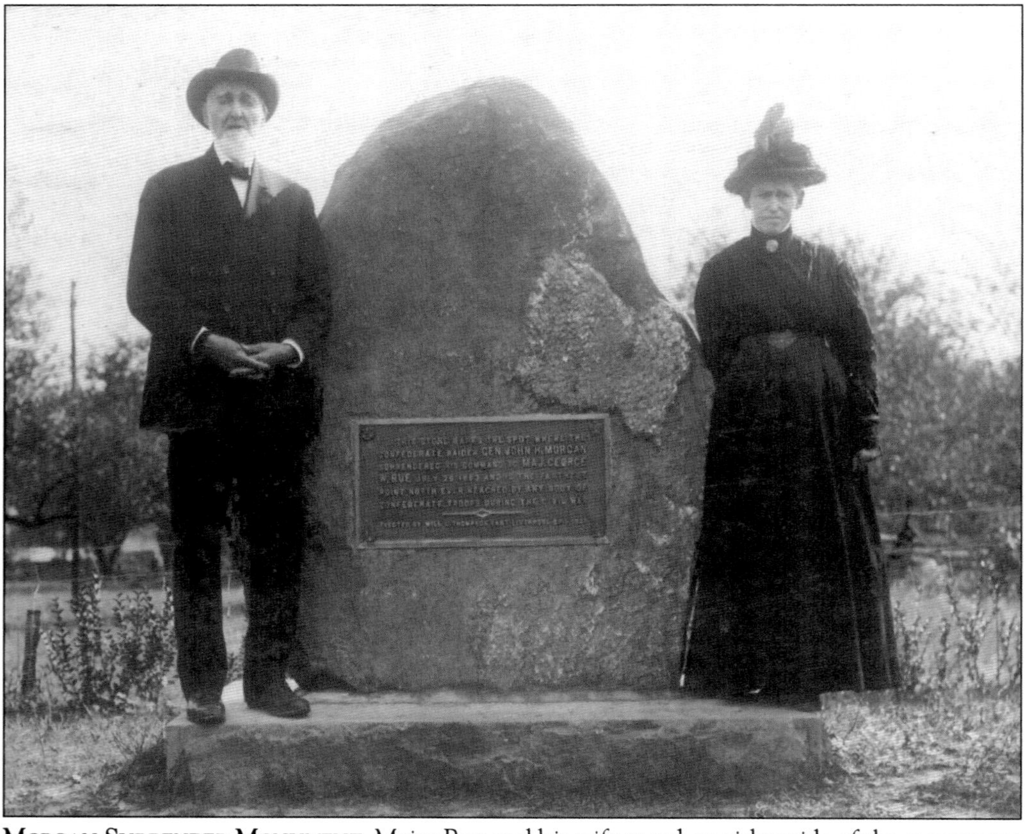

MORGAN SURRENDER MONUMENT. Major Rue and his wife stand on either side of the monument that marks the actual surrender of General Morgan. This was the dedication day for the marker south of Lisbon. Rue was the military officer who actually accepted the surrender, although General Schackleford arrived shortly afterwards. Morgan was taken prisoner but later escaped a Columbus, Ohio, prison and made his way south, where he was killed in 1864.

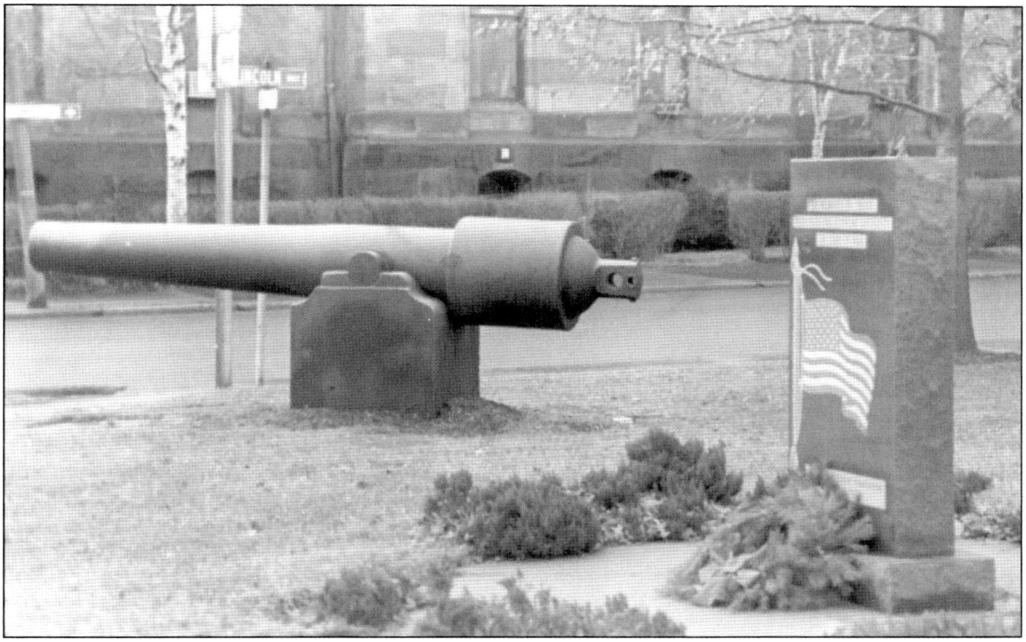

CIVIL WAR CANNON. Pres. William McKinley, Civil War veteran, made arrangements for Lisbon to obtain this naval cannon that sits in the northwest quadrant of the village square. Lisbon also participated in the Spanish-American War. Prof. W.H. Van Fossan's book *The Story of Ohio* describes the leadership in 1898 that strongly involves Lisbon connections: Pres. William McKinley, the commander in chief at the time, and Marcus A. Hanna, a Senate leader.

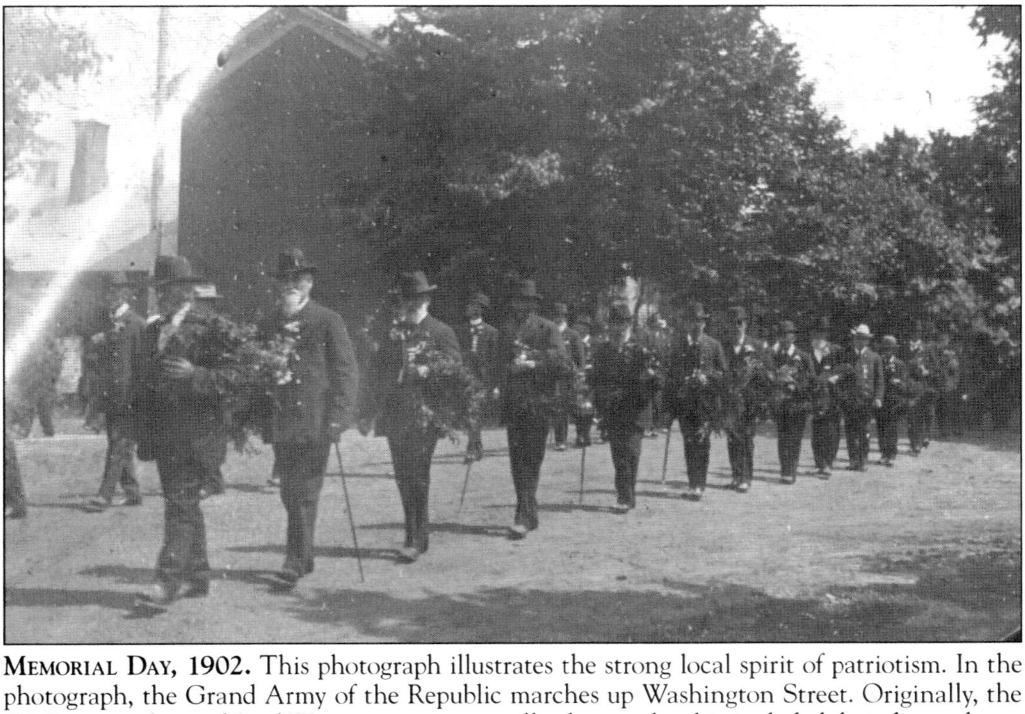

MEMORIAL DAY, 1902. This photograph illustrates the strong local spirit of patriotism. In the photograph, the Grand Army of the Republic marches up Washington Street. Originally, the GAR was made up of Civil War veterans; eventually, the membership included their descendants. The traditional Decoration Day parades continue to the present time.

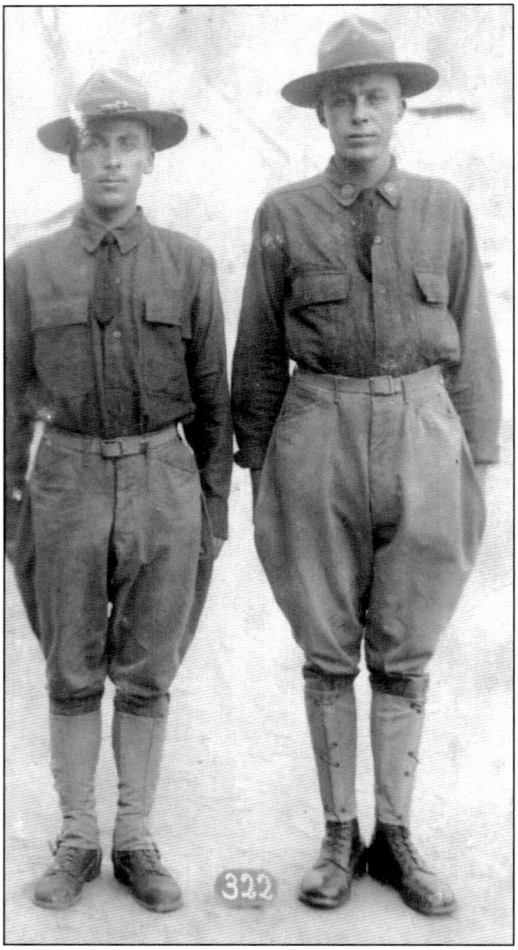

THE DOUGHBOYS OF WORLD WAR I. Bill Swaim (left) and Russell Peppel (right) are representative of the young men who went to war as World War I became a part of American life in the early 20th century. Mary Firestone's book lists 170 soldiers plus two war nurses in France who were from Lisbon. Of these, 17 gave their lives.

MEMORIAL DAY PARADE, 1920S. As World War I ended on November 11, 1918, the veterans came home, and organizations to commemorate their service began. This parade marching past the corner of Market and High Streets includes Carl Bowman, Clarence Ball, Wallace King, William Briggs, Allen Ramsey, Ross Fox, Rev. P.M. Kendall, Louis Binsley, Lawrence Baker, C.C. Connell, Lester Farmer, and Rev. D.E. Scott.

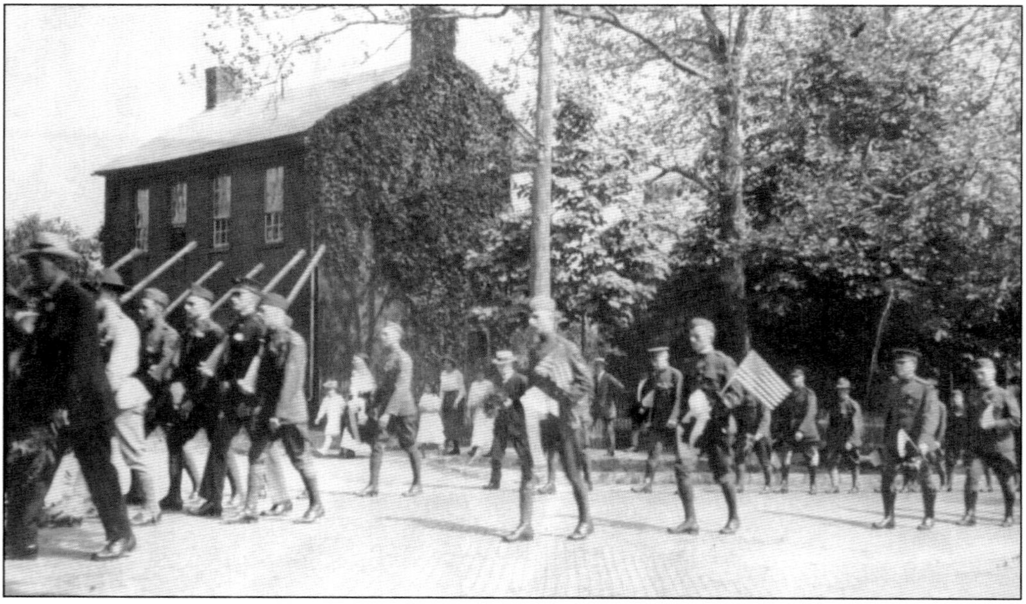

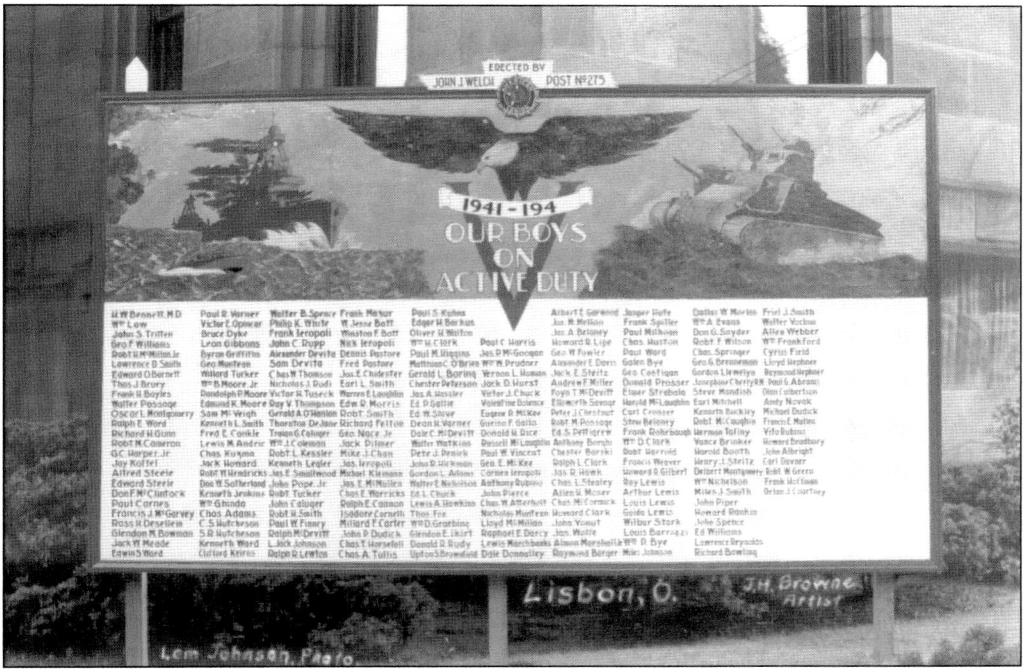

"Our Boys on Active Duty." This sign was posted in front of the courthouse during World War II. J. Homer Browne hand lettered this important military roll. Again, Firestone's sesquicentennial book lists approximately 874 in service, with 20 losing their lives. After the war, there was great celebration for the hard-fought victory, and organizations for veterans became quite active.

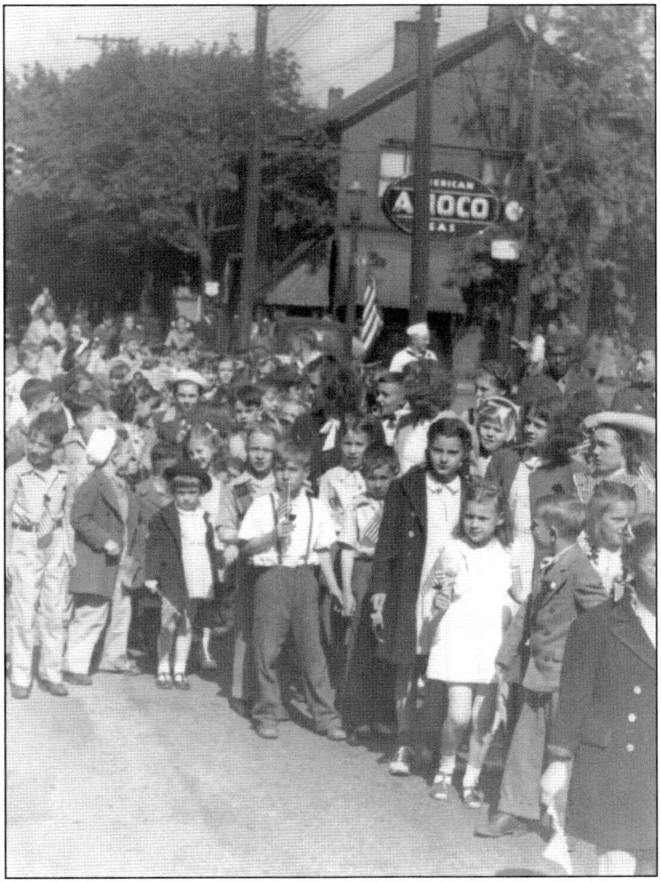

Schoolchildren at the War's End. Children during World War II were often acutely aware of the great conflict through the service of family members and the rationing in food and fuel. These children are lined up for a parade on Memorial Day, May 30, 1945, undoubtedly caught up in the excitement.

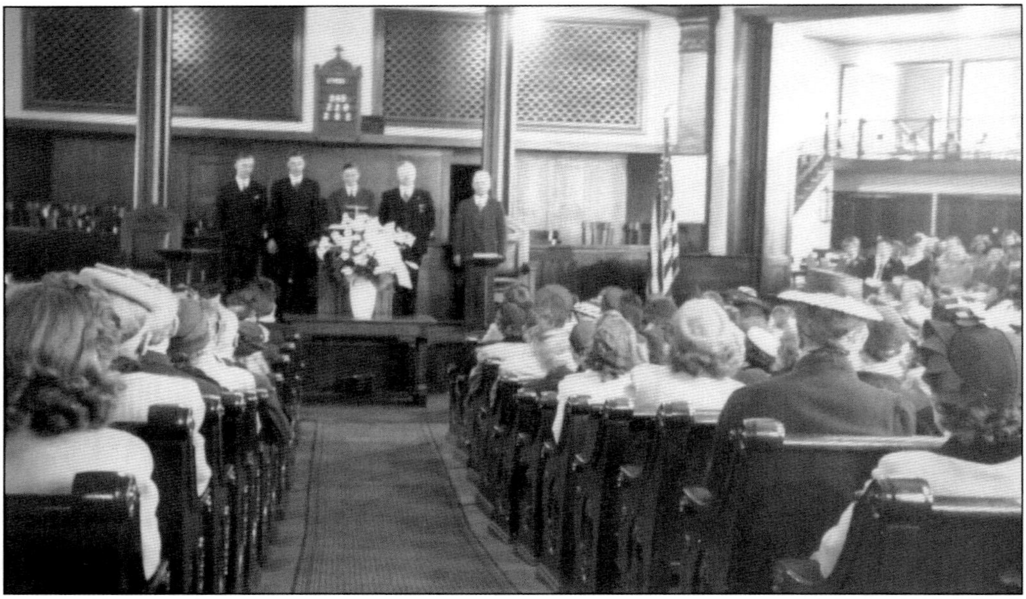

SPONTANEOUS THANKSGIVING SERVICE. As the news came of VJ Day on August 14, 1945, there were celebrations in the village square followed by a spontaneous service in the First Presbyterian Church sanctuary. Considering the capacity of the church, there must have been 500 to 600 in attendance. The pastors participating are, from left to right, Reverend Cord (Disciples of Christ), Reverend Reynolds (United Presbyterian), Reverend Cox (First Presbyterian), Reverend Jones (Church of the Nazarene), and Reverend Cope (First Methodist).

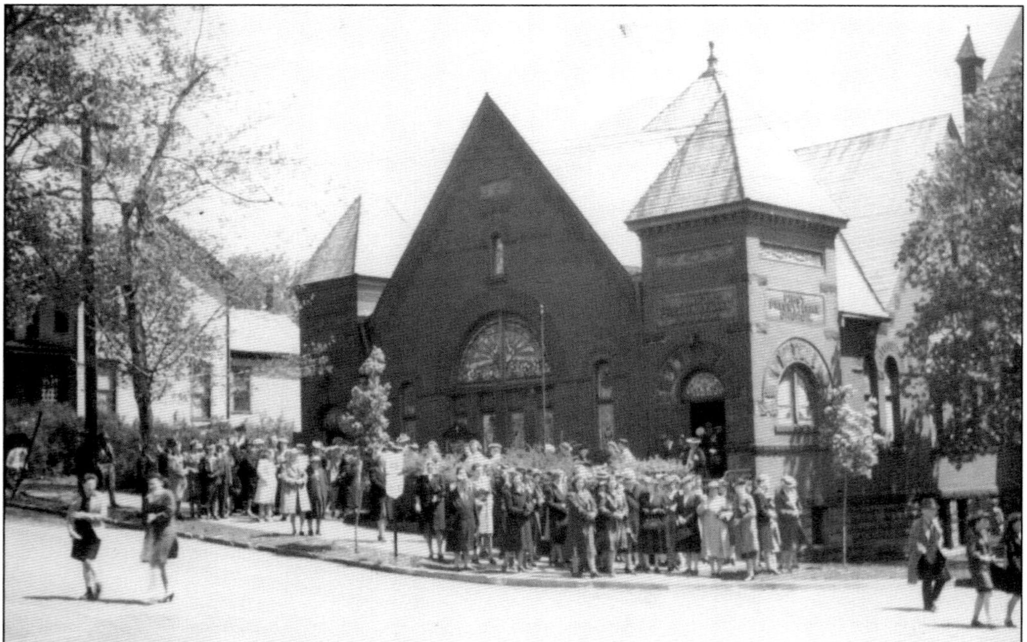

LEAVING CHURCH AFTER THE SERVICE. The crowds from the VJ Day service, which helped mark the official end of World War II, are seen leaving the church. Other views of the interior show women in their Sunday best complete with church dresses and hats while the men wore suits. This good news required respect and gratitude however hasty the preparation must have been.

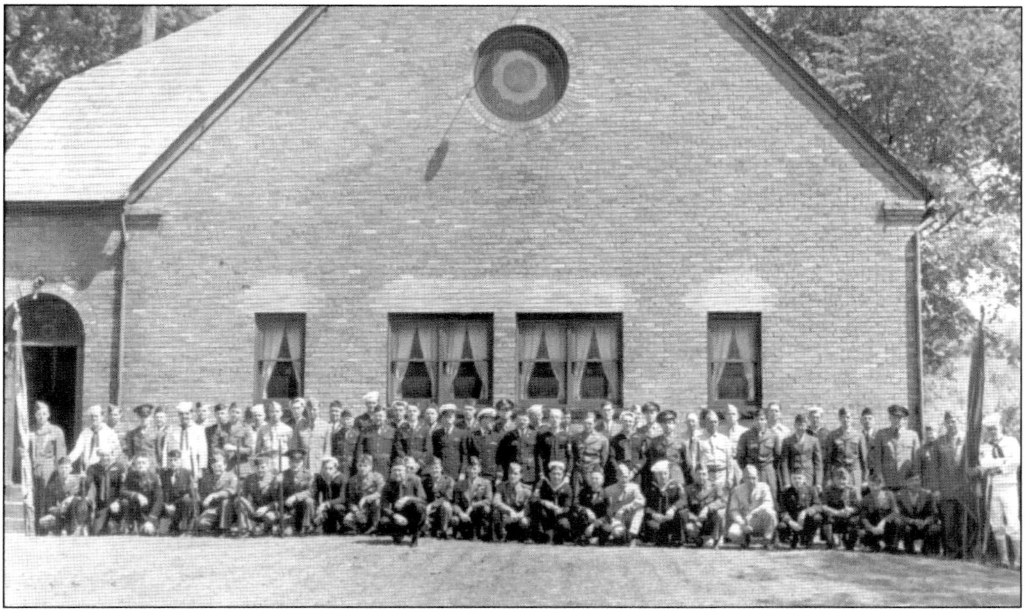

Gathering of Veterans. As the servicemen returned home, the American Legion and the Veterans of Foreign Wars became very important organizations in the postwar years. William Sexton was junior vice commander, and attorney Howard Cole served as state commander of the VFW of Ohio. In this photograph, men in uniform from both the American Legion and the VFW gather in front of the American Legion post to show their unity and patriotic gratitude.

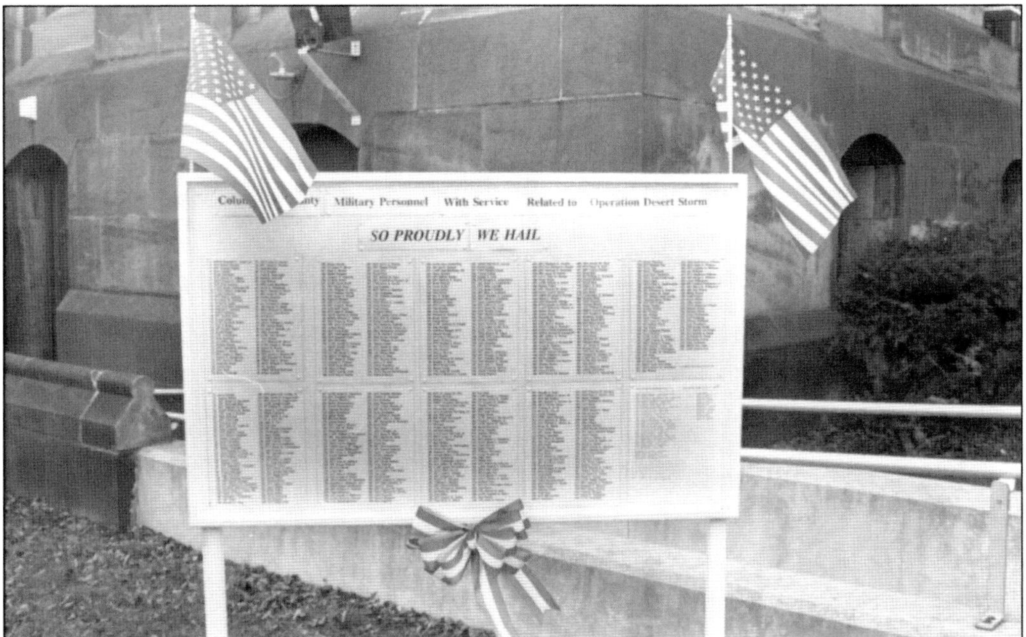

Operation Desert Storm Participants. With involvement in two more conflicts after World War II, Korea and Vietnam, the United States again gave service in the Desert Storm Operation in the early 1990s. The local community erected this sign in front of the Columbiana County Courthouse to indicate those involved from the county in the service of their country.

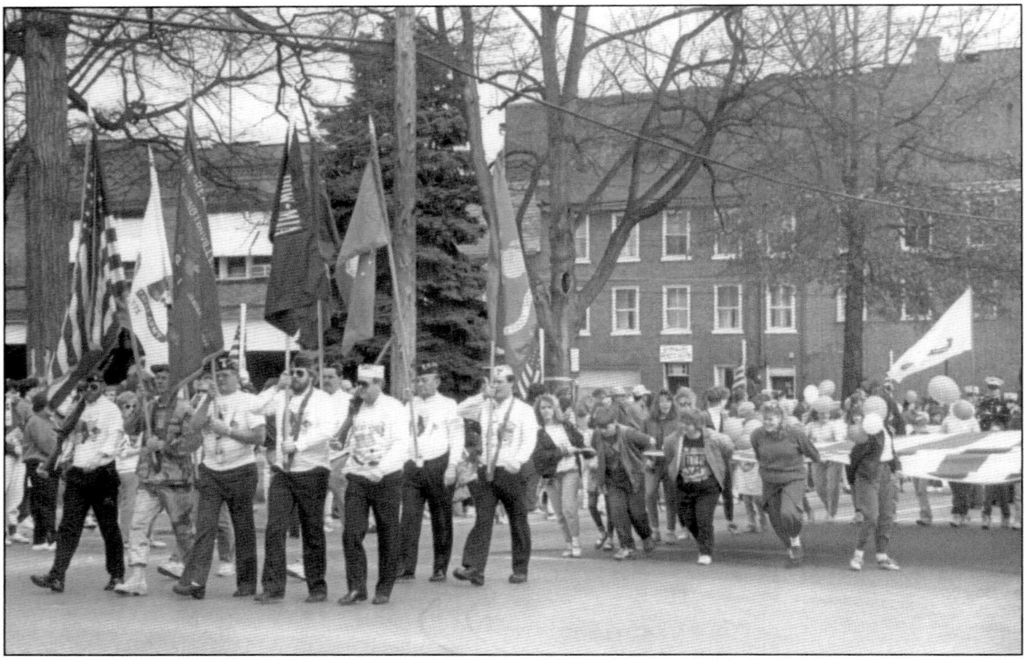

DESERT STORM WAR PARADE. With this short operation ended nationally, the local community again celebrated in downtown Lisbon. Heading west on Lincoln Way is the official color guard followed by citizens displaying the American flag. In the background can be seen the village hall and the Round Corner buildings.

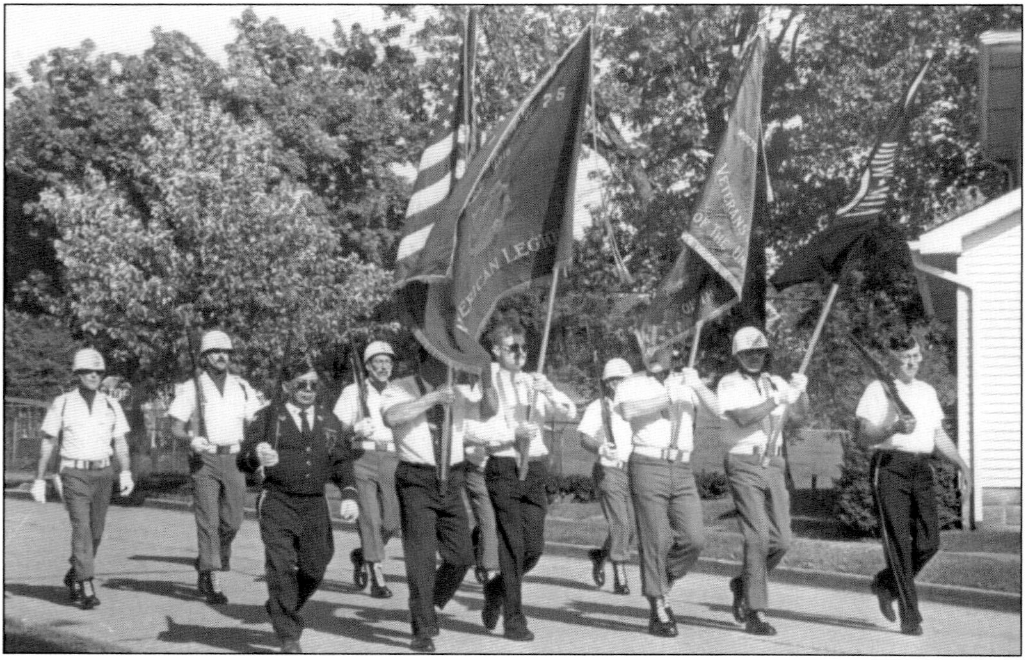

A RECENT MEMORIAL DAY. A combination of American Legion Post 275 and VFW Post 4111 marches as Lisbon's color guard. Some of the members of the unit are Dave Williams, Jeff Dorrance, and Don Morris. This is a time-honored tradition through the years, actually centuries, that continues without fail each year.

William M. Hostetter. Hostetter, whose patriotically decorated home appears on the cover of this book, was the marshal of the centennial parade in 1903. He was a Civil War veteran and president of the Columbiana County Insurance Company. Involved in the community and its centennial celebration, he is remembered as a leading citizen.

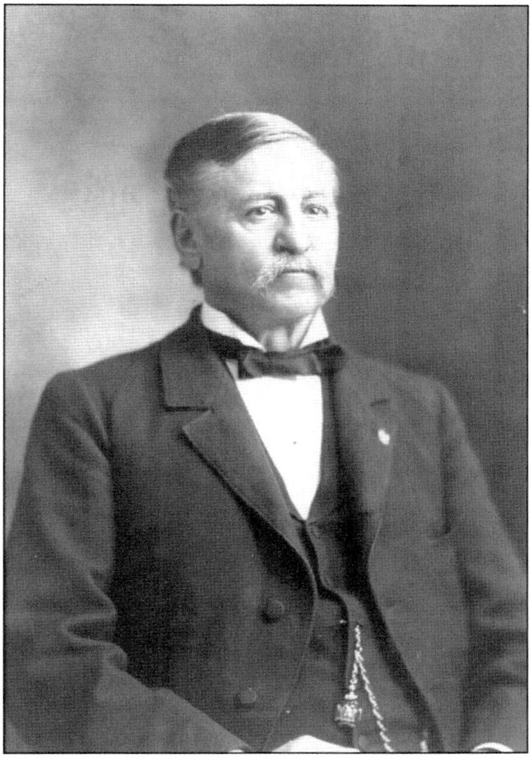

Lisbon's 1953 Sesquicentennial. This covered wagon sat in the village square during the July 1953 sesquicentennial celebration. Representative of the early roots of the community and contrasted with its progress, this was truly a vivid week of pageantry, contests, imported drum and bugle corps concerts, crowning of a queen, a grand ball, and a new publication on Lisbon's history. Throngs of people returned to celebrate their town.

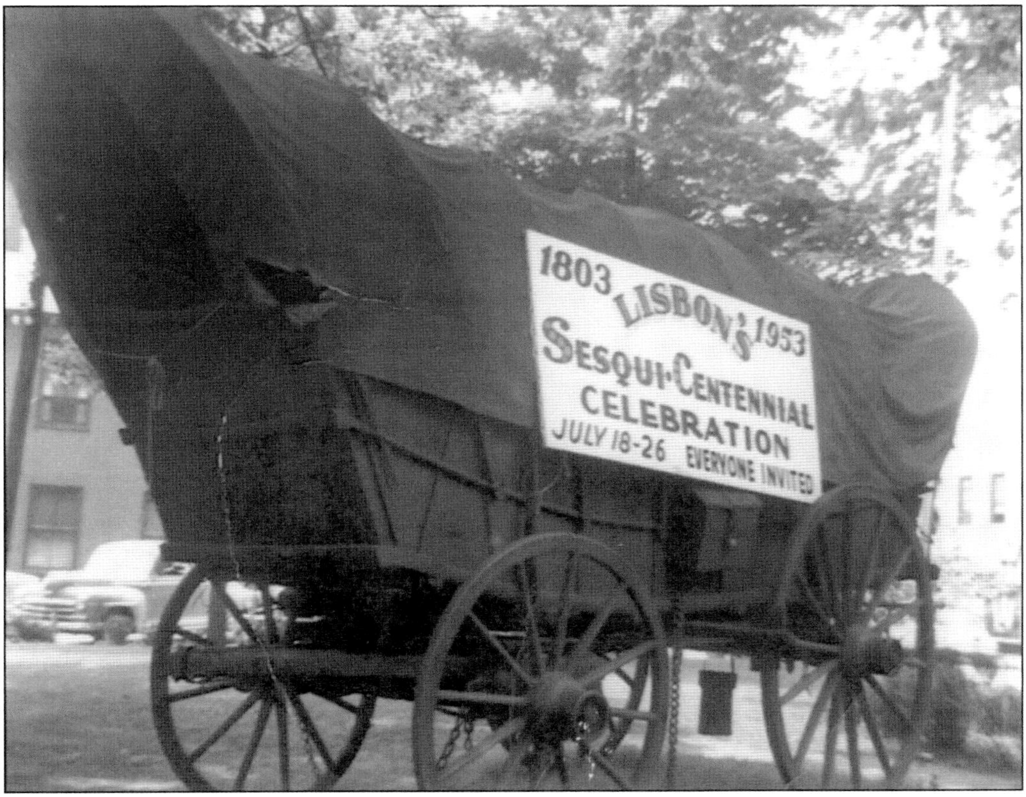

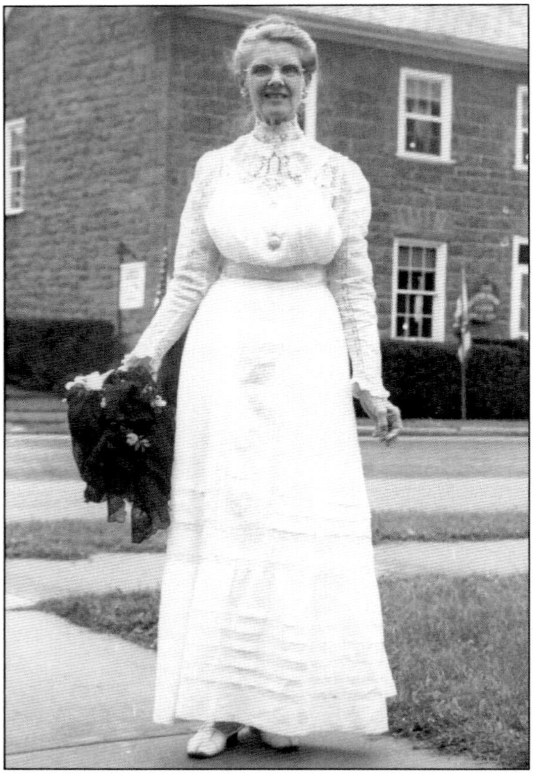

A SESQUICENTENNIAL COSTUME. Frances Lafferty, a member of the Binsley family and wife of attorney George Lafferty, is gowned in an old-fashioned costume complete with a traditional hat. She stands in front of the Old Stone House, which had been restored to its historical roots by this time. She and her family were quite involved with Lisbon history.

MEN OF THE SESQUICENTENNIAL. The employees of the Lisbon Post Office pose in July 1953 for the sesquicentennial. They are, from left to right, (first row) Earl Richardson (postmaster), John Snyder, Howard Hochmann, Malcolm Bricker, Louis Binsley, James Shattuck, and James Carlisle; (second row) Paul Flugan, Raymond Ketchum, Kenneth Robert Williams, Louis McKenna, Robert Vance Brinker, Galen Kenty, Carl Bowman, Paul Burnip, Albert Webber, and Lester Maple.

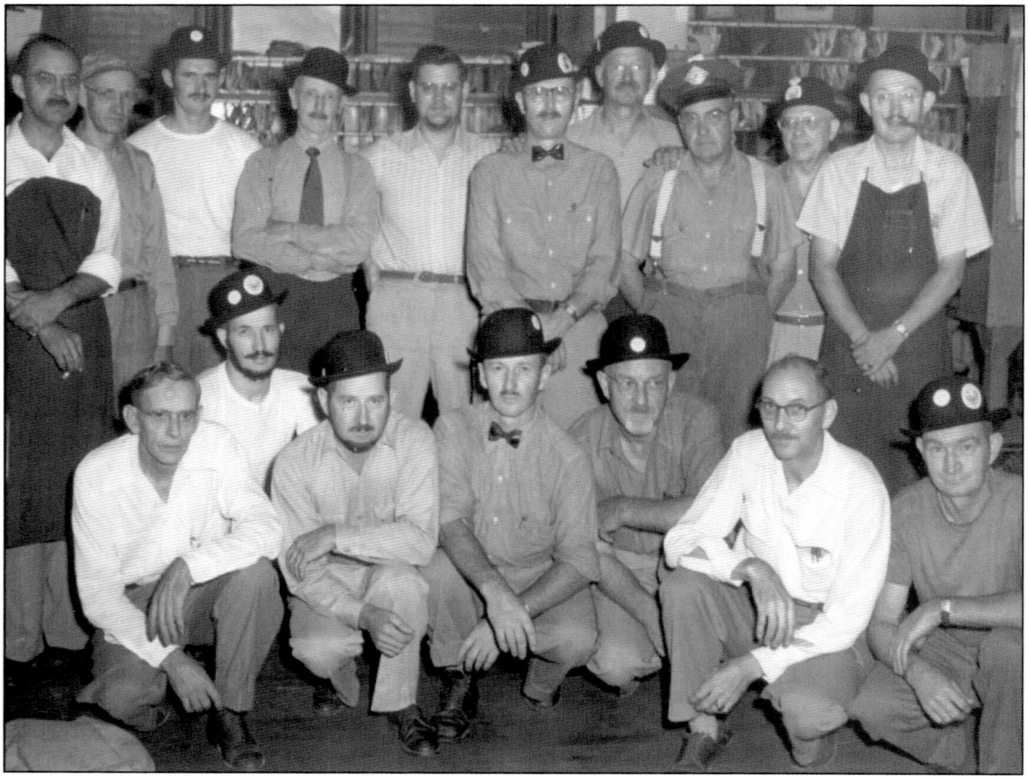

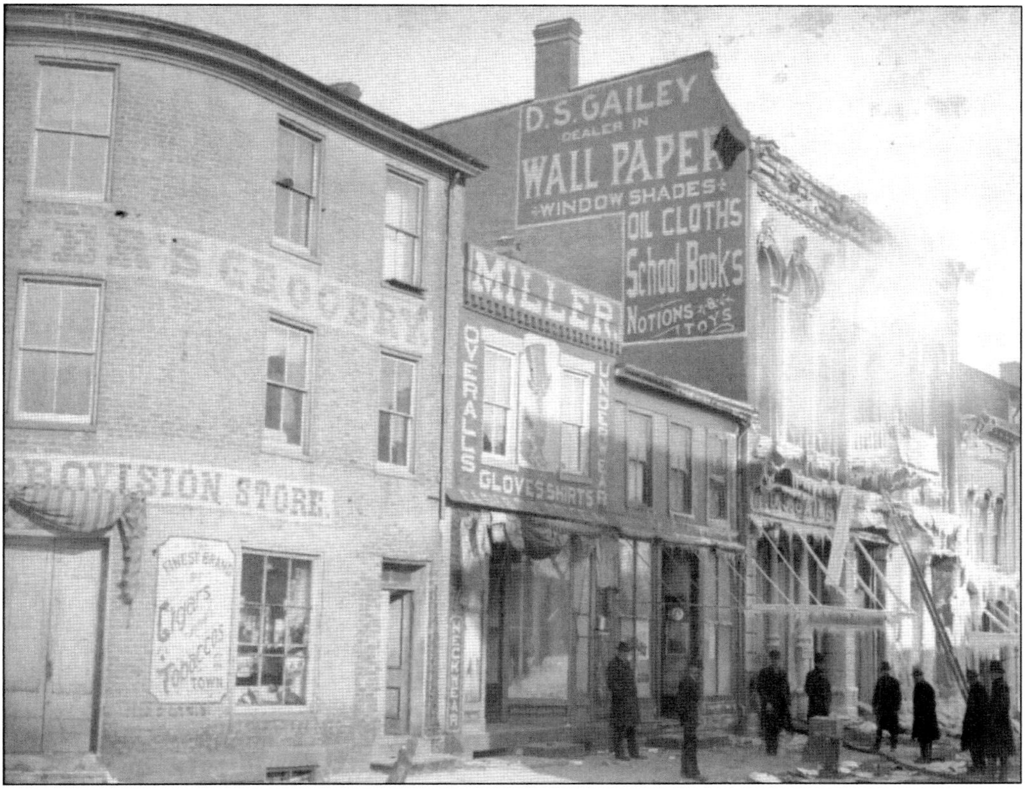

Old Opera House. One of the early historic building losses was the old opera house. Such structures were prevalent in 19th-century towns, and this edifice—one of two opera houses in Lisbon—stood in a major downtown block of buildings. After the fire, the Gailey-Firestone Building was constructed on that site, midway between the Round Corner and the Cross Keys Hotel.

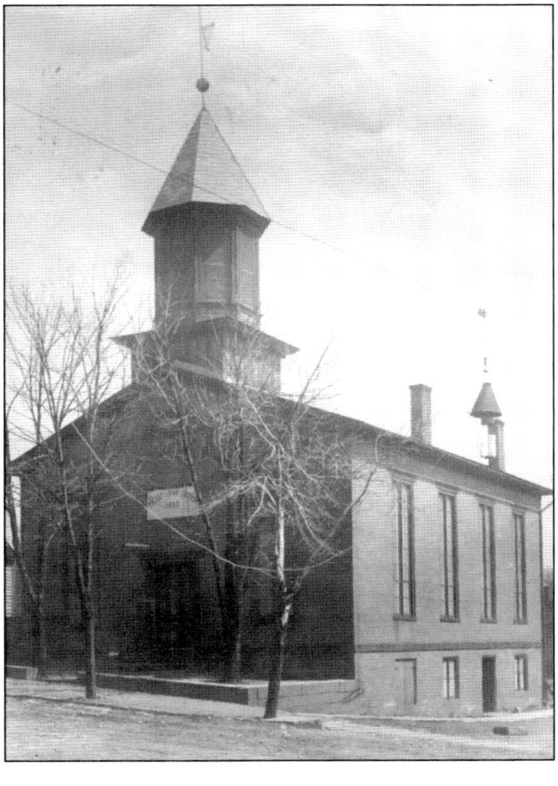

Old Presbyterian Church. This was the Presbyterian church of 1840, its second home on the corner of North Market and East Chestnut Streets. The building, not too large as a structure, sold pews to its members. It not only housed the congregation, but also served as a school; high school classes were taught in the basement level.

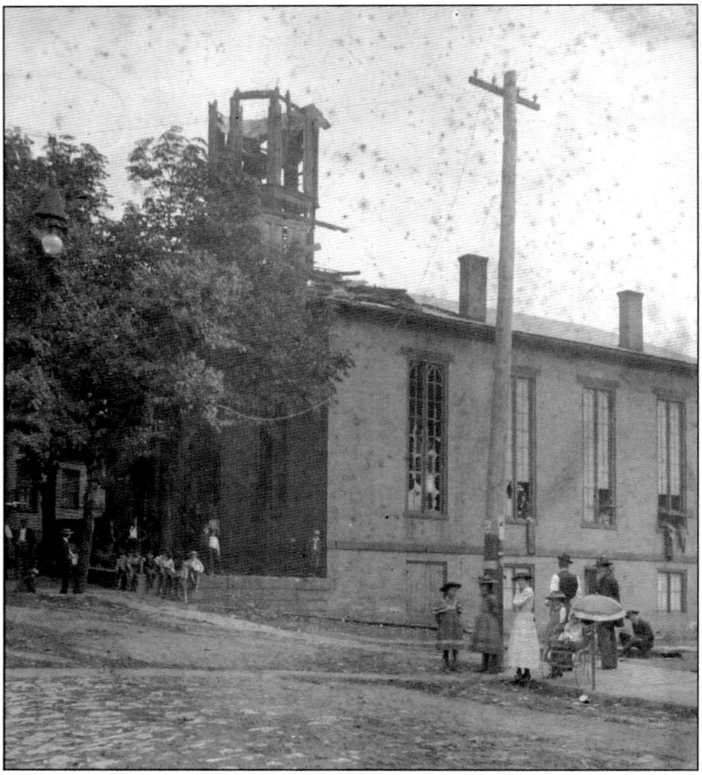

Burned Presbyterian Church. This structure, the same First Presbyterian Church built in 1840, burned in 1894. Housing the sanctuary and church needs as well as public school classrooms, locals ran and screamed: "The church is burning!" Shortly after this fire, the church began construction of the 1895 building that is still in use today.

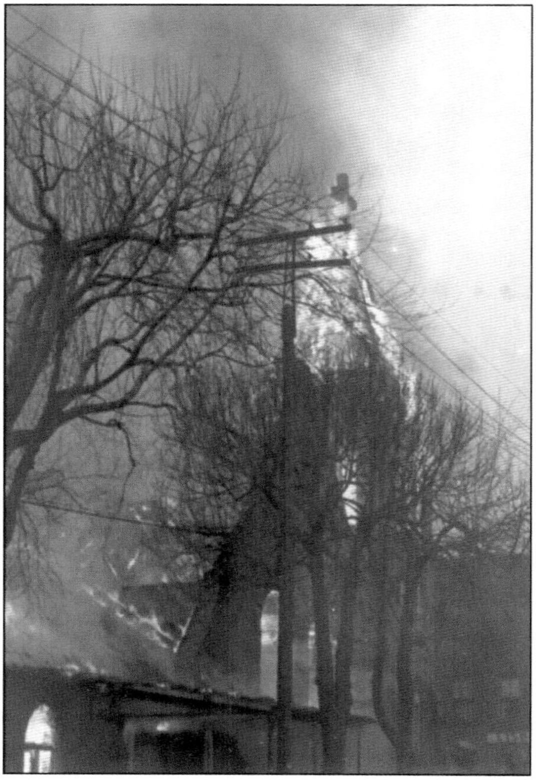

Lisbon Methodist Fire. Fire raged through the beautiful old Methodist church on February 28, 1944. As evidenced here, the building was a total loss, but the congregation moved forward to replace their church building. By 1950, they were worshipping in a new brick building with all of the characteristics of a traditional, yet practical, church.

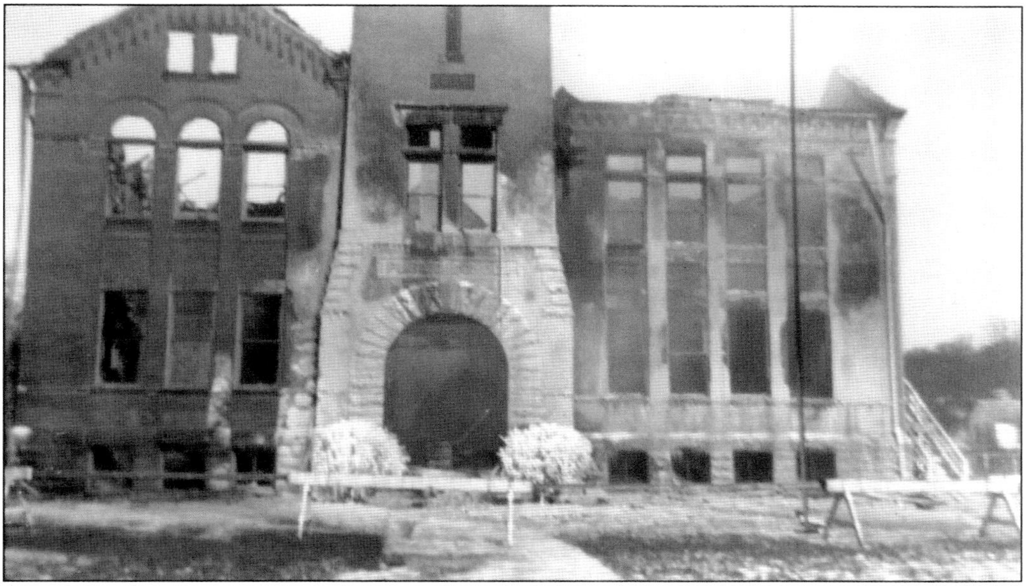

Fire-Ravaged McKinley School. On March 3, 1950, the strong, square, fully brick McKinley School building was completely burned. Only the walls stood as the bell fell from the tower, the roof went up in flames, and the floors and furnishings burned. Inches of ice from the fire hoses watering through the night blanketed the fire escapes. The loss of memories and facilities was devastating, but a new building rose by the September 1951 start of school.

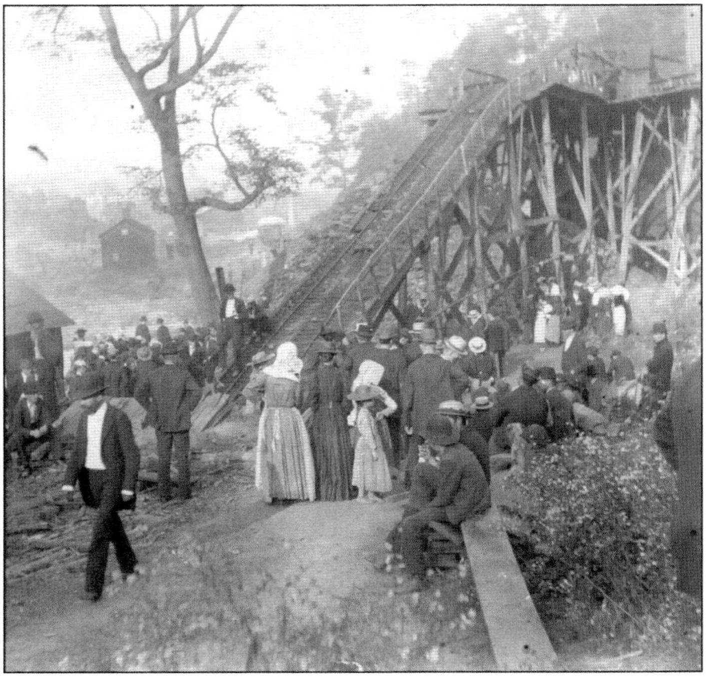

The Mine Disaster. While no specific information is given concerning this particular mine disaster, it can stand as symbolic not only of the potential but also the reality of mining disasters. In February 1881, the *Ohio Patriot* headlined: "Havoc and Death among the Miners," referring to the great disaster of the Rock Hill Mine at Robinsville, four miles from New Lisbon. Five deaths are listed along with dreadful injuries.

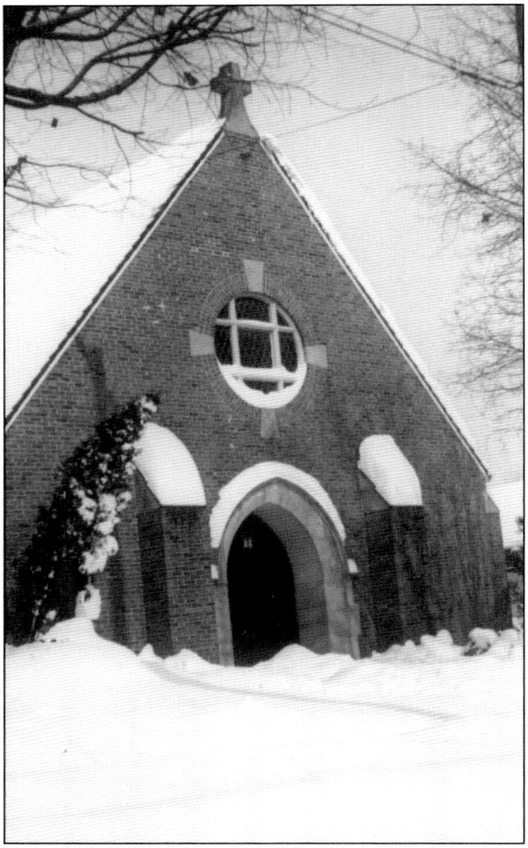

St. George's in 1950s Snow. The day after Thanksgiving in 1950, upwards of three feet of snow fell upon Lisbon. This was always known as the "Big Snow," which closed churches, businesses, and schools for a week. Digging out from this was a major project; mining equipment came to the rescue in some cases, including opening Route 30 from Lisbon to East Liverpool, 17 miles.

St. George's Rectory. The rectory standing next to the church is also, of course, blanketed in feet of snow. Such casualties bring the community together as happened again with the downburst, not officially qualifying as a tornado, in the summer of 2014 that destroyed homes and trees.

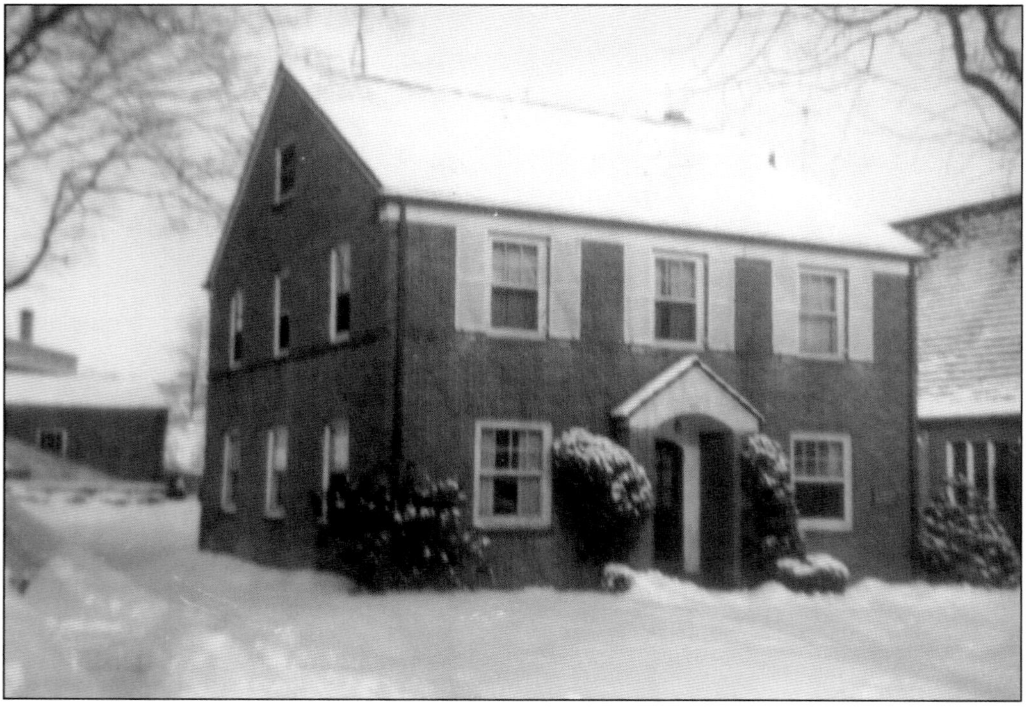

Six

FRAMED IN TIME

Perhaps some of the greatest charm in Lisbon is the sense that the past is ever so present. Those who drive through the town often comment upon the buildings, the square, and the rolling hills that encompass the village. Indeed, it is framed in time.

However, that framing in time has led to some interesting paths. One would be the restoration that occurs periodically among the landmarks. While numerous old buildings remain as they always have been, others are in the process of restoration to former appearance or new repurposing. This gives an interesting pattern to community in both its immediate impact and its future life.

Another framing in time is the transition northward that places the village in a new world, a new era. Progressing north on Market Street, there are new buildings in harmony with past appearances as well as modern businesses and conversion of older homes to apartments. Just beyond the village limits, both government and commercial interests have acquired much land for building purposes. The county maintains offices, and the various social agencies operate there. The county municipal courthouse is nearby. Several group homes are nestled in the hills as well. Businesses have acquired space from a company headquarters to a supermarket and a variety of stores from everyday items to a pharmacy to automotive in nature. The portrait is a different one, a 21st-century world.

The entire frame of time is the overall imprint of the world of the 19th and 20th centuries captured in buildings, names, and traditions. The landmarks remain with a sense of nostalgia, the alumni return for reunions and events, and the local services are provided as they are in most American small towns. The chamber of commerce is very active.

For every visitor and every former and current resident, this little village maintains a certain sense of a world of the past yet still a place to live, to be. The covered bridge draws a conclusion that the America of the past was real and is real as the fast-paced electronic world of the 21st century dominates in a new and different lifestyle.

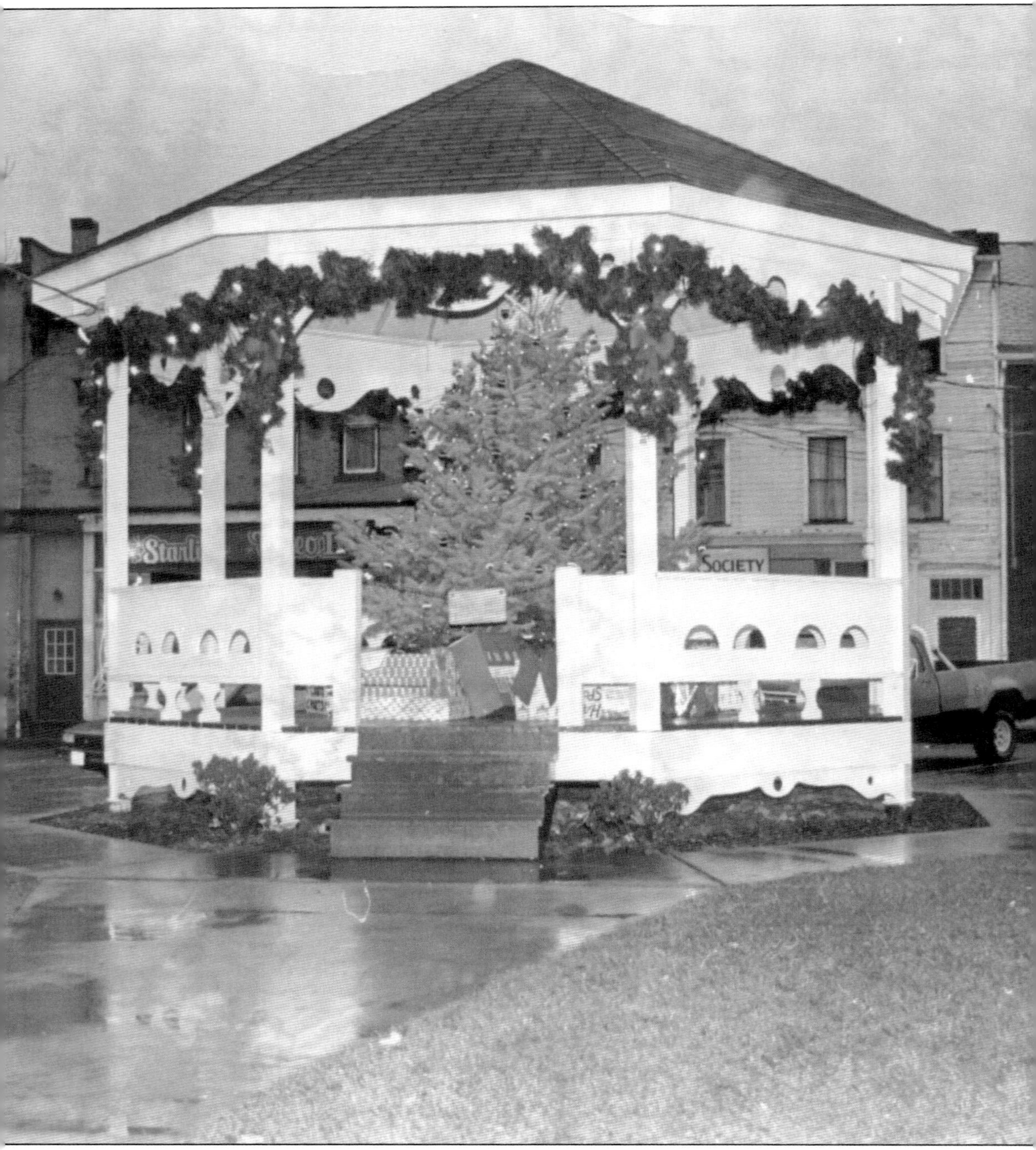

Lisbon's Original Gazebo. The gazebo stands in the center of the southeast quadrant of the village square. The wooden structure is used for speeches, announcements, weddings, and musical events. Today, a replacement gazebo occupies the traditional spot of the one pictured. Built by youth from the Columbiana County Career and Technical Center, the new structure is more modern in appearance yet retains the significant purposes of the original. A gazebo is an important way to mark the community gatherings, the transitions of time, the charm of the past, and the progress of the future. The new gazebo is an excellent marker of the transition of time in village life but the pride in the past.

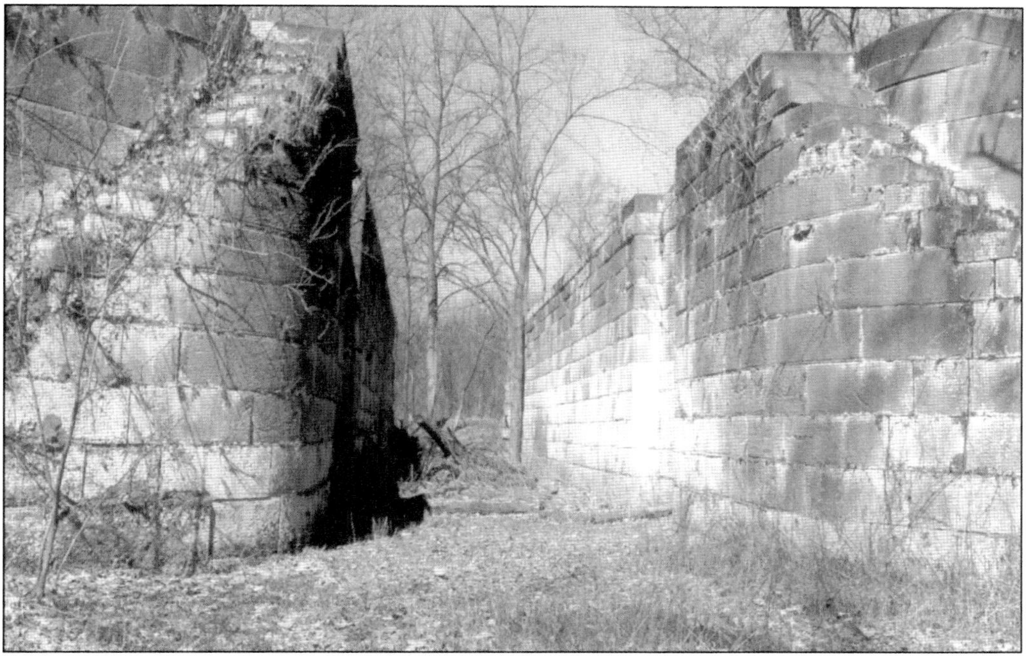

The Sandy and Beaver Canal. This canal was the great economic hope of the community in its dreams of becoming an important city. Sadly, that did not happen, but this dramatic illustration of the remaining Lusk's Lock gives a sense of the large project and the significant representation from the past. Today, the area is simply nostalgic beauty.

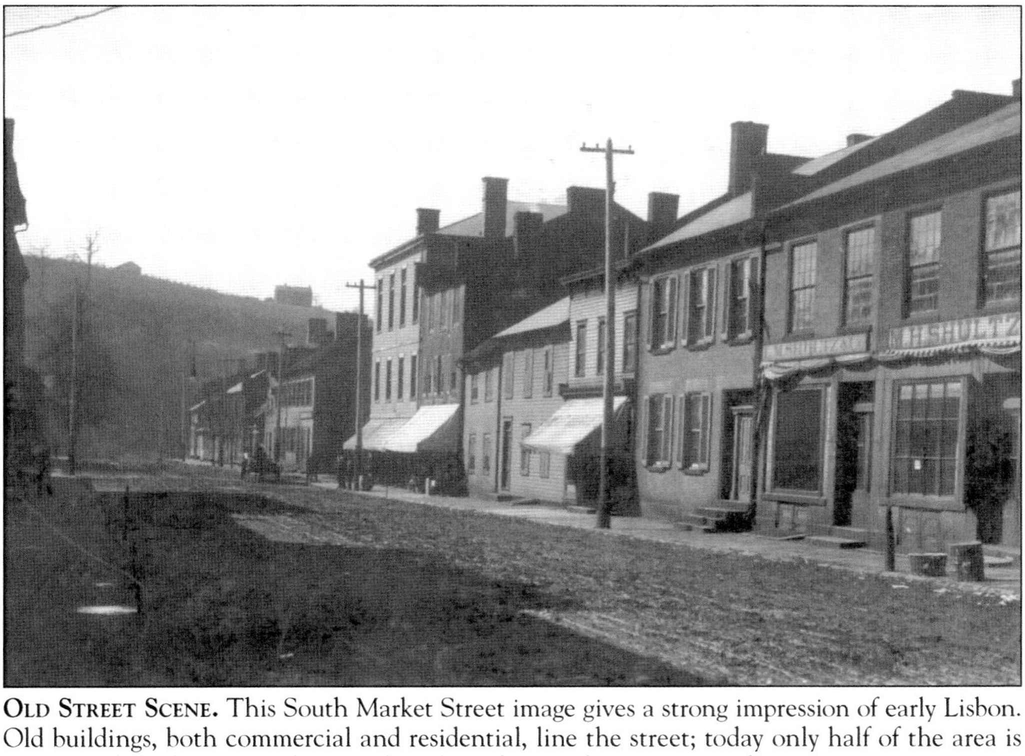

Old Street Scene. This South Market Street image gives a strong impression of early Lisbon. Old buildings, both commercial and residential, line the street; today only half of the area is business while the rest is a large parking lot. There is the transition of time.

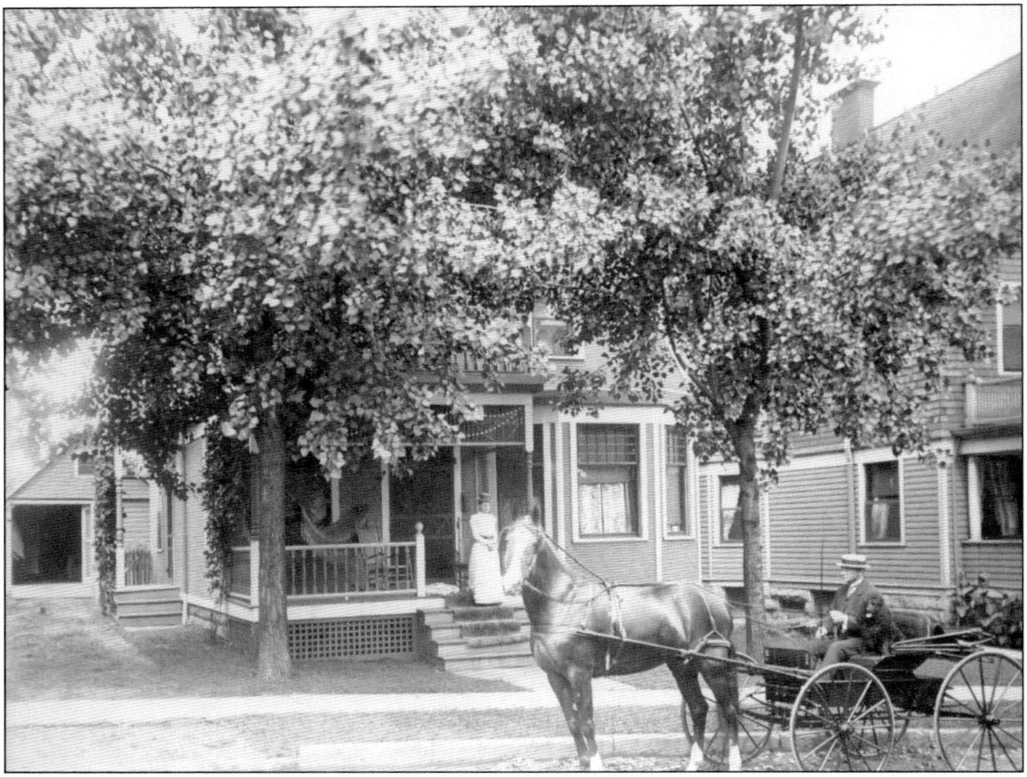

HORSE-AND-BUGGY DAYS. A Mr. Ruhl is seen driving his horse and buggy past a West Lincoln Way residence. The house illustrates the Victorian characteristics of bay windows and carpenter's lace porches. There is a certain romantic look to the Victorian house and the 19th-century transportation; it could well be the genesis of a painting.

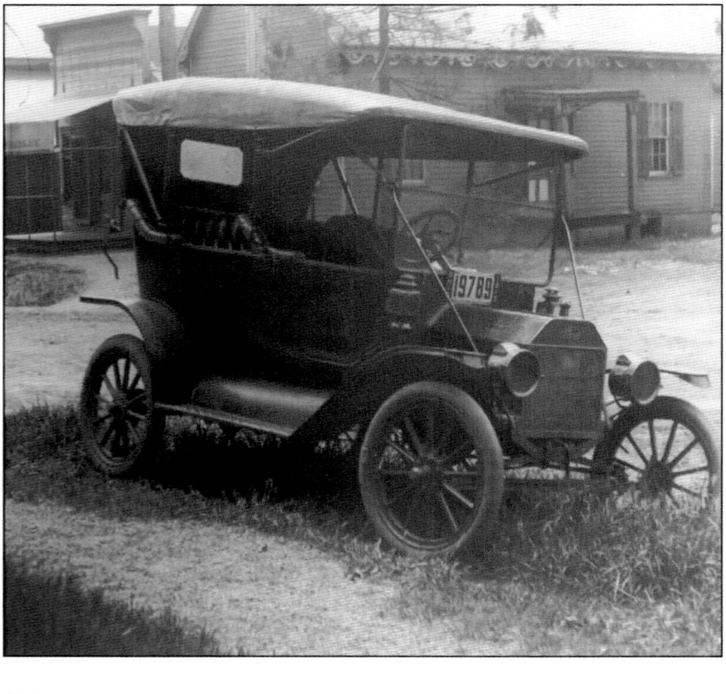

THE COMING OF THE AUTOMOBILE. Early in the 20th century, the automobile changed the culture of the United States forever. Lisbon was no exception, as this classic car, dubbed the horseless carriage, stands in front of an old building of the times. The automobile, of course, spawned new businesses such as the longtime community staple Pilmer Auto Parts.

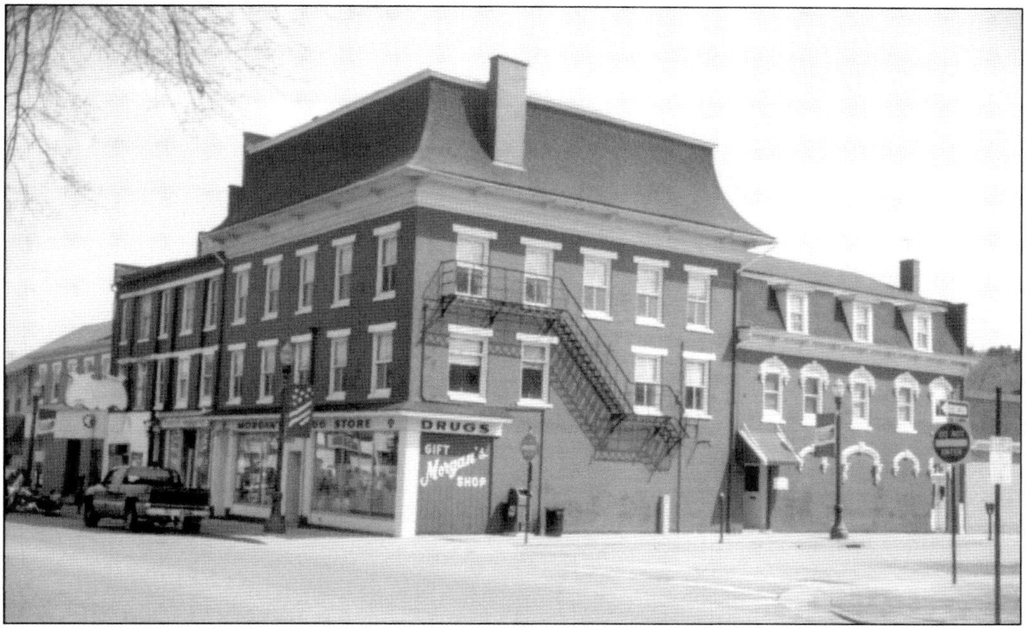

MORGAN'S DRUG STORE. A primary landmark of the village square, Morgan's Drug Store, founded in the 19th century, still maintains its place in the community. Although other places exist, the charm and friendliness of the establishment thrives. (Photograph by Wendell Cole.)

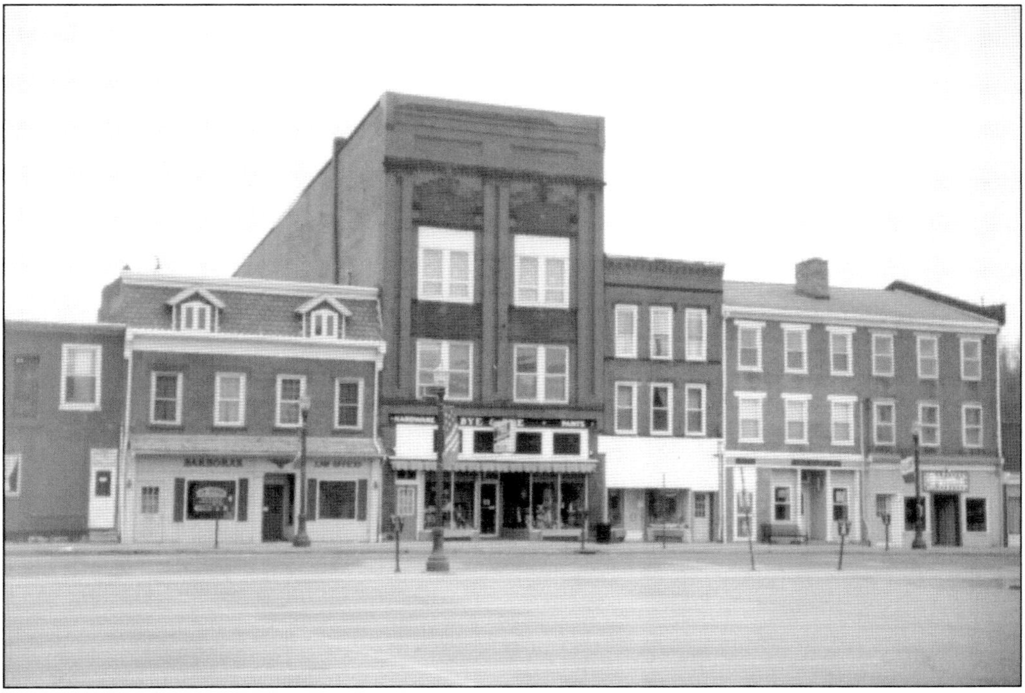

BYE AND BYE HARDWARE. Founded by the Bye family and still in the family, this business occupies a prominent South Market Street location. With a traditional look in oak drawers and traveling ladder, the store features modern appliances, boutique items, and a florist as well as just a few nails or the practical tool. Locals and visitors frequent the shop. (Photograph by Wendell Cole.)

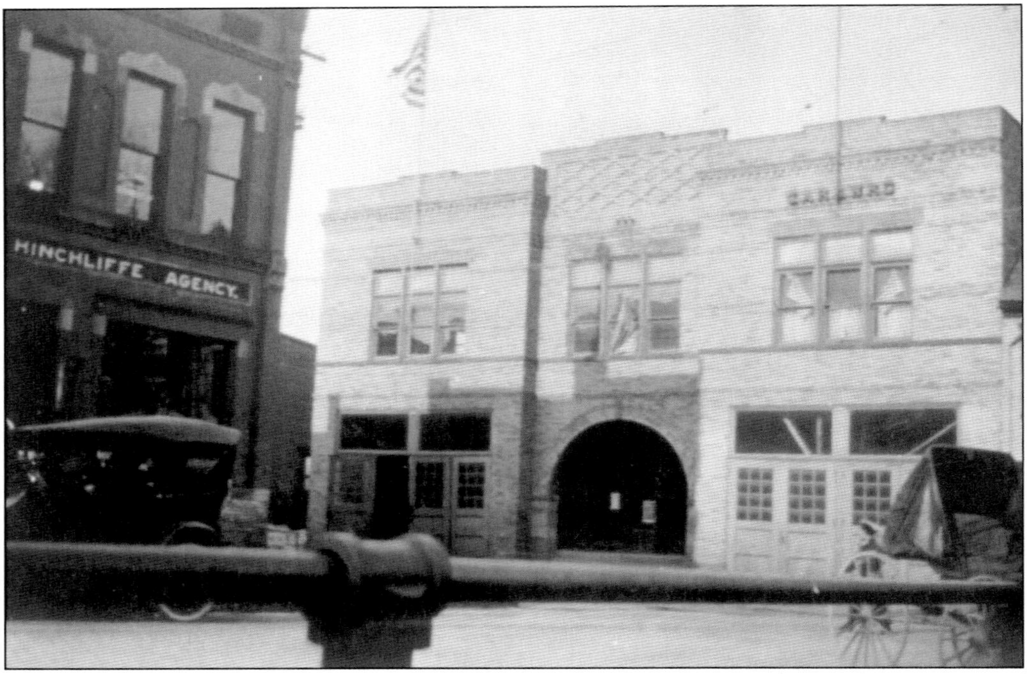

PREVIOUS VILLAGE HALL. This village hall served for many years on the northeast corner of the village square, originally housing the fire department. Visible in the front are the old cars as well as the hitching rail for horses; the replacement of the hitching rail in the 1950s was quite a change and cause for concern as the town acquired parking meters.

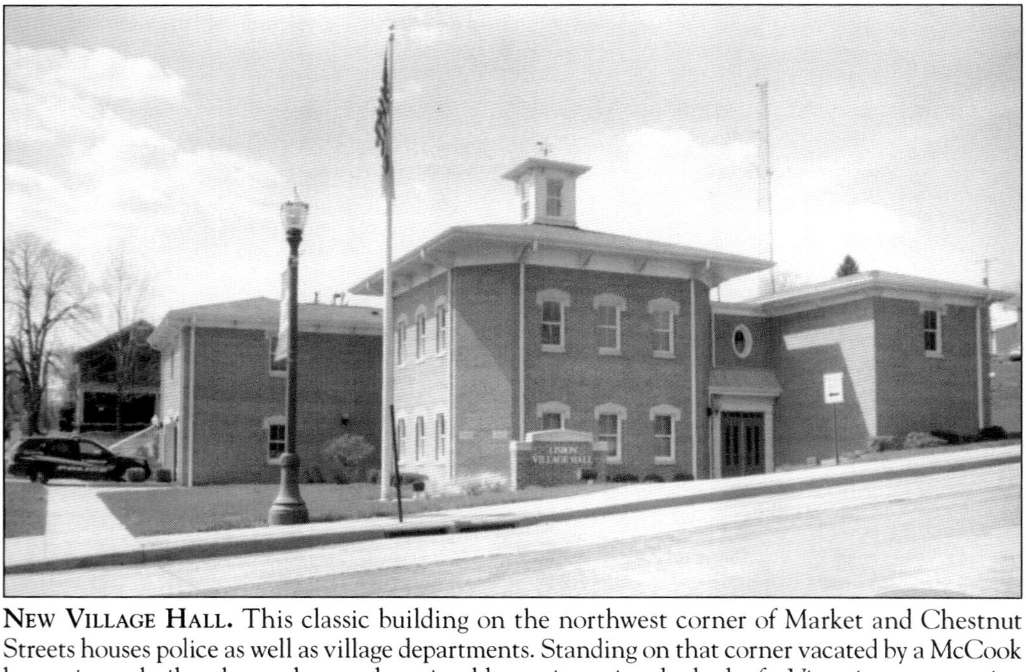

NEW VILLAGE HALL. This classic building on the northwest corner of Market and Chestnut Streets houses police as well as village departments. Standing on that corner vacated by a McCook home, it was built to be modern and serviceable, yet it retains the look of a Victorian community. (Photograph by Wendell Cole.)

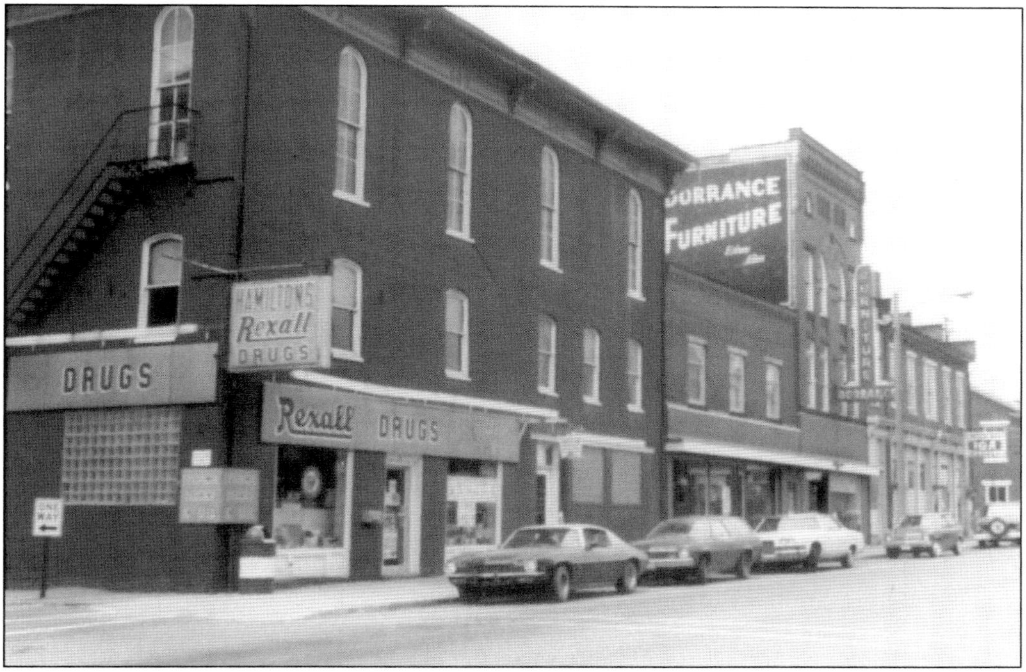

HAMILTON'S STREET SCENE. Hamilton's Drug Store, considered the oldest brick building in Ohio, was built early in the 1800s. Early on, the second story housed the law offices of Edwin Stanton, who later became Lincoln's secretary of war and A.D. McCook, who served as a major general in the Civil War. Also visible is the long-surviving Dorrance Furniture Company, family owned and known for its quality furnishings.

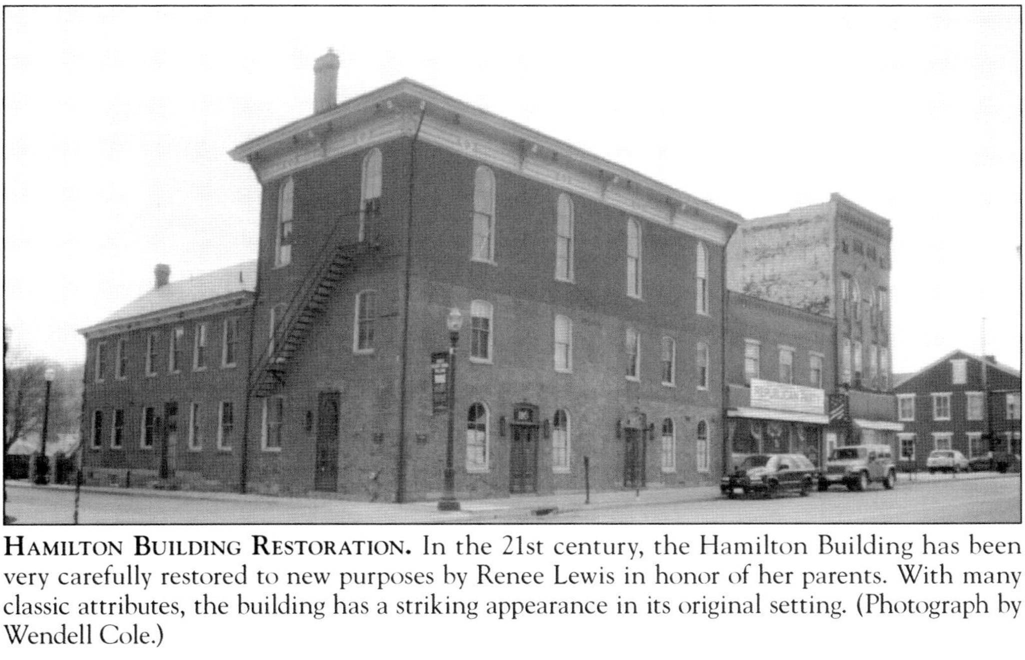

HAMILTON BUILDING RESTORATION. In the 21st century, the Hamilton Building has been very carefully restored to new purposes by Renee Lewis in honor of her parents. With many classic attributes, the building has a striking appearance in its original setting. (Photograph by Wendell Cole.)

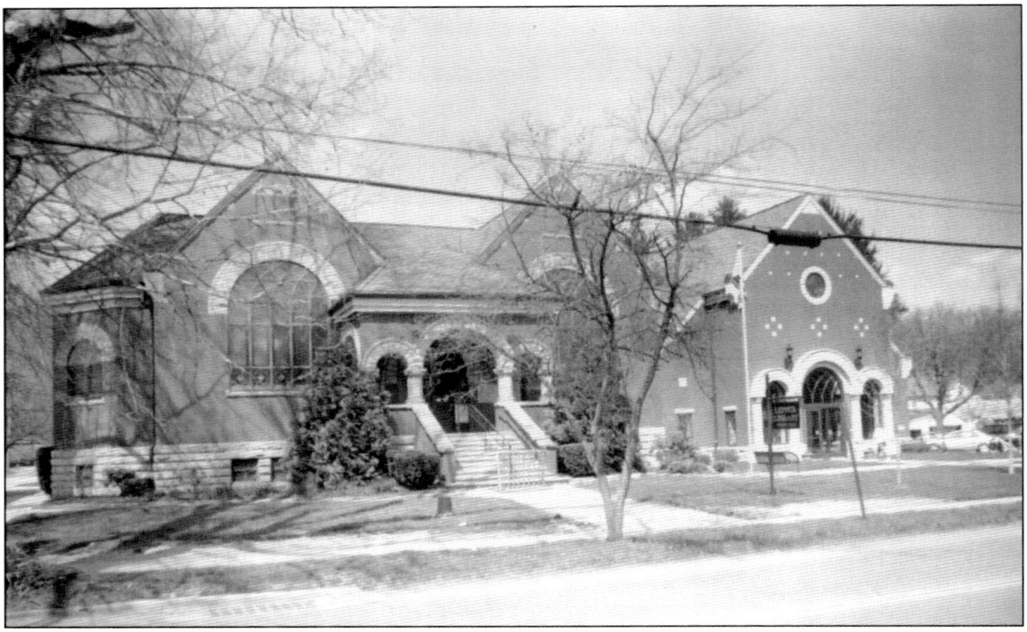

Major Lepper Library Addition. Many years ago, the Lepper Library acquired a new wing through the generosity of attorney George Lafferty. In recent years, there has been the major addition to the east of the building of a complementary wing equal in size and matching in pattern to the original structure. This traditional building meets many local and county needs to this day. (Photograph by Wendell Cole.)

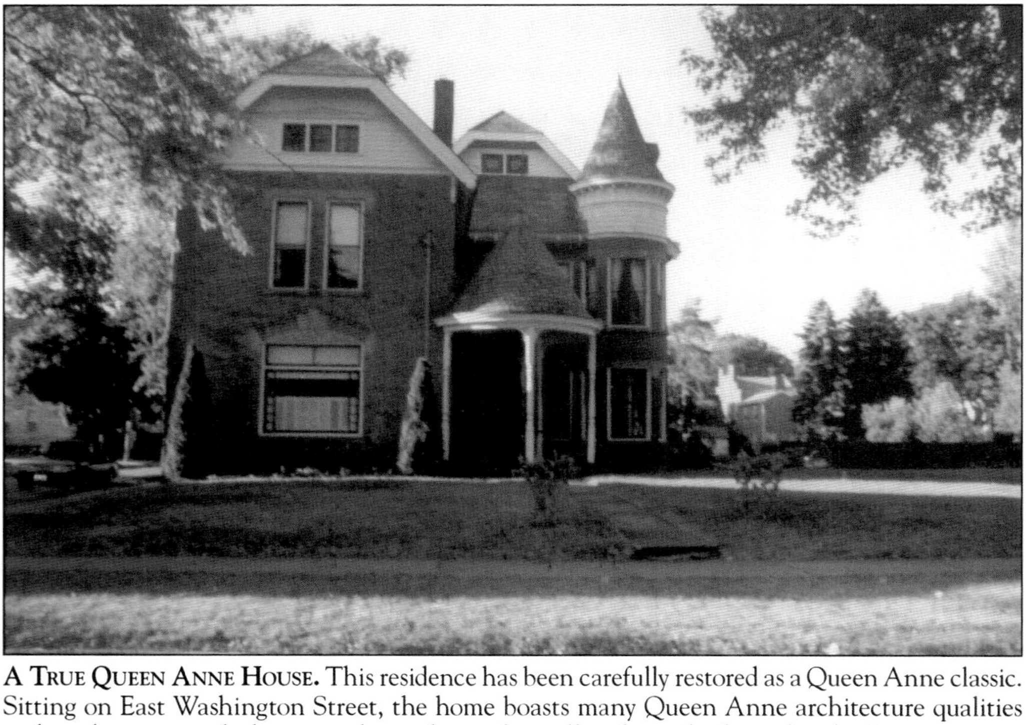

A True Queen Anne House. This residence has been carefully restored as a Queen Anne classic. Sitting on East Washington Street, the home boasts many Queen Anne architecture qualities such as the tower with the pointed, circular roof as well as the multiple roof peaks. In more recent years, it has been home to the Neill family and, currently, the Halverstadts.

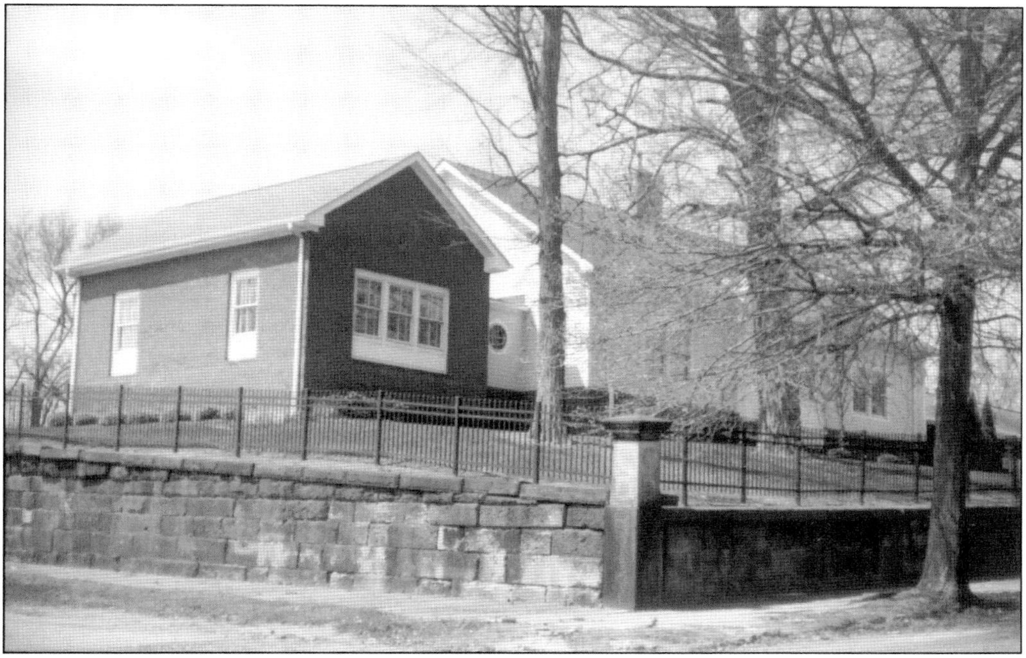

Current Board of Education Building. As the McKinley School expanded, the house occupied by the board of education was razed. This new building, in architectural harmony with the village, sits on North Market Street, land of the old Lincoln School. It retains the stone wall that has always been a symbolic educational boundary. (Photograph by Wendell Cole.)

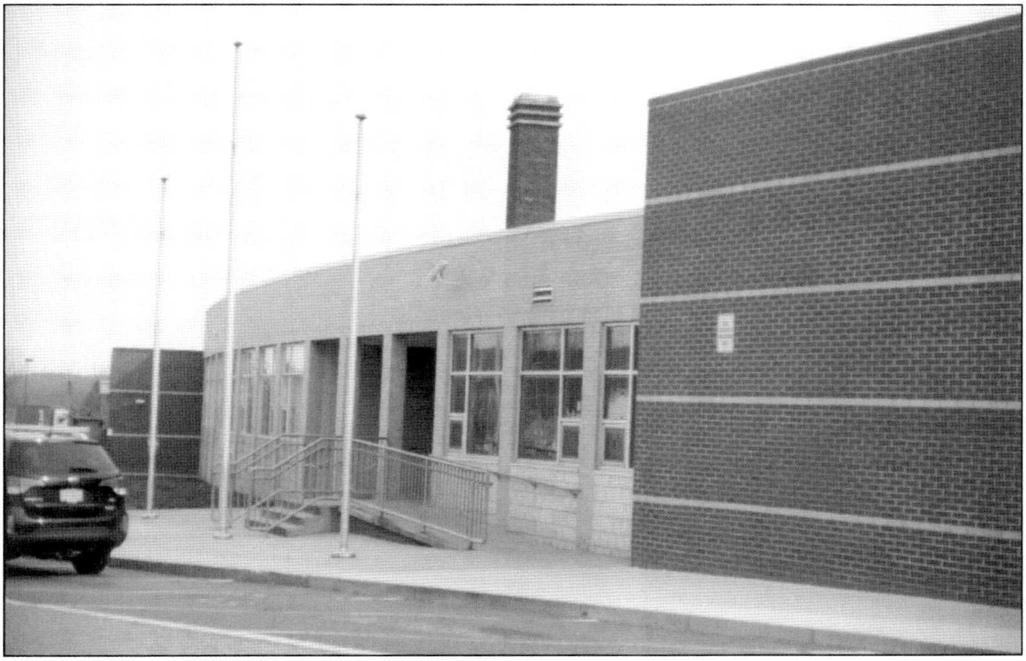

Current David Anderson High School. Beginning its existence as the Lincoln School, this building houses grades six through 12. The original section was opened in 1952, and multiple additions have been made. Today, it is the active center of the local school system in numbers and opportunities begun at the McKinley School. (Photograph by Wendell Cole.)

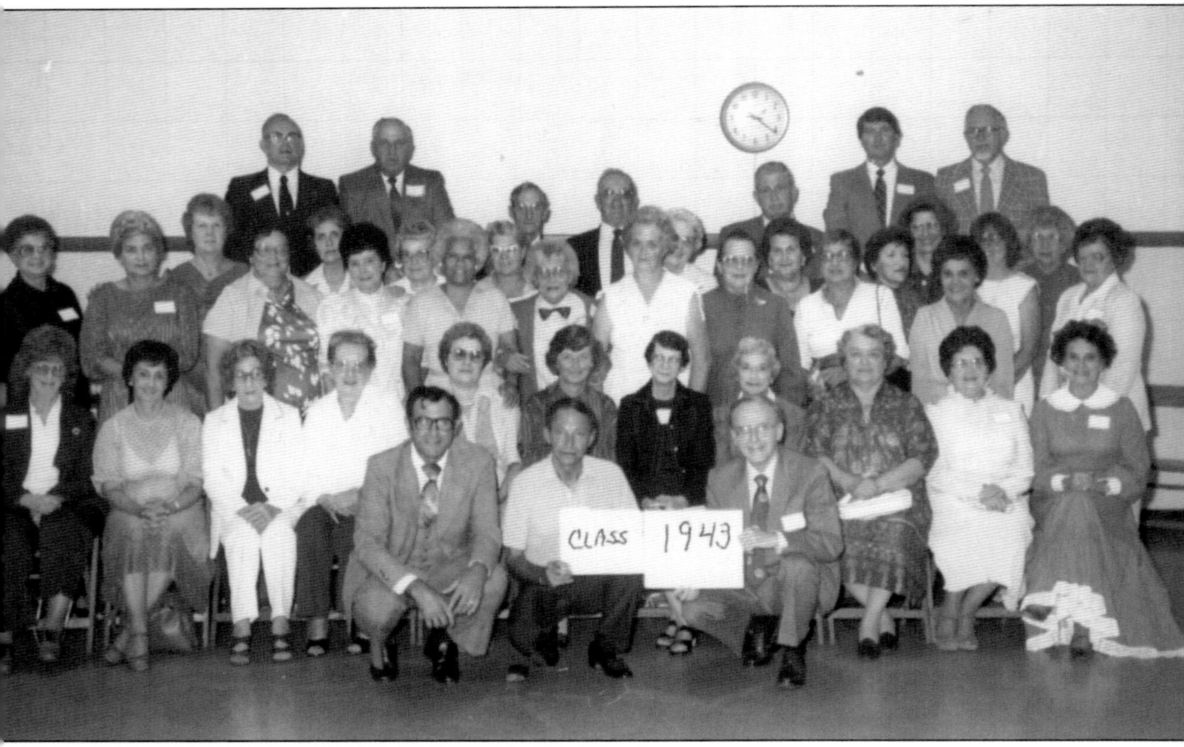

CLASS OF 1943. The annual class reunion to share memories and life experiences is a Lisbon tradition. At their 50th reunion in 1993, the following classmates, from left to right, gathered: (first row) Charles Senanefes, Fr. Lewis O'Neil, and Robert Farrell (second row) Lucille Lewis McIntosh, Margaret Dudick Novak, Viola Wells Reynolds, Doris Carlisle, Mary Valentino Newell, Dorothy Lewton Brown, Jean Todd Foster, Alice Jean McGrew, Rita Smith Snyder, Pauline Armstrong Cook, and Mary Smallwood Schnader; (third row) Mary Higgins Saporito, June Chevrent Mansfield, Eris Rouse Smith, Opal Holliman Hresbovcin, Doris Dillard Grice, Mary Capoziello Eckols, Ruth Armstrong Dotson, Frances Evans Brenner, Dorothy Biscan Jacobs, Beulah Deland Cultertson, and Dorothy Ketchum Copeland; (fourth row) Marjorie Ward Mitchell, Catherine Hadley Miller, Doris McDevitt Figley, Helen Miller Jarman, Helen Horner Taylor, Sue Novak Belaney, Mary Louise Estock Glavin, Anne Novicky Shilling Doris Stafford Irvin, and Naomi Hawthorne Sebrell; (fifth row) Lester Smith, Harold Lewton, Gail Wallace, King Strudoff, Ralph "Mickey" McDevitt, Foster Lewis, and Rev. Wilbur Cook.

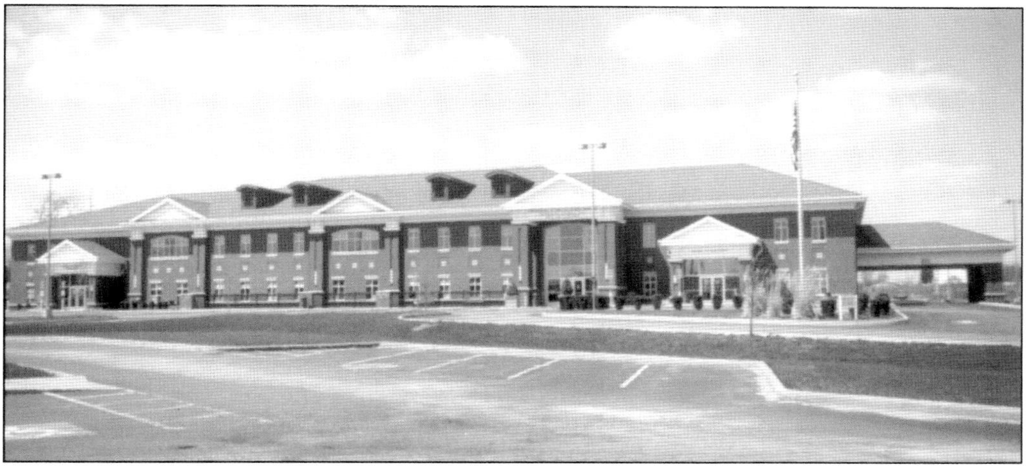

Jobs and Family Services. Replacing buildings downtown and illustrating the northward migration to the township edge of the village, this large new structure houses numerous social service agencies as well as the board of elections and county commissioners. Traditional in style but contemporary in services and technology, the offices employ a large number of individuals. (Photograph by Wendell Cole.)

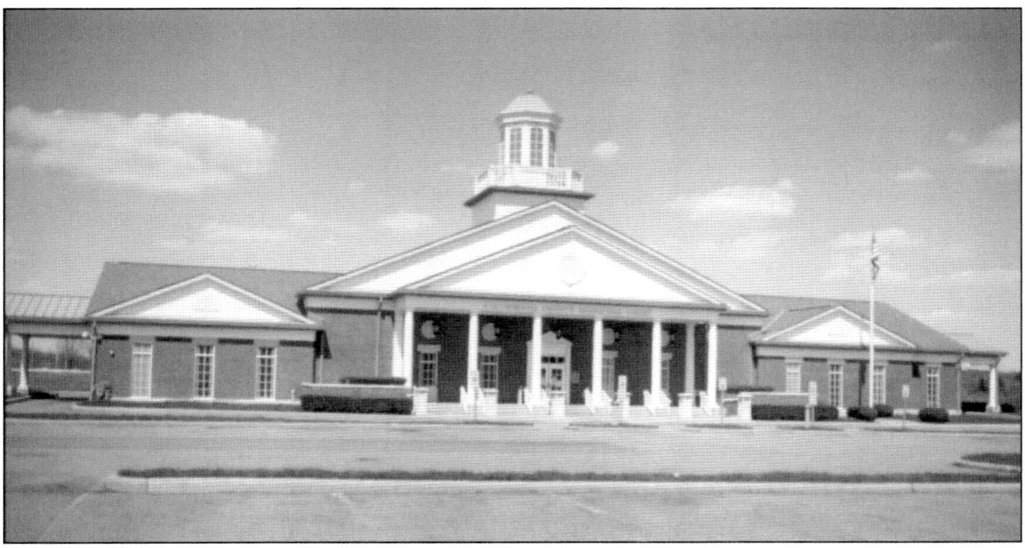

Columbiana County Municipal Court. A short distance away from the jobs and family-services complex as well as the Dickey Drive businesses and social services stands this large new county court. While the original courthouse occupies its time-honored position and functions downtown, this Saltwell Road edifice houses many county duties. (Photograph by Wendell Cole.)

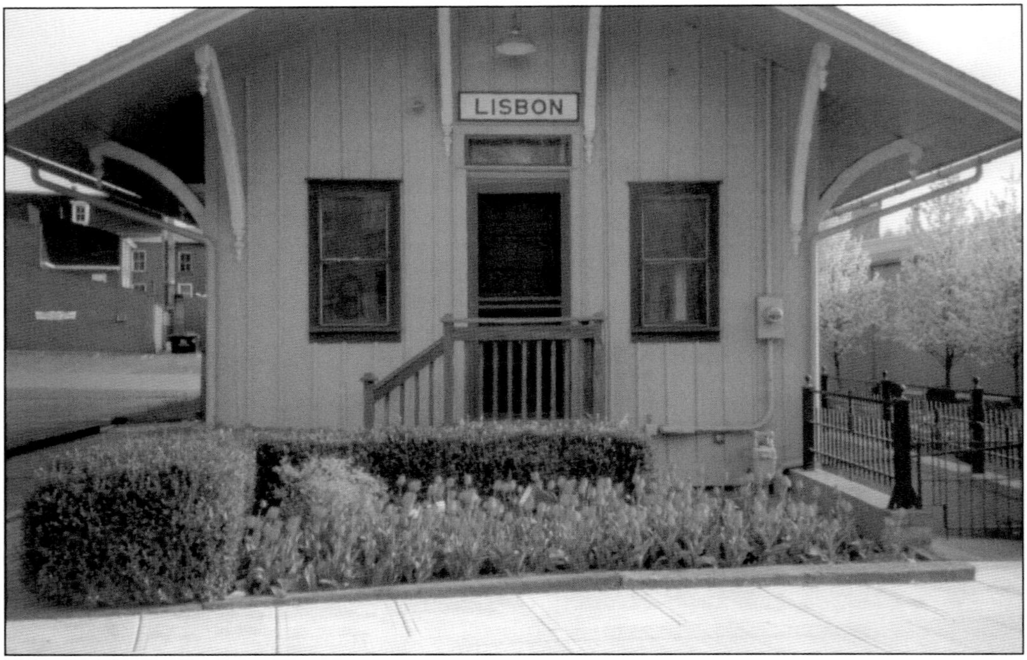

Lisbon Historical Society Museum. This former train station was moved to a site near the center of Lisbon and the other historical society buildings in 1986. The main floor houses meeting facilities and many interesting artifacts from the village's 200-plus years. This is also an important site for record checking for visitors and locals.

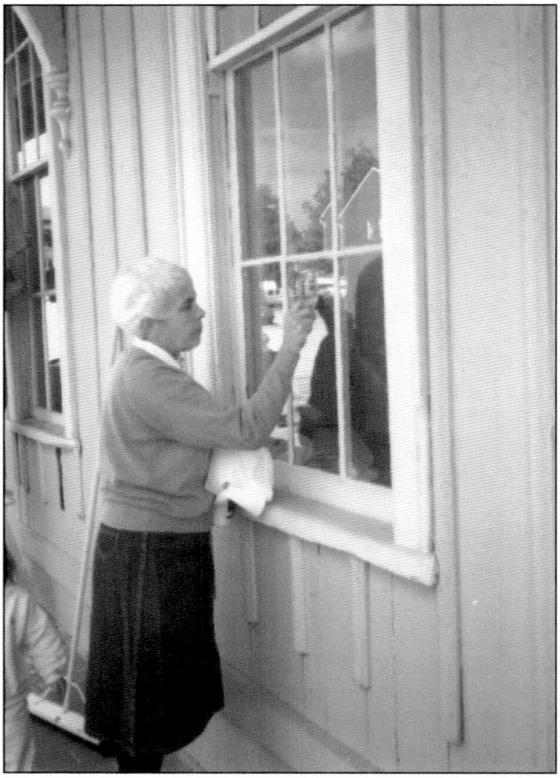

Serving the Historical Society. Jewyl Hina, daughter of Annie and Dr. James Gruber, a local medical doctor, has given many hours of service to the society. With a thorough knowledge of Lisbon from her family and her research, she was instrumental in establishing much of the local society's original direction.

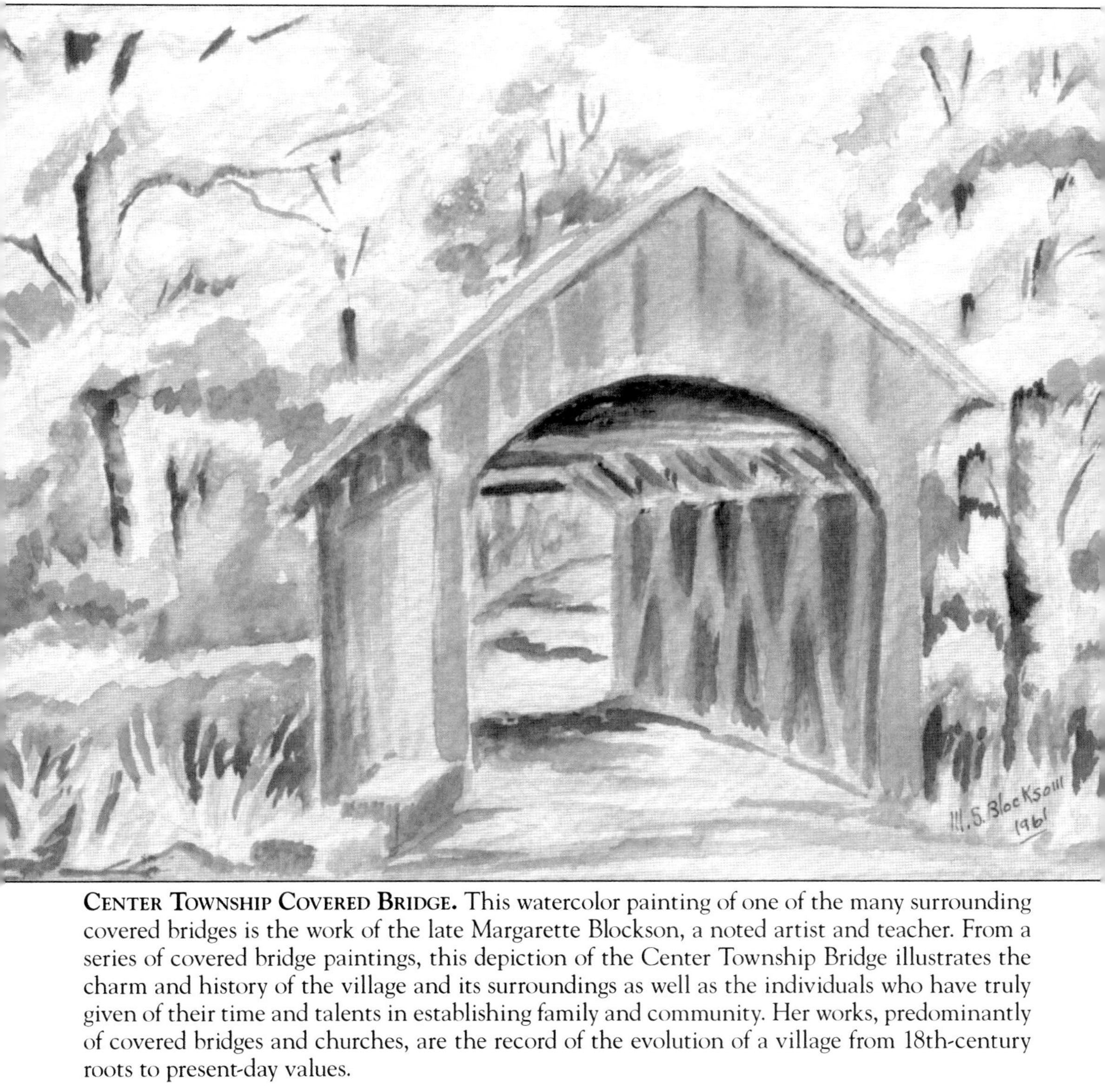

Center Township Covered Bridge. This watercolor painting of one of the many surrounding covered bridges is the work of the late Margarette Blockson, a noted artist and teacher. From a series of covered bridge paintings, this depiction of the Center Township Bridge illustrates the charm and history of the village and its surroundings as well as the individuals who have truly given of their time and talents in establishing family and community. Her works, predominantly of covered bridges and churches, are the record of the evolution of a village from 18th-century roots to present-day values.

Bibliography

Buildings and Sites in Ohio Historical Inventory. Columbus, OH: Ohio Historical Society, 1979.

Firestone, Mary. *Historical Sketch Compiled for the Sesquicentennial Celebration of Lisbon, Ohio*. Lisbon, OH: Buckeye Publishing Company, 1953.

Frantz, Tina, ed. *Reflections of a Village: Lisbon 1803–2003*. Lisbon, OH: Gray Kodrich Supply, Inc., 2003.

History of Columbiana County. A Reproduction sponsored by Lisbon Historical Society. Lisbon, OH: Gray Kodrich Supply, Inc., 2002.

Marquis, May. "Lisbon History." Compiled and read by the author for the Lisbon Day Celebration in mid-1940s.

Speaker, C.S., C.C. Connell, and George T. Farrell. *An Historical Sketch of the Old Village of New Lisbon, Ohio*. Lisbon, OH: J.J. Bennett, Printer, 1903.

Thorp, David. "Havoc and Death among the Miners." *Ohio Patriot*. Lisbon, OH: February 17, 1881.

"To Raid: To Surrender, General John Hunt Morgan." Souvenir Program, Lisbon Historical Society. Lisbon, OH: Gray Kodrich Supply, Inc., 2013.

Van Fossan, William Harvey. *The Story of Ohio*. New York: The MacMillan Company, 1937.

About the Lisbon Historical Society

Chartered by the State of Ohio in 1939, the Lisbon Historical Society has been and remains a very active part of the community. The first president was attorney George Lafferty. In its earliest days, preservation of records and artifacts donated to the society was its primary mission. By 1952, under the leadership of Ollie Rogers, the society acquired the Old Stone House, which has been carefully restored to its 19th-century roots and remains an important site in the society's East Washington Street area. In 1986, the old Erie Station was moved near the house; the society's records and multiple artifacts are stored and used there along with meeting space. Finally, in 2004, the Bye Barn, an estate gift of Galen and Betty Bye, was constructed with space for large artifacts.

The society, under the leadership of its 12-member board of directors, remains very active. Tuesdays are regularly scheduled and staffed for individuals to come to research. Frequently, they are directed to the Columbiana County Archives and Research Center, a block away, for further information. Three times each year, the society and its 100 members are invited to participate in a dinner meeting with a relevant program.

Special events sponsored by the society include programs in the local schools and cemetery tours. A major commemoration in July 2013 was the 150th anniversary of General Morgan's Raid complete with food, speeches, a church service, and a booklet. Authentic Victorian teas staged in the Train Station Museum are often the base for further touring of the community. The spirit and generosity of the society as well as the expertise of the leading members is amazing. Their resources are abundant, their knowledge is strong, and their possibilities are growing.

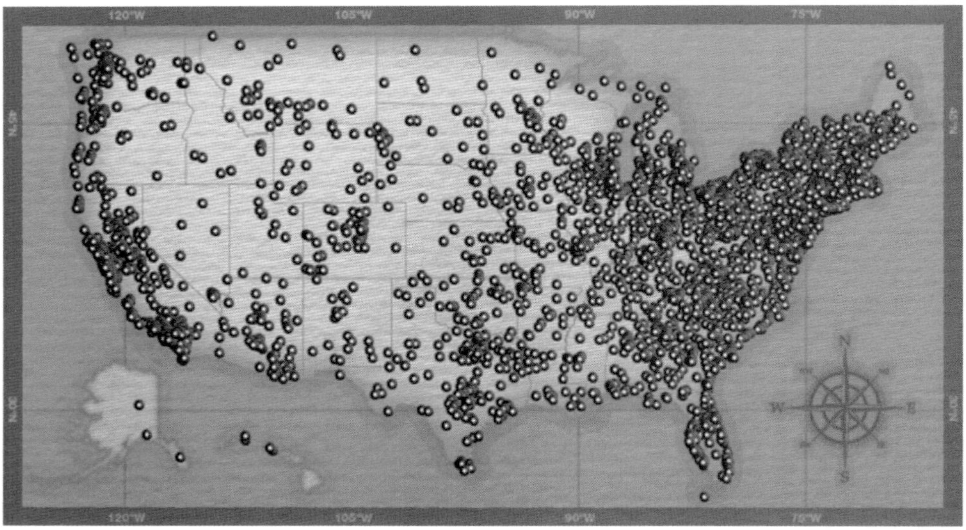